The Complete Allotment Guide

Volume 1 – Getting Started

Jason Johns

DEDICATION

This book is dedicated to my amazing wife, Nicola, for all the support and love over the years.

Visit me at www.GardeningWithJason.com for gardening tips and advice or follow me at www.YouTube.com/OwningAnAllotment for my video diary and tips. Join me on Facebook at www.Facebook.com/OwningAnAllotment.

If you have enjoyed this book, please leave a review.

Look out for the other books in The Complete Allotment Guide series available online or from any good bookstore:

- Volume 2 – Growing Fruit
- Volume 3 – Growing Herbs
- Volume 4 – Growing Vegetables
- Volume 5 – The Allotment Cookbook
- Volume 6 – Preserving and Storage

Table of Contents

Introduction 8
Chapter 1 – Introduction to Allotment Gardening 9
Why Own An Allotment? 10
How To Get An Allotment 13
Creating A Mini Allotment In Your Garden 19
Essential Equipment 20
Allotment Etiquette And Rules 22
Chapter 2 – Getting Started **26**
Assessing Your Plot 27
Creating An Action Plan 29
Tackling An Overgrown Plot 31
Organic or Non-Organic? 33
Allotment Health And Safety 34
Allotment Security 35
Clearing The Rubbish 36
Overcoming Weeds – The Perennial Problem 38
Saving Water On Your Plot 44
Raised Beds vs. Growing In The Ground 46
The Importance Of A Shed 48
Building Paths 50
Greenhouses, Polytunnels and Coldframes 51
Allotment Management And Events 52
Coping With An Average British Year 56
What To Do First 57
Chapter 3 – Creating Your Own Compost **58**
The Composting Process 59
What You Can And Cannot Compost 60
Building A Compost Heap 62
Compost Tea 64
Worm Farming 65
Chapter 4 – Working Your Allotment **67**
Allotment Pests And How To Deal With Them 68
Potential Allotment Problems 72
Buying Seeds And Plants 77
How To Grow From Seeds 78
The Difference Between F1 Hybrid And Heirloom Seeds 80
Growing In Containers On Your Allotment 81
Feeding, Fertiliser and Manure 82
Soil pH Levels 85
Keeping Chickens On Your Allotment 88
Keeping Bees On Your Allotment 89
Companion Planting Explained 91
Crop Rotation Explained 94
Making The Most Of Your Space 96
Maintaining Your Allotment 99
Amending Your Soil 101
Making The Most Of Your Allotment With Children 102
Running An Environmentally Friendly Allotment 103
Basic Gardening Techniques 105
How To Save Seeds 108

Chapter 5 – Your Allotment Month By Month 112

   Seed Sowing Chart...112

   Allotment Jobs..116

Endnote 154

Appendix A - Useful Resources...156

Appendix B – Glossary of Gardening Terms 157

Other Books By Jason...161

About Jason 165

Want More Inspiring Gardening Ideas? 166

Introduction

Taking on an allotment is a big commitment, but something many people aspire to. With waiting lists often being years long, when you get one, you want to hit the ground running and make the most of it. It can be very overwhelming when you first walk onto a plot waist deep in weeds and you need to know what to do. The majority of new allotment holders give up in the first year or two either due to it being more work than they thought, not knowing what to do or struggling to cope with unseasonable weather (which is getting increasingly common).

A before and after shot of one of my allotments.

This book series has been created to introduce you to allotments and everything you need to know about them from choosing an allotment to how to get started and what to do to tame the wilderness. But there is more. Later books in the series will go into detail about growing fruits, herbs and vegetables plus what to cook with them and even how to preserve them.

The first book, which you now have in your hands, introduces you to your allotment and talks you through everything you need to know from how to get an allotment to choosing a plot when you are offered one to getting started working on your allotment.

You will be talked through how to get started on your allotment as, let's face it, being presented with a couple of hundred square feet of weeds and rubbish can be very overwhelming, particularly if you are new to gardening on that scale. Managing an allotment is very different to growing a few vegetables in your back garden. I'll talk you through what to do, how to tackle the weeds, ways to minimise the amount of work you need to do plus how an allotment society works including etiquette and dealing with other people on the site.

It can be very overwhelming starting on an allotment and I regularly hear from readers who have taken on a new allotment and have no idea where to start. With some allotments, it can be a mammoth task. The cover of this book shows a before and after picture of one of the allotments I took on. The plot was shoulder deep in weeds and so bad that I didn't realise it had raised beds until I (literally) tripped over one while clearing weeds. I'll talk you through how to make clearing an allotment as easy as possible and how to get your plot productive right from the start.

There is a lot covered in this book and it is basically everything I wish I had known when I had got my first allotment (another patch of weeds). The aim is for this book to help you go from allotment newbie to allotment expert in as short a period of time as possible!

You will also learn gardening techniques including how to improve your soil and use tools, plus there is a handy seed sowing chart to help you know what to plant and when to plant it.

This book is written from my personal experience as someone who has grown food at home for over twenty years and has been on various allotment sites for over ten years. I've written this to help you get started with all the information you need to make the most of your allotment and successful grow your own fruit and vegetables.

That first day on the plot can make you feel like you have taken on the impossible, but with the information in this book, you can get started from day one and turn those weeds into a productive vegetable plot.

Many people give up their allotment in the first year because they take on what looks like an unmanageable patch of weeds and rubbish and don't know what to do or how to cope. This book helps you understand the best way to tackle a new plot and not to feel overwhelmed, even showing you how to grow something in your first year, which is incredibly motivating to keep working on your allotment. I hope that you will be able to enjoy your allotment for many years and get as much from your allotment as I do.

After some hard work it starts to look good.

Chapter 1 – Introduction to Allotment Gardening

An allotment is an area of land that you rent from your local council or a private landowner to grow fruits, flowers and vegetables on. What you can, and cannot do, on an allotment varies significantly between sites, as does the actual size of the plot you are given. Rules vary from site to site, so you need to make sure you are aware of what you can and cannot do on the site you choose.

Allotment gardening has a long and illustrious past. When Bourneville was built in Birmingham to house workers for the Cadbury factories, each house had fruit trees and a vegetable patch in the garden for the workers to grow their own fresh produce. Of course, this wasn't an entirely selfless act by the owners of Cadbury's; they knew that workers who ate fresh fruits and vegetables were healthier and more productive!

Allotments can trace their history back to the industrial revolution in the 19th century which led to a nationwide shortage of food. At the time, there was no welfare state so the government allocated land for the working classes to grow their own food, which because the allotments we know and love today.

In 1908, allotments were formalised by the Small Holdings and Allotments act which made local councils responsible for providing sufficient allotment space for their residents. In 1919, the Land Settlement Facilities Act made land available to everyone, not just the poor, mainly to help people returning from fighting in the First World War. In 1925, the Allotments Act was passed which protected allotments by ensuring councils could not sell off the land or develop it without permission from the Government.

In both World Wars, allotments took on an increased importance as growing your own fruits and vegetables helped the war effort and fed the populace. After the Second World War, allotments became more popular as rationing was still in force. Growing your own was a good way of getting extra food and staying healthy. As the 1980's happened and technology took a greater role in our lives, the popularity of allotments waned as people preferred to stay indoors to enjoy television and the new computer games. This continued into the 2000's when allotment gardening saw a boost in popularity, partly from TV shows promoting growing your own vegetables and partly from an increased need by people to be healthier. The increased cost of living was also an influencing factor, yet councils were trying to shut down and sell off allotments all over the country as they became more desperate for money.

My new plot, fortunately it is in good condition.

Allotments are very popular as people have realised the many benefits of owning one. Some areas will have waiting lists running into the years, yet other areas will have empty plots begging for someone to take them. Typically, urban areas have the longer waiting lists due to the lack of green space and many houses having small or non-existent gardens. Rural areas tend to have shorter waiting lists as many of the houses have their own gardens so people can grow vegetables at home.

Now, there are around 330,000 allotments across England and Wales with people of all ages, races and beliefs drawn together by the common love of growing their own produce. At the peak of their popularity, it is estimated there was over 1.5 million, and current demand calls for at least another 90,000 allotment plots to be created across the country. If you have been thinking about taking on an allotment, have just taken one on, or have even had one for a while, this book will take you through everything you need to know about owning an allotment from choosing your plot through to managing it, so it becomes a productive area of land. Don't worry if you work or have a busy life, you can set your allotment up so it is minimal maintenance. Don't worry if you don't have an allotment, they are not expensive to maintain, and you don't need much more than a fork, spade and hoe to get started

Why Own An Allotment?

There are a multitude of reasons to have an allotment, and everyone has their own reason or reasons for getting one. There are some common benefits and advantages of having an allotment:

Health

There are many health benefits from owning an allotment. Numerous studies have shown that elderly people who have an allotment live longer, more active and healthier lives. The increase in vitamin D from being outside in the sun is incredibly beneficial, not to mention the vitamin and mineral benefits from the fruits and vegetables you grow.

Recent research has shown that there are beneficial bacteria in soil which can help combat depression. The very act of being outside and gardening allows you to practice mindfulness and has a beneficial effect on your spirit. I know many gardeners, myself included, who will happily tell you that their allotment is their therapist.

For many, it is an escape from the hustle and bustle of our stressful, modern lives. Being able to escape the television and games console gives you space to think, reduces the stress hormone levels in your system and allows your mind to work through your problems. It is almost a break from modern life!

Exercise

Allotment gardening involves a lot of exercise, though you can make an allotment suitable for someone with a disability, in a wheelchair or with a bad back. For most people, the exercise is a real benefit. How many people do you know pay for a gym that they don't visit as often as they should? A couple of hours at the allotment every week provides you with an excellent full body work out that a gym would struggle to provide! It helps keep your joints supple, improves your lung capacity and generally improves your sense of wellbeing. As a bonus, you get fresh fruit and vegetables too! With many people living sedentary lives, the exercise from working an allotment is a welcome boost to your health and does your heart the world of good.

Community

The sense of community at most allotments is wonderful. This are small, independent communities that draw people together with a common interest. You can get as involved as you want, from being on the committee and working communal areas to just getting on with your plot, if you prefer.

For many elderly or single people, it provides a much needed meeting place where they can talk to people and socialise. It's a great place to meet people who are friendly and more than willing to chat. I have had regular conversations on one allotment site with all sorts of people from retirees to a PhD student to a University lecturer to a scaffolder! The lovely thing is, all of these people are happy to share their knowledge, though sometimes their opinions may be unwelcome. I have learned some wonderful, time saving techniques (which are in this book) from a delightful, 84-year-old pensioner who has had two hip operations, survived prostate cancer and still manages to put my plot to shame with how well tended his is! This transfer of knowledge is wonderful!

Plus, people are always willing to share seeds, excess plants and even excess produce. I built a strawberry bed the other year and another plot holder gave me the runners from their plants. I worked out it would have cost several hundred pounds to buy the amount of plants I put in, but was given them for free by another, kind plot holder. The level of involvement you have is entirely up to you, but it's lovely to be able to chat to the other plot holders and meet new people, it always surprises me who you find on an allotment site; it's an incredible cross-section of society.

Fresh Fruit and Vegetables

One of the main benefits of owning an allotment, quite obviously, is that you get fresh fruits and vegetables from it. While it is unlikely to work out cheaper than buying the produce from the supermarket, you will be growing food that is mostly organic and benefiting from the exercise associated with it. With an allotment, it is the process of growing rather than the end result that is important.

One of the biggest benefits is that the vegetables you grow at your allotment actually taste of something! Carrots and tomatoes, to give just two examples, bought from a supermarket are often very watery and tasteless. Open a bag of carrots and they don't smell like carrots. Pull up a handful of fresh carrots on your allotment and the aroma is unmistakable.

Commercial growers do not grow vegetables for their taste; they are grown based on their ability to survive transportation without damage, to look pretty and for high yields. Because of this, commercial growers will only grow one or two varieties, so unless you are buying the expensive, 'finest' varieties, you will find your store-bought vegetables tasteless by comparison.

Many commercial crops are picked before they are fully ripe and stored at low temperatures so they can be transported without damage. My youngest daughter loves strawberries, but only those she picks from the allotment or from a pick your own farm. Out of season, buy strawberries and she won't eat them because they taste of nothing! I served my in-laws carrots from the allotment that I had picked that morning; they all commented on how tasty the carrots were and had wondered what I had done with them! Although you can buy cheap fruit and vegetables from the supermarket, the taste of home-grown produce is so much better. The satisfaction of serving a meal where you have grown most of the vegetables is indescribable.

Growing Unusual Vegetables

In a supermarket you are limited to very few varieties and shopping around will not increase the amount of varieties available to you unless you buy the expensive ones. With an allotment you can grow the types of vegetables you like that are either hard to get hold of or expensive to buy in stores.

I love greengages, for example, and gooseberries (I adore gooseberry jam), but you can never find greengages in a shop and gooseberries are a rare find when they are in season. I have a greengage tree and several gooseberry bushes because I really enjoy them. I also like coloured tomatoes, particularly yellow and black ones, but you won't find black tomatoes in the shops and yellow ones are hideously expensive for the smallest handful. I grow these each year and love

serving salads with a variety of coloured tomatoes in. The same with carrots, I love yellow and black carrots as they taste so much nicer, in my opinion, than orange ones. You will struggle to find them in the store, but they are as easy to grow on your allotment as the orange ones.

You can grow different coloured cauliflower, peas, beans and all sorts of vegetables that are a change to those you find in the store. I have a policy that every year I will plant at least one bed of a vegetable I've never tried before; some work, some fail, but we get to try new things. I grew petit pan squashes one year, we didn't like them so I've not grown them since, the same the cape gooseberries, tried them and didn't like them. However, I grew spaghetti squash and it was a big hit with the family, so that is now regularly grown. An allotment gives you the flexibility to experiment with vegetables and to grow varieties that have more taste than those bought from a shop and varieties that you will never find in a supermarket.

Growing Show or Giant Vegetables

I will admit that growing giant vegetables is a passion of mine. The first time I grew a 120lb pumpkin was one I'll never forget, everyone wanted to see it and the kids were fascinated. Since then I've grown giant onions, cabbages, more pumpkins and many other unusual, large vegetables purely because I like the challenge. Some people grow giant vegetables to show or regular vegetables to show at exhibitions. There are vegetable competitions at church halls and county fairs all over the country and it's a surprisingly competitive environment! After a few years of growing your own produce you may decide to try exhibiting it and you will soon be hooked!

Enjoying being Outside

This is perhaps my favourite reason to have an allotment, I've got a good excuse to get outside. Research is showing that being outside and working the soil is good for your health. Being out in the sun increases your vitamin D levels, something that is low in a shocking amount of people, plus working an allotment appeals to some primeval part of you. Perhaps the most important part of having an allotment s being away from modern life. You are not sat in front of a computer or television, can put your mobile phone in your pocket and just get on with enjoying a simpler life.

Being back in touch with nature really improves your mood and mental state. Most retired people who own allotments live longer and healthier lives than those that do not. Many younger allotment owners will tell you they feel much better and more alive when they are at their allotment and it helps them 'get through the week'. I regularly talk to people on our allotment site and to a person, they have all said that their allotment makes them feel much better.

How To Get An Allotment

The process for getting an allotment varies from area to area and site to site. There are all sorts of rules and criteria with no standards across the country. For example, I live a mile and a half from an allotment site, but after applying for it I was told I was not eligible. Why? Because the boundary marker for the council that runs that site is two hundred yards on the wrong side of my house. However, I am eligible and was given a plot on a size seven miles away on the other side of town from me! The rules can be completely bonkers, but you need to be aware that to be given an allotment, you must live, or sometimes work, in the right council area. Some allotments are run by a parish and you have to live within that parish to have a plot. Move out of the parish and you will be asked to give your little patch of heaven up.

Putting raised beds into an area not worked for 10-15 years.

The first step is to find out whether an allotment is council or committee run. The Internet is your friend here, so search for terms such as "YOUR AREA allotment" and that should give you a good set of results. Also check your local council website as there may be details on there, though you can phone the council and ask to speak to someone about allotments who can help. The best way is to drive around your area, find the allotment sites (some of which are well hidden) and look for a contact number of any information display boards. Some sites will at the least have the name of the site displayed, which makes searching online easier, whereas some will have no information at all, not even a contact number of anyone involved with the site.

If you are visiting the site, then see if you can find someone there to talk to. Even if they cannot directly help you, they will be able to provide you with a name and telephone number of someone who can. When I got my latest plot, I visited the site and got chatting to a gentleman who was just going onto his plot. I told him I wanted to get a plot there and he gave me a tour of the site and took my contact details to put me on the waiting list. It turned out he was the chairman of the committee and my appreciation of his garlic and knowledge of allotments got me a full-sized plot surprisingly quickly!

Once you are on the waiting list, you have nothing more to do than wait. When you get put on the list, find out how long the wait usually is so you can manage your expectations. Although they may say the waiting list is four years, it can be longer or shorter than this. There are many factors that influence how fast an allotment waiting list moves, including how militant the site management are on evicting people for non-cultivation of plots. I have also found that any variation in the weather also helps the waiting lists move along. Hot summers put people off as it is harder to grow plants and more watering needs doing. Wet summers put people off because it is hard to get anything to grow and cold winters also cause people to give up because it kills off their plants.

If the site is managed by the council, then you need to contact the council to be put on the waiting list. It is worth contacting them once a year to find out where you are on the waiting list and to remind them that you are there as sometimes people are 'forgotten'. Councils often purge their waiting lists and if you have missed and email or letter, you can find yourself taken off the waiting list.

If the site is run by an allotment society, then you need to contact the committee secretary who will put you on the waiting list. Remember to ask for a rough idea of how long you will be waiting, but once you are on the list there is nothing else to do except wait and pray for some bad weather to get the waiting list moving!

There are three types of allotment found in the UK:

1. Statutory Allotments – these are protected by the 1925 Allotments Act and cannot be sold or developed with permission from the Secretary of State for Communities and the Local Government. These are the most secure type of allotment as it is very difficult for the council to close them down.
2. Temporary Allotments – the local council own these, but they are not protected and can be sold off with plot holders given notice by the council.
3. Private – these are completely under the control of the land owner and your rights will depend on the covenant between the allotment committee and the land owner. Usually, the area is signed over for 99 years or more, so there is a degree of security.

Council owned allotments can be applied for on

your local council website or through the Directgov website. Privately owned allotments or self-managed allotments are often found through the National Allotment Society (https://www.nsalg.org.uk/) or the Federation of City Farms and Community Gardens (https://www.farmgarden.org.uk/). The amount you pay for an allotment will vary significantly and depends on the council or land owner, it can be anything from a few tens of pounds to a couple of hundred or more. What it includes will depend on the site and the allotment management. Sometimes it will include water, sometimes the water rates are extra and sometimes no water is included.

If there are no allotments in your area, then you can apply to your local council for land to become allotments. You will need six or more people to make the application to your council who have a legal duty to consider it. The downside is that although they have to provide land if they recognise the demand, there are no legal requirements on them to specify a timeframe and they often drag their heels. Getting together more people and identifying a piece of council owned land that could be used will help, but it is no guarantee of a successful application.

Choosing a Plot

After months or even years on the waiting list, the day comes when you get a phone call or letter and are told that you have reached the top of the list and a plot is available for you. Sometimes you will be given a specific plot, but often there are several available and you may be able to choose which one you take. It's a big decision as you will be working your allotment for many years, so you need to make sure you choose the best plot for you.

It is very rare that you will be offered a plot that is in pristine condition and ready to work immediately. If you do, then jump at the chance as it is a fantastic opportunity. When I was offered a plot that had been worked and needed almost nothing doing to it beyond pruning a few trees, I accepted then and there without any hesitation. Usually, the plot you will be offered will be anything from a bit weedy to a jungle that is neck deep in weeds. For many new allotmenteers, one allotment covered in weeds looks pretty much the same as the next, so what do you look for when choosing your plot?

Remember this is a long-term project, so whether it is full of weeds or not isn't particularly relevant to your decision. You are more concerned about other factors such as location, proximity to water, exposure to sun and so on which have more impact longer term than some weeds that can be removed. These are the key points to look for when choosing your plot.

Most new allotments are covered in weeds after a year or more of neglect

Weeds

Weeds should not be the major influencer in your decision, but it certainly is a factor you need to consider. A plot covered with weeds is not necessarily a bad thing, but if the weeds are perennial weeds such as dock, nettle, comfrey, bindweed or mare's tail, then they are much harder to get rid of. I took on a plot covered with nettles, dock, and comfrey once; it took years to get them under control and no matter how much I weeded, they never really went away.

Weeds can be removed, so really the other factors are much more important when deciding which plot to have. A good application of weed killer in the autumn will get rid of most of them and then the residue should be gone by spring when you start planting. If you want to be more organic, cut the weeds down to ground level, remove perennial weed roots and cover. Which you choose is up to you and does depend on your available time.

Structures

You may be fortunate enough to be offered an allotment with a shed and/or greenhouse on it or other structures. Depending on the site policies, these may come with the plot or you may have to pay the previous plot holder a fair price for them. It will depend on the rules for that particular site so enquire with whoever is showing you the plot. These will be in various states of disrepair and sometimes on a more neglected plot are literally scrap that just needs tearing down and disposing of, which will be your responsibility, so bear that in mind.

Having a shed or greenhouse on your plot is really helpful, and we'll discuss them more later in the book. If you can get one that comes with your plot then that will help you a lot, but if they are derelict, you have to consider how you are going to dispose of them, particularly if you do not have access to a car. You may be able to repair them, but that does depend on your DIY skills.

Check the condition of a shed, look for damage to the panels or the roof and check the floor inside. Mice will make a home beneath a shed and wreak havoc on anything you store in there, so look for evidence of vermin as you may have to get rid of them before you can use your shed properly. Pay particularly attention when looking inside for any wet patches which will indicate leaks. If there is any damage, you will have to factor in the cost of repairing it into your allotment budget.

There is a shed, potting bench and small greenhouse under those weeds.

Look at the condition of the greenhouse too. Is the frame straight? Are the panes of glass in good condition or broken? Are any clips missing from the glass? What is the floor made of? Replacing a few panes of glass isn't too expensive, you can often pick up spare panes for free from Freecycle or similar sites. You can buy horticultural glass or polycarbonate cheaply enough. If the greenhouse has oddly shaped or curved panes, then these are going to be much more difficult and expensive to replace. Clips and rubber glass seals can be bought cheaply from eBay, so are not too much of a problem. We will talk about greenhouses in more depth later on, but you will need to factor in the cost of any repairs to your budget.

There could be other structures on the plot such as polytunnels, coldframes, compost bins and more. Look at all the structures, check what state of disrepair they are in and whether or not they are repairable. Any that are not, you will have to demolish and remove.

Check to see if any of the structures on your site have water butts to collect water. Have a quick look to ensure they are in good condition as these are essential if there is no water on your site.

Proximity to Water
One of your first questions to ask is whether or not water is provided. Some sites do not have any water provided and you are responsible for either bringing your own or collecting it from the rain. Although this sounds easy enough, during very hot weather you will go through a lot of water. However, lack of water should not put you off a plot as there are steps you can take to reduce your water dependency.

Look for the nearest water tap, ask your guide if you

have to. In the summer, when it is hot and everything is growing, you will have to water your plants. Few sites permit the use of hoses except to fill water butts, so you may have to carry watering cans full of water from the tap to your vegetables. This is easy enough for a few plants, but when you've got a couple hundred square metres of plants needing watering twice a day, it soon becomes very tedious!

I like to choose a plot close to a tap and ensure I have water butts on my shed and greenhouse to collect water. This helps to reduce the amount of time I am walking back and forth with watering cans, though it is very good exercise! Trust me, when you get a very hot summer, you will be so grateful to be near to a tap!

Clearing the weeds back and a water butt to catch water from the shed.

Trees and Obstructions
Look at what surrounds the plot you are viewing. Is it surrounded by other plots, backs on to houses or is it surrounded by trees? If it is the latter, then that may well be a problem!

As well as casting shade on your plot, which many of your plants may object to, trees also suck up nutrients and water from the ground and deprives your vegetables of them. Pine trees are particularly bad because they discourage anything growing underneath them and the fallen needles makes the soil acidic which many vegetables will not tolerate.

Look at where the sun tracks across the sky and see how much of the day your plot will be in the shade as this will impact your plants. One plot I worked had trees down one side as it was next to the site road. Fortunately, they didn't obstruct the sun until the evening during the summer months. However, they also dropped lots of leaves and seeds on the plot in the autumn. I was forever digging up baby oak, ash and other trees and moving barrow loads of leaves. It also had the effect of making the whole plot damp in the winter because there was very little sunlight hitting the ground.

However, while these are a problem and annoying, they shouldn't be a deal breaker if there are no other plots on offer. If you've been waiting for a plot for several years, it is better to have an imperfect plot than never have a plot at all! You can minimise the impact the trees have on your plot. For example, if the trees are on one end of your plot, use this end for your shed, compost bin and storage, which is what I do on my current plot. You could, depending on site rules, use this end of the plot to keep chickens so they are not in the sun all day long. So you can see, trees shouldn't put you off a plot, but if you have a choice of one with trees at one end and one without, you'd usually choose the one that hasn't got trees near it.

If the plot is on the boundary of a site, then see what is growing at the boundary point. Sometimes there can be brambles or other difficult to control weeds which will continually encroach on your plot. Again, these don't need to be deal breakers, but you need to be prepared to manage them and stop them from growing where you don't want them to grow.

Also look at what is on the other side of the boundary. If you are next to a fence, is someone's house on the other side or a public area? You can find rubbish being thrown through from a public area, but this can be minimised by growing something substantial such as blackberries, raspberries or gooseberries there. If a plot is against a boundary, avoid putting any structures near the boundary as it could help people gain access to the site climbing over the fence.

Parking and Paths

If you drive, which I am assuming you do for this section, you will need to see where you can park for your plot. If the plot is miles away from the car park and you cannot get your car nearer, then you need to consider how you are going to transport items from your car to your plot and vice versa. You may think that isn't a problem but wait until you have to shift ten rows of potatoes or a two-hundred-pound pumpkin! Or what if you get a ton of manure delivered that you then have to wheelbarrow to your plot.

I cannot park next to my current plot, which I could at the previous site I occupied. However, my plot is adjacent to the site road so I can park on the road to load or unload my car when necessary. Obviously, I can't leave my car there as it will upset other plot holders, but it does mean I am not carrying heavy loads too far.

Neighbouring Plots & Site Facilities

Look at the plots that surround the one you are being offered. Are these neat and well-kept or are they unkempt weed farms? This will give you an idea of how well the site as a whole is worked, but if the plots next to you are covered in weeds then you may struggle to keep the weeds at bay on your own plot as they come across from the overgrown plots. Be aware that weed seeds will blow from unattended plots on to yours. If they look untended, you can ask your guide whether or not those plots are available if they look better than the one you are being offered. They may say yes and offer you one of those instead.

As you are walking around, look at the site security in general. Is the site fenced with secure gates? Does everyone have padlocks on their sheds? Is there secure storage available? Ask your guide about site security as you don't want to store any valuable tools or equipment in your shed if there is the risk of it being broken into.

Look at the general condition of the site as you walk around. If it is, on the whole, in good condition, then you know it will be a good site as people care enough to look after it. An untidy, poorly maintained site is often an indication of one that is struggling. This could be due to problems with getting a committee or other issues. If the site does seem poorly maintained, you can always ask your guide about it and try and find out more about what is happening on site.

Some sites have manure and wood chip delivered free of charge, have communal chickens or bees or even a communal orchard. Ask your guide about manure and wood chip as they are handy if the site buys them, otherwise you will have to pay for your own to be delivered. Check out the communal facilities as part of your tour to see what is on offer. Some sites will also have an allotment shop selling discounted items that you will need such as compost, onion sets, canes, seed potatoes and more.

Good neighbours with well looked after plots.

Ask about toilet facilities on the site too. Some sites will have them, others will not. It is helpful if a site has them because it means you can stay on the site much longer. However, many plot holders are very inventive and a bucket in the shed solves a lot of problems!

Sun Exposure

Plants need sunlight in order to grow and is important for you to assess how much sunlight your potential new plot would get. Too much shade can cause damp conditions that encourage fungal diseases, making it difficult to have a productive plot. Too much sun can easily be shaded against through careful planning and planting as well as the judicious use of shade netting.

From a single visit you will not be able to determine how much sun your plot will get throughout the year, but you will be able to estimate the quality and quantity of sunlight the plot will receive.

You are looking for a plot that gets plenty of sunlight. The more you can get the better it will be. If it is in partial shade, then you need to be more careful with your planning so that shade loving plants are put in the shadier areas and sun loving plants are not. It is very unlikely you will be offered a plot that is always in the shade as these are known to be no good for growing and are usually assigned to communal spaces if there are any at all.

Size

The size of an allotment varies considerably as you travel from site to site. Some are massive and some are smaller. As demand has increased, many allotment committees have taken the decision to divide large plots into two or more allotments in order to meet demand. Many allotment groups recognise the fact that people are very busy and that most people who work are not able to manage a full-sized plot adequately.

If the plot is too big for you, then you may end up struggling to manage it which causes conflict with the allotment committee or council which can result in written warnings and eviction notices. If you feel the plot you are being offered is too large for you to manage, then you can ask about sharing the plot or splitting it in half and them offering the other half to another new tenant. However, experience tells me that no matter how much space you have on an allotment, it will never be enough to grow all the plants you want to grow! The first couple of years you may struggle to plant your allotment fully, but once you get into the swing of things you will have many more plants than space. This is when techniques such as vertical gardening and succession planting become vital, both of which you will learn about in a later chapter.

Depending on the site you are visiting, you may be offered to choose between plots or you may be shown the only plot that is available, in which case you don't have a choice. If you do have a choice of plots, choose one that is of a size you can reasonably manage to work bearing in mind your other commitments such as your job and family. We'd all love a large plot of land to work, but you don't want to struggle with it and potentially lose it. It's better to have a smaller plot that you can work, than a larger plot that will be neglected.

The Rule of Inheritance

Allotments will often come with good things and bad things. The general 'rule of inheritance' is that if it is on your plot when you sign the lease, it is yours. It is assumed that the previous plot holder has removed anything they want from your plot before you take over.

Once you have signed the lease, no one should remove anything from your plot, including the previous plot holder. However, sometimes other plot holders do not realise that the allotment has been taken over and will help themselves to items on what they think is an abandoned plot. On rare occasions, the previous plot holder returns and removes items they have now decided they want, but as most allotment sites are secure, this should not be possible.

The best thing to do is to make sure you are visible. Ensure it is obvious that people are working the plot and that it is 'inhabited'. Be seen down at the allotment, so go in the evenings and at weekends when there are lots of people there so everyone knows you have taken on that new plot. Should things go missing, then you need to report it to the committee who will investigate and take appropriate action.

Depending on what is on the site and the site policies, you may be asked to negotiate with the previous plot holder to buy structures that are on the allotment such as greenhouses and sheds. This does not often happen, but it can occur occasionally. In this case, you discuss a price and come to an agreement. I would recommend paying the plot holder in the presence of a committee member and getting a receipt from them so there can be no future arguments about the agreement.

However, you are under no obligation to buy these items. If you cannot afford them or cannot negotiate what you consider a reasonable price, then you can request that the previous plot holder removes them and give them a fixed deadline. Again, this can be done in writing and witnessed to protect yourself. In some cases, people can be cheeky and want unreasonable sums of money for basically scrap wood. When you tell them you do not want the structure and that they need to remove it, they capitulate and either give it to you for free or negotiate a better price.

However, in most cases, the structures, tools, plants and anything else on the plot is yours to keep for free … and that includes any rubbish that has been left behind! This can be beneficial for you, I inherited a shed and greenhouse that look like they were built just after World War II, dozens of car loads of rubbish, several pairs of Wellington boots and a good half dozen wheelbarrows in various states of disrepair.

When you are looking at plots, ask what comes with the plot and what, if anything, the previous plot holder is taking with them. This will help you to understand what you need to buy and if there are any additional costs you need to factor in to taking on a new allotment.

Just a small selection of 'treasures' from my allotment!

Creating A Mini Allotment In Your Garden

While you are waiting for an allotment, you can start growing some fruit and vegetables at home. Whether you have a large garden, a concrete yard or live in a flat, there are still some things you can grow to get started and hone your skills ready for a full-sized allotment.

While you are waiting, begin to invest in gardening books and join gardening groups online on sites such as Facebook. Starting following allotment owners (like myself @allotmentowner) on social media such as Twitter and Instagram. This helps to keep your enthusiasm up while you are waiting for your allotment and give you the opportunity to learn more about owning an allotment so you can hit the ground running when you finally reach the top of the waiting list.

A corner of the garden to grow vegetables.

Herbs grow very well in pots and can easily be bought from any supermarket, repotted and grown throughout the summer. These are ideal on a kitchen windowsill where you can grab a handful of fresh herbs to use while cooking. Chilli plants will also grow well on a sunny windowsill and can produce some fiery peppers to challenge your palate! If you have a small garden, you can grow vegetables in containers or buy a walk-in plastic greenhouse to grow tomatoes or other vegetables in. Larger gardens can have vegetables planted in the borders, create raised beds or even dig over an area to become a vegetable plot.

How much you do is entirely up to you and will depend on your budget and available space. I live in a house with a concrete yard and have three plastic walk-in greenhouses in the garden. In these I grow chillies and tomatoes every year in pots, rather than grow them down at the allotment. I also use the greenhouses to start off my seeds every spring, so they are close at hand for regular attention. Come late spring, there is lots of transporting of seedlings from the house to the allotment and the greenhouses are turned over to other plants.

When I lived in a house with a much larger garden, I turned a large portion of it over to vegetables, removing the lawn and creating raised beds to make what the neighbours jokingly referred to as 'the farm'. What you do will depend on the space available to you. It is a good idea to get started at home and start learning the ropes so that when you finally do get an allotment you are not overwhelmed and trying to learn everything from scratch.

Growing a few plants in your garden helps you get used to growing and gives you an idea as to whether you are going to be committed enough to have an allotment, or whether you do not have enough time or energy to do it. I have seen too many people take on allotments, spend money on them and then lose interest as they realise just how much work is involved, and it is quite considerable. After growing at home for a year or so you may decide you definitely want an allotment, or you may decide that it is not for you. Better to find out before you take on several hundred square feet of land as you can always remove yourself from the waiting list if you need to.

While waiting for your name to creep up the waiting list, start growing what you can at home. You will enjoy it, get a taste for growing your own fruits and vegetables and start learning, ready for your full-sized plot.

Essential Equipment

There is a mind-blowing amount of equipment that you can buy for your allotment. You could easily spend thousands of pounds and still not have everything you 'need'. However, don't panic, there is surprisingly little that is essential equipment and even that doesn't need to cost you a lot. Here we will discuss the equipment I feel you cannot live without at an allotment as well as how to use them effectively.

Many of these items can be obtained for free via sites like Freecycle or you can buy them cheap in supermarkets towards the middle of summer when they start to sell off their summer stock ready for Hallowe'en and Christmas. These don't have to cost you a fortune, but if you are buying tools, always buy the best you can afford as usually they will last longer and are of much better quality.

A couple of tools on the plot

Fork

An absolute essential for turning your soil and breaking up lumps. It is helpful for shovelling manure and digging up some larger vegetables or moving plants. It will be a godsend when weeding your allotment as it allows you to dig up weeds with tap roots, such as dandelions, without breaking the root (which causes new, deeper rooted plants to grow). There are ladies forks, which are slightly smaller than larger forks and are ideal for people of a smaller stature.

Spade

Not so useful as a fork, in my opinion, but handy for digging holes or trenches (for potatoes) where you don't want the soil falling back into the hole. Handy for chopping through tree roots and levering out larger weeds/plants when a fork is too weak.

Hoe

Probably the most essential tool on the allotment. Hoe your allotment two or three times a week and knock the tops of the weeds. They will die before they can establish themselves and you will have a lovely, weed-free allotment. A smaller, hand hoe is useful when you want to keep narrower rows of plants weed free.

Rake

Useful for levelling soil and breaking up large chunks after digging. A hand rake is helpful if you have smaller raised beds.

Trowel and Hand Fork

Very useful for planting as well as removing smaller weeds, particularly those growing near to your plants. Avoid plastic tools as, although cheap, they break far too easily.

Wheelbarrow

Vital for carting around weeds, plants, bricks, manure, wood chip and ripe vegetables. Moving anything heavy in your wheelbarrow saves your back. I use mine to move piles of bricks around my plot, transport manure and even transport my harvest to the car. Buy a good quality, robust and rugged wheelbarrow. This is going to be your workhorse and spend a lot of time being abused on your plot, so get a decent, sturdy wheelbarrow that isn't going to develop a puncture at the first bump! You can get puncture proof tyres and these are often worth it at an allotment where it is very easy to get a puncture from a variety of debris left on site.

Seed Trays

Vital in spring to start off all your seeds. Try to buy hard plastic ones rather than the flimsy plastic trays as they will last longer, resulting in less plastic being disposed of. Look in stores such as Wilco or larger supermarkets around July/August time and you can often find these heavily discounted as the retailers clear the shelves to make way for other seasonal stock.

Pots

Useful for transferring your seedlings to before you plant them out or starting off larger plants such as squashes, cucumbers and tomatoes. Buy a selection of different sized pots ranging from three inches across up to eight or nine inches in diameter as you will pot on your plants into larger pots before you can plant them out. These can often be found on Freecycle, though are also sold off cheap in many stores in July or August.

Watering Can

An essential for the summer months when you need to keep your plants watered. These can be bought very cheaply nowadays. As these have a hard life at the allotment, it isn't really cost effective to buy an expensive, metal can. I buy the cheap plastic ones and they last for many years without leaking. Although you want a large watering can so that you don't need to make as many trips to the water tap, you need to be able to comfortably carry the watering can when it is full. I have two on my allotment so that I can take two full cans per trip to the tap, which halves my watering time!

Bucket

Another essential item. I use it for collecting weeds in as I am weeding my vegetable beds and then empty it on to the compost heap when full. It stops me dropping weeds everywhere and is a bit easier to use than a wheelbarrow if you are only pulling up a few weeds. I have several on my plot, including one with a hole in due to old age. The holey bucket is used for stones and rubbish I find when digging.

Weed Membrane

Use a good quality weed membrane to cover unused areas of your allotment. Some people use tarpaulins, but these are not permeable, so you end up with puddles of water on top of the covers. This is absolutely essential and a mistake many beginners make. When you have finished weeding an area, cover it to prevent the weeds from growing back, unless of course you really like digging and weeding! Many people complain that no sooner have they finished weeding an area than it is covered with weeds again. Covering it with a heavy weed membrane will stop the weeds from growing back and give you a chance to get your allotment under control.

Secateurs

Useful for pruning fruit bushes and trees. Buy a good quality pair as they are more likely to last longer.

Penknife

Handy for all sorts of things. I have a good quality Swiss army knife I use at my allotment. I use the saw for cutting pipes and branches and the knife is useful for many tasks. You will be surprised how useful one of these is. You can buy a multi-tool or something similar instead as it does most of the same jobs.

There are many other tools that you can buy for your allotment and we will talk about these more as the book progresses. When you get started, these are the most important tools, some of which you may already own for your garden at home. Eventually you will want a duplicate set so you can have one at the allotment and one in your garden to save you transporting them. I did keep all my tools in the car boot, but this soon became impractical when I had to put shopping in it! Now I have a second set of tools at the allotment which I am not overly worried about if someone breaks in and steals.

Allotment Etiquette And Rules

Every site will have a set of formal rules which are detailed in the contract that you will have signed when you took on the plot. However, every site will also have a set of informal rules. These are generally fairly common between sites as they are mostly based on common sense and good behaviour. Here are some of things you need to be aware of when taking on a plot so that you don't rock the boat and upset the community. An allotment site is meant to be a pleasant place to be and you don't want to cause unnecessary conflict.

Sometimes you will encounter people who will want to give you advice even if you don't want it or have an unwelcome opinion about what you are doing. I recommend just smiling, nodding and getting on with it. On the rare occasion you will find someone who is out to cause conflict and they are best avoided completely. If you do have continued problems with an individual and are feeling harassed or threatened, then you need to contact the allotment management immediately to report it so they can take action. At no point should you feel bullied to leave your plot.

Generally, the allotment will be a nice place to be. In the many years I've owned an allotment on three different sites, I have never encountered anyone who was objectionable, though I know people who have. I have met a few people who I have felt it was better to avoid rather than potentially create conflict, but the majority of people have been friendly, welcoming and helpful.

Familiarise Yourself with The Site Rules

This is probably the most important thing you can do. People will get upset if you break the site rules and, in some cases, you can get formal warnings with continued rule breaking resulting in an eviction notice. Read through your contract and make sure you are aware of all the rules, most of them will be common sense, but there could be odd rules that you need to be aware of. One site I was on had a strict rule that no tree could be taller than six foot which was militantly enforced. I actually saw a committee member with a tape measure measuring trees! A plot owner was instructed to lop the top off their apple tree as it was over six foot even though it was the wrong time of year and would have caused damage to the tree to do so. Some sites do not allow sheds or greenhouses, some have limits on sizes and some let you do pretty much anything you want. Some sites allow you to keep chickens, others don't, so do your research before you apply for an allotment to make sure you can do what you want to do.

If you are in doubt about anything, then ask someone on the allotment management committee whether or not what you want to do is allowed. Most sites will allow you to have greenhouses, polytunnels, and sheds, but some have limits on sizes, positions and even quantities. Generally, it is good etiquette to ask permission and check that where you are going to site your structure is acceptable. I would always recommend doing it by email because then you have written evidence that you were given permission in case of any future disputes. The last thing you want to do is have to demolish and move your greenhouse because someone has taken umbrage at its location.

Most of the allotment rules are common sense but read through the agreement carefully so you don't inadvertently break a rule and cause a commotion.

Never Take Anything from Another Plot

This isn't always written into a contract but is a very strict rule that should never be broken. Never take any item or any produce from another plot, even if it is empty, as this can result in your eviction from the site and, let's face it, you wouldn't appreciate it if someone did it to you. It is heart breaking to have your hard work disappear because someone else has helped themselves to it. You will be surprised the number of people who help themselves to fruit and vegetables from someone else's plot. Many people now have cameras on their plots and people caught stealing from other plots are usually evicted immediately.

On one site, I had a large, very productive strawberry patch that was a few days away from being ripe. I promised my daughter, who adores fresh strawberries, that we would visit at the weekend and pick them. When we visited the entire bed had been stripped bare of strawberries, there wasn't a single one left. As you can imagine, she was devastated, and we had to go to a pick your own farm instead. It wasn't long after this that I gave up that plot because things constantly went missing even down to an empty spray bottle I'd left on the plot.

Most allotment holders will be happy to share their produce with you or even lend you tools, if you ask. If you are curious what a particular fruit or vegetable tastes like, ask them and they will usually let you have one. My allotment neighbours and I often share excess produce or lend each other tools. I commented once about how lovely one plot holder's dahlias were and a few days later he gave me a handful of tubers he had dug up, so I could plant some on my plot! In general, other plot holders are lovely and friendly.

Do Not Step on Another Plot Without Permission

This is much more of an unspoken rule that should be obeyed. When you are talking to another plot holder, you stay on the path or road next to their plot. Only step on to their plot if invited or if you ask so you can get closer to them to hear them better or show them something. Then only walk where directed and stay on any paths they have made. As you don't know what they have planted where, you need to be very careful not to tread on their plants, seedlings or compact soil that they have just dug over. It's a little thing, but it shows you respect them and their plot. People will get very upset if you accidentally tread on their precious seedlings they've been raising for weeks.

Be Friendly and Sociable

In life in general, you get what you give. If you are friendly and sociable, people tend to be friendly and sociable back to you. If you are stand-offish and don't get very involved with other people, then you will find you get treated the same way. I always make a point of saying hello to anyone I pass while on the allotment, whether I know them or not. I have developed some great casual friendships with some fellow plot holders where we can have a good chat about a wide variety of things.

My other, personal rule, at the allotment is to always take time to talk to the elderly people at the allotment. Many of these retirees live alone and for some, going to the allotment is the only time in the day they will see or talk to another person. Therefore, talking to them is very important and makes a big difference in their lives. I spend time helping one of my neighbours where I can as she has very bad arthritis and the allotment is her haven to get out of the house.

By being friendly and sociable, you will generally find people will treat you nicely. When I am not in the mood to talk to people, I work on the part of my allotment furthest from the paths so that people can't see me to talk to me. However, even then I will always be polite if someone takes the time to come over to talk.

Get Involved with The Site

One of my top tips for getting on with everyone on the site is to show some interest in being involved with it! This doesn't mean volunteering for the committee and taking on lots of work, but it does mean showing support for the allotment site. This can be as simple as following the rules, being polite and holding the site gate for people who are arriving or turning up for community days and events, whether they are barbecues or work parties.

Showing your face at these sort of events shows people that you are keen to be a part of the community and you are more likely to be accepted and forgiven any minor transgressions of the rules. Even if you don't have a lot of time, at least turn up and support community events, even if you are just there for half an hour or so, it will be remembered!

Keep Your Plot Well Managed

Most sites will have some sort of rule regarding the cultivation of plots. This can be something as general as "keeping it tidy" to something more specific such as "50% of the plot must be cultivated and planted". The details will be in your allotment contract of how your plot needs to be managed. If you are having any problems due to your personal life, then speak to whoever manages your site and they are generally going to be lenient. If you don't talk to people when you have a problem, then you are more likely to have a problem if your plot gets out of control.

However, here's what you do to very easily ensure your plot looks good. Firstly, strim down the weeds to ground level, cover with cardboard, manure, and then weed membrane. This will keep the weeds under control so you are not continuously battling them, giving you time to sort the rest of your plot. Then start at whichever end of your plot is nearest to the path/road where people will look at your plot from. Start building beds, planting or whatever you are going to do with it. If you are really struggling, dig over the required area of the plot and plant potatoes … then you can argue that the plot is tended and planted! Depending on how militantly rules are enforced on your site, this should give you some breathing space, though you are usually given a year to get the plot under control, particularly if it is very weedy.

I was assigned a new allotment on one site and happily took it on, though it was in a bit of a state. It was long and thin, being about four metres wide at the allotment road. The previous tenants had planted parts of it and about a third of the way down the plot from the road were some brassicas that had grown to about six foot tall and flowered. Between them and the road it was generally overgrown. One day while on site I was approached by the chairperson of the committee who told me they were concerned by the lack of work I had done on the plot. I was very confused as I had been down there almost every day, built compost heaps and done lots of work, so I asked them why. They told me that my plot was unworked and overgrown and then I had a lightbulb moment. I led them onto my plot, past the six foot high brassicas and showed them the other two thirds of the plot which were weed free, planted and looking great. The committee had not looked beyond the tall barrier and thought I hadn't done anything with the plot! Naturally, my next job was to remove the brassicas and clear about a metre from the road so they could see things were happening.

Keeping your plot well managed is polite to your neighbours too because they don't have to deal with weeds coming from your plot to theirs. It drove me mad to be next to a messy plot where I was battling dandelions and bindweed coming from their area. If you are struggling for time, at the very least remove spent flower heads from the weeds before they seed; leave the flowers for the bees though and remove them when they have finished flowering.

You will find other plot holders will be much more congenial to you when they realise that you are taking good care of your plot and you are serious about being a good allotment owner.

Do Not Let Trees or Structures Shadow Other Plots

You will be keen to make the most of your plot and may end up erecting a shed or greenhouse or even planting trees. If you do, then you need to think carefully where you are putting them so that they do not cast shadows on anyone else's plot. The same with trees, keep them under control and prevent them from shadowing your neighbours. I grow all my trees as espaliers simply because they are easier to keep under control, take up less space, and aren't going to annoy my neighbours by growing out of control.

There is nothing worse than planting your new strawberry patch to realise that your new neighbour has put their shed in the direct path of the sun so your strawberries are now in the shade for most of the day. Yes, it did happen to me and I wasn't happy! Depending on your site rules, you may well be told to move the shed or greenhouse, which if you have spent time and money putting down a proper base will not be welcome news. It is always best to ask your neighbours if they are okay with your plans to erect a structure where you are planning and to also ask the allotment management. That way, there can be no complaints later from anyone that will cause conflict.

If you want your trees to grow large, then plant them where they will not cast any shadows on other people's plots. You are best buying dwarf rootstock trees, so they do not grow too big and are easier to keep under control. Keep them well pruned and stop them growing too high; if they do grow too tall, then you will struggle to reach the fruit anyway. Your allotment space is valuable, so you do not want to be wasting it on large trees!

Do Not Litter

Simple isn't it? Just do not. I am constantly finding chocolate bar wrappers and even empty soft drink cans on my plot, particularly near the road where people walk by and it really winds me up as I have then got to remove it from site and dispose of it!

But it's not just about regular litter. Avoid dropping weeds or anything else on communal areas if you are carrying them to and from your car. Be careful if you are wheelbarrowing wood chip or manure around the site that you do not drop lots of it everywhere from where you have overfilled your wheelbarrow. It's really common sense but keeping the site tidy benefits you and everyone else too!

Obey Fire Rules

Different sites have different rules about burning waste on your allotment which need to be stuck to as you can face eviction if you don't follow them. Your allotment contract will tell you the rules about fires but be sensible with them too. The application of a little common sense will save a lot of problems and potential conflict. The last thing you need is local residents complaining to the council or committee that you are burning stuff.

A quick way to get rid of some rubbish.

I heard of one allotment owner who lit a fire directly under a tree, which of course then caught fire resulting in the fire brigade being called out. Said allotment owner was given his marching orders there and then! Another was being paid to take rubbish from a local shop and burn it on his plot, he too was evicted. Another was burning tires and plastic, which caused smoke clouds to cover the adjoining houses and complaints made to the committee. He was another who didn't last much longer on his plot even though he had been on the site for years. Don't risk your plot for the sake of burning some rubbish. Be sensible about it!

Here's some good rules of thumb to follow which should help you avoid annoying anyone!

- Check the wind direction – look to see which way the wind is blowing and if it is going to blow the smoke towards houses then it may be best not to light a fire, particularly if they have washing hanging out or children playing in the garden.

- Isolate your fire – light your fire in a bare area of your plot with no trees nearby and nothing flammable within five to ten feet of your fire. The wind can cause the flames to leap quite a distance plus plastic items such as a polytunnel will melt if they get hot.

- Keep it under control – buy an incinerator to burn in so you can keep your fire small and controlled. This can be moved around your plot as you work it so that it doesn't damage anything you are growing, plus you can move it to keep the smoke away from houses.

- Be prepared – have a bucket or two of water to hand so that if the fire does get out of control you can quench it. Keep a long stick to hand to poke the fire so you do not need to go too close to it.

- Don't light it in dry weather – in extreme dry weather, even grass can become flammable and in heatwaves you must not light a fire as you could potentially cause a serious incident. Pile everything up you want to burn and burn it when normal weather conditions are resumed.

Obey Pet Rules

Dog owners may like to bring their pet to the allotment with them. Some sites will permit this, whereas others will have a strict, no pet rule, so check your allotment contract first.

If you are permitted to bring dogs to the site, then you need to keep them on a lead and under control at all time. Not everyone likes dogs and some people are terrified of them. A dog jumping up at an elderly plot holder could knock them over and cause a serious injury. Build a fence around your plot to contain the dog or use a ground stake and extendable leash so that your dog can roam but not leave your plot.

It is nice to have your dog on site with you as it gives the dog some exercise and fresh air, but you have to consider other plot holders to avoid causing conflict.

Park Considerately

Another very common-sense rule, but make sure you park in designated areas and do not park on any plots. Avoid blocking anyone in and avoid parking on access roads for any length of time. If you have to unload equipment from your car, do so and then move your car to a parking area so it isn't causing an obstruction. Again, this will go a long way to avoiding any potential conflict and help keep the allotment site running smoothly.

On one site I was involved in, one gentleman insisted on parking his car on the road by his allotment. While it was convenient for him, it meant that no one else could get down that road to access their plots to drop things off and it causes all sorts of arguments. Make sure that you park so people can not only walk past your car (with a wheelbarrow) but can get their cars past if they need to.

Keep the Site Secure

Site security is taken very seriously as, sadly, many allotment sites are broken in to and vandalised. Follow the site security rules and make sure that you lock gates properly and secure any buildings when you leave. You can help keep the site secure by not leaving any tools or equipment in plain sight where someone can see them from outside of the site. Also, be vigilant and keep an eye on what is going on when you are on the site in case you see anything suspicious. Should there be a security incident, then immediately contact the allotment management and inform them. If there has been a break in, don't touch anything in case the police wish to fingerprint and look for evidence. If you see unauthorised persons on the site, then be careful about approaching them as you should not put yourself at risk.

Generally, your allotment site will be safe and secure providing everyone locks the gates and keeps buildings secure. Avoid putting anything near a perimeter fence that could help people scale fences or break in, i.e., keep structures at least six feet from perimeter fences so they cannot be used to climb the fence.

Chapter 2 – Getting Started

Before you so much as a lift a spade, you need to assess your plot and decide what you are going to do with it. If you have never owned an allotment before, it can be incredibly overwhelming to survey your domain and realise that you have no idea what to do with it! Or to be full of ideas with no idea how to execute them or if they are even practical on your plot. If you have been growing at home, then you may have more of an idea, but it is still a big leap forwards to be presented with a large area of overgrown land that you are expected to magically turn into a productive vegetable patch. Often you can feel pressurised because of site rules or when you see your neighbour's plots. You have to put this all to one side and focus on working your plot and getting it under control.

One of my first allotments before I started!

This chapter is all about determining what approach to take towards your new allotment. You will learn everything you need to know to take on an unmanaged, overgrown plot and turn it into a good looking vegetable garden producing delicious fresh fruits and vegetables. It can be very overwhelming when you stand on your new plot, spade in hand, ready to start. Perhaps it is six-foot-deep in weeds, piled with rubbish or, if you are very lucky, it is relatively neat and ready for you to work.

As you read this chapter, you will be walked through the process of understanding what you have taken on and determining the best way to move forwards with it so your plot becomes productive as soon as possible. It is quite de-motivating when you have to spend months clearing and tidying your plot before you can grow anything. I always recommend people start growing as soon as they physically can, i.e. within a few weeks (season dependent) so that they can see some results from their allotment and stay motivated. When you are doing nothing but clearing weeds and digging for weeks, it takes away some of the enjoyment, but if you can be harvesting some vegetables in the first couple of months, the allotment bug bites, and you get addicted. It also gives you something to show your family and friends and it really does convince you of how good an allotment is! Unfortunately, there will be naysayers, and these can sap your enthusiasm. In the next pages, you will learn what to expect from your allotment, how to design your plot and how to manage an overgrown plot without it becoming too overwhelming.

It does not matter what time of year you take on a plot, you can still make it productive relatively rapidly, even if you work full-time or have children, providing you take the right steps. Having a plan is the first step and vital so you make the best use of your time on site and get maximum return for the hours you spend there.

Assessing Your Plot

The first thing you need to do is to look at your plot and determine what you are facing. If you are very fortunate, your plot will be ploughed and new, though this is very rare. It is much more likely that you will be facing a weed infested jungle filled with who knows what rubbish! Be careful exploring your new plot as you do not know what trip hazards or dangers are lurking beneath the weeds (seriously, I have fallen over hidden objects on an overgrown allotment and know people who have stood on rusty nails buried under weeds!).

My new allotment with shoulder deep weeds.

So, before you start digging, look around your plot and determine what is there. Are there any raised beds? Where are the structures located? What items are located on your plot and what rubbish has been left by the previous tenant? Is any of the rubbish usable by you or any other plot holders? The fun part comes from looking to see what plants are already growing on your plot, apart from weeds. There will be something left by the previous owner, though what it is will depend on the time of year you are taking on your allotment.

Look out for currant bushes, blackberries and raspberries. The latter two are pretty easy to identify at any time of year, though currant bushes are harder to identify until they have flowered and are producing fruit. Look out for rhubarb too as most people will have some of this on their plot. If you are taking over in winter, then this may have died back, though you should be able to still see the crowns poking up above the soil. You are likely to find a strawberry bed too, though it may be in poor condition. Sometimes there will be other vegetables that the plot holder planted before they gave up, it depends on how long ago they gave up and why.

I found these raised beds when I tripped over them in the weeds.

Once you have had a good look around, I recommend measuring your plot so you can draw a plan of it out on paper as this will help you a lot with creating a plan of action. Make sure you measure any structures too so they can be included.

Take stock of what is there and what you will need to clear away. On my current plot, I was lucky enough to find raspberries, blackberries, redcurrants, a ridiculous number of potatoes, a cherry tree, some sad strawberry plants and a well-established asparagus bed. There was a dilapidated greenhouse and shed, and more rubbish than you'd believe … there was eight pairs of wellington boots in the greenhouse providing the local spider population with homes, a first aid kit dating from the late 1990's, rat poison and six wheelbarrows in various states of disrepair! It took me four trips to the tip to empty the greenhouse, and I have a large, seven seater car! The shed was another story involving giant spiders, wasps and several mouse nests lurking in debris left in the bottom of the shed. Let's not mention the bags of rubbish, the rotten cardboard and so much more. I have given away a lot of the items left on my plot to other plot holders who had a use for them and made over thirty separate trips to the tip with rubbish in the first year.

Burning and clearing rubbish.

Few allotments have the facilities to dispose of rubbish due to the costs and time involved, i.e., the council charge for rubbish removal and someone has to be present to give the council access to remove the rubbish. What you cannot burn, you will have to take to the tip or take home and dispose of yourself. (Check your allotment regulations for rules concerning fires – they do vary considerably). Of course, if you have not got a car, disposing of rubbish can be tricky, but you can hire a man with a van to take the rubbish to the tip for you if necessary.

It depends on who owned your plot before you as to how much there is for you to get rid of. My current plot had a lot of rubbish on it and a greenhouse full of logs as the previous owner was drying them for his log burner at home. Fortunately, another plot holder wanted the logs as they had a wood fired stove in their shed, but all the rubbish had to go to the tip. I have kept anything I think could be useful and given many items away to other plot holders that I am not going to use, but it certainly gave me a challenge clearing all of that away! A lot of the 'rubbish' left on my plot were things that I would not personally use, but other plot holders have made good use of it! I have made several new friends and got to know people from giving them items from my plot that I have no use for, which is much better than taking them to the tip.

Once you have assessed your plot, then it is time for the next step.

If you are very lucky, your new plot will look like this!

Creating An Action Plan

An action plan is essential to get your plot under control. Not everyone can spend several weeks working their plot all day long to tame it, so a plan helps you focus your efforts for maximum results. The more you can achieve with less effort, the better! My entire plot has been set up to minimise the amount of time I spend digging and maximise the amount of time I have for the fun stuff like planting, harvesting and sitting in the sun enjoying the peace and quiet!

What is it you want to achieve from your plot? Are you planning on growing vegetables, fruits or flowers? Would you prefer raised beds or to just grow in the ground? Are you going no-dig or planning to dig? This book will explain all the different aspects and options for your allotment, so if you are not sure, finish reading this book first before making your action plan, but the next few sections will give you some ideas on what to do first and where to start. Everyone approaches their allotment in a different way, and if you are new to growing vegetables, you will learn many of the possible options as you read on.

Before you take a trip to your allotment, think about what it is you want to achieve when you get there. Whenever I visit my allotment, I always have some goals in mind of what I am going to achieve. I will clear this area, move that tree, fill those beds, harvest those beds and so on. I found that if I went without a plan, I would spend far too much time pottering around and then leave without really achieving much. Any planned work always starts with some weeding. I spend the first 20-30 minutes (or less) removing any weeds that have invaded my beds. Keeping them down like this stops the weeds from becoming unmanageable and helps keep your plants healthy and pest free. Leave the weeds and they quickly become overwhelming. There is nothing more motivating then spending hours clearing an area to find it full of weeds a couple of weeks later. A quick weed on every visit stops the weeds from taking over and reduces the time you have to spend pulling these invading menaces up.

On top of this, though, you need a long-term plan and to know how you are going to develop your plot over the coming years. Hopefully, you have measured your plot and drawn it out on a piece of paper. Do not worry if your artistic talents are limited, mine certainly are, this is just a rough plan to help you determine what is going to be planted where. It is better to do this right at the start as you do not want to be putting sheds or raised beds in place and then decide you have to move them as you prefer them elsewhere. There are a number of online tools that you can use to plan your plot if you prefer, but I like old fashioned pen and paper as it is easier to make changes and do it quickly, plus you can easily see the whole thing at once.

Draw out a large rectangle which is roughly to scale for the size of your plot, use squared paper if you have any as you can assign easy square a size, e.g. one metre or half a metre, so you can draw a scale model. Having your diagram to scale helps a lot because you know if everything is going to fit rather than just guessing if you are not working to scale.

Next, draw any permanent structures such as greenhouses or sheds on to your plan in roughly the right location and any permanent beds that are already established such as asparagus, rhubarb, raspberry and so on. After this, you can draw in any beds that will be permanent for perennial plants such as trees, currants, asparagus, strawberries, rhubarb, raspberries, blackberries and so on. If you are putting in any more structures, draw these on to your plan too. Once you have determined where these will be, then the rest of the space is allocated to annual plants that you will grow each year.

Draw out beds for the plants based on how much space the plants you want to grow in them need. Personally, I tend to make all the beds roughly the same size, usually 4x6 feet or 4x8 feet as that is a manageable size where you can reach the whole bed without standing on your plants. If you are planting in rows, then leave sufficient space between rows so you can get between fully grown plants (this looks odd when the plants are young as there is masses of space available, but you will be grateful for it as the plants mature). Remember to factor in space for paths so you can get around your plot without damaging plants. Paths need to be wide enough to accommodate a fully loaded wheelbarrow (assuming you own one) and take into consideration plants dangling over the edge of the beds or rows. We will discuss raised beds versus marking out beds on the ground in a later chapter.

When the growing areas have been marked out on your plan, then you can start to decide what you are planting where. This will depend on the time of year as in autumn you are much more limited in what you can plant, but you can certainly prepare for the spring. If you are starting in winter, then you can prepare your beds for spring so that next year's crop has a good head start with healthy, well-maintained soil. However, as you will learn, there is something that can be planted at almost any time of the year.

Take some time here to sketch out a plan for your plot. Once you are happy with your plan, then you can start work and planting. However, you can still be clearing weeds or rubbish and generally tidying up your plot while you are creating your plan. I would not recommend building structures or beds unless you have got a plan in mind as you don't want to have to redo your work later on when you decide something is in the wrong place! Sheds and greenhouses often have permanent bases, and these can be extremely difficult to move, so planning is essential.

The first thing on your plan is to decide where your compost piles will go as you are going to generate a lot of weeds to compost initially. These are going to be the first thing you use and moving compost piles around is messy, difficult work. Put them somewhere out of the way in an area which is not going to be very good for growing. Mine is located by the perimeter fence, under the trees that line the fence which is not somewhere I would have planted anything anyway due to the shed, invasive weeds and the shade from the trees. Get this built first because then you have somewhere to put the weeds as you are clearing your plot. I made the mistake on my first plot of piling the weeds up as I was clearing them and found I was forever moving these piles around as they were getting in my way. Once I had built some compost heaps, they were put out of the way and my work reduced.

Tackling An Overgrown Plot

Most of the time, you are going to be taking over a plot that has been neglected and is covered in weeds. If you are lucky, then it will only be knee deep in weeds, though I've taken on plots that have been six-foot-deep in weeds (seriously, I could lose myself in them). These plots are a challenge, but unfortunately, they have been neglected which is why you have been assigned it. Only if you are extremely lucky or taking a plot on a brand new site will you find your plot even vaguely dug over. Some allotment sites will at least strim the weeds down before you start, but they are the exception rather than the rule and you are lucky if they do.

A before and after picture – worth taking so you can see what you have done!

It is daunting when you take on a plot like this and very off-putting. I have seen people take on an overgrown plot, battle valiantly against the weeds for a couple of weeks and then give up. However, if you persist, then you will end up with a lovely plot that is your own.

When you dig the soil and turn it over, you are exposing any weed seeds that are dormant under the ground to the air and light so they will burst into life and start growing. So many people will cheerfully dig over their plot, come back a few days later and find it covered in weeds where these dormant seeds have sprung up. This is a common mistake people make when starting out with their allotment, but don't worry, you can avoid this problem!

With your new plot, start by cutting or strimming the weeds down to close to ground level. Remove all the debris and put it in your compost heap, burn them when they have dried, or bag them up and take them to the tip. Now the weeds are down at ground level, cover your plot with good quality, black plastic weed membrane or plastic tarpaulins. You may be tempted to use carpet, but don't! Many allotment sites have banned the use of carpets as older carpets will leach harmful chemicals into the soil. More importantly than this is that after a couple of months on the ground, the carpets start to rot, weeds grow through them and they break down. They then become incredibly difficult to remove and are very, very messy. I inherited a site where someone had used carpets and they were disgusting to move and dispose of. I had to take them down to the tip and then get my car valeted afterwards as it was such as mess!

Carpets and weeds inherited on this allotment.

If you have time, before you cover an area, dig out any perennial weed roots such as dock, dandelion, comfrey, wild blackberry, and so on. This will stop these from growing back as comfrey will continue to grow, even when covered. The long tap roots will often continue to grow deeper plus they can become brittle and break, which is a problem. It also means that if the leaves die off when covered, you are not then struggling to find the roots when you start to clear that area. Use your fork to remove the roots, being careful to get all of the root out. If they break, then new plants will grow from each piece, so it is important you get them out as whole as possible. Be patient and dig down as far as you can. If you have not got time to do this now, then cut them down to ground level and deal with them when you work each area.

Now start clearing an area at a time. Remove the weed membrane, then dig out all the weeds and once you have finished, put the weed membrane back to cover the soil. This allows you to get control of the weeds, so you don't need to continually go back and re-dig areas you have cleared. Leave your allotment covered until you are ready to plant an area, then remove the weed membrane, dig up any new weeds and plant it. I keep any area of my allotment that is not actively growing covered. This means that when it does come to planting, I just have to remove the cover and start planting rather than spend hours digging. To me, this is a very efficient way to run your allotment as you are spending less time digging and more time doing the fun stuff like planting.

An area partially cleared, weed membrane down and raised beds in place.

You may be tempted to use a rotavator on your plot, which is a great way to turn the soil, particularly if it hasn't been worked for some time. Before you do, remove all perennial weed roots otherwise all the rotavator does is chop the weed roots up and distribute them around your allotment where they grow into new plants. After rotavating your plot, make sure you cover it to prevent the weeds growing back.

If you know you are not going to work an area for a while, then you can suppress the weeds even more. Put a layer of cardboard down on the ground, having removed any sticky tape or plastic labels. Then cover it with four to six inches of manure and cover the manure with your weed membrane or tarpaulin. This helps to keep the weeds down, but the manure then breaks down and feeds the soil. If you have a heavy clay soil, digging in some manure before covering it will help a lot in improving the soil condition.

Organic or Non-Organic?

This is an ongoing debate amongst gardeners, and everyone has their own opinion on the matter. Many people are very militant about their decisions here, but I want to present you with both sides of the argument so you can make up your mind whether you are going to be an organic gardener, a non-organic gardener, or somewhere in between.

Organic gardeners will not use chemicals on their plots. This means that they do not buy chemical weed killers and will often by certified organic seeds. This is a great concept, but you have to remember that when it rains on your allotment, the rain brings down chemicals into the soil. Your neighbouring plot holders are likely not fully organic, so they will be using chemicals which may leach or blow on to your site.

Organic gardening is a great concept, but finding organic seeds and plants is difficult and expensive, plus you are very limited in the varieties you can grow. I don't buy organic seeds as I refuse to pay the premium, but I do grow my plants organically, which is in my mind a happy compromise. By buying regular seeds, I can get the varieties that I want, rather than having to make do with the few organic varieties I could buy.

This is something that you must make your mind up on what you want to do. If you are facing a seriously overgrown plot, then you may be tempted to get it under control with weed killer rather than digging. There is no right or wrong answer to whether you should be organic or non-organic, it is something you have decide based on your personal beliefs and opinions.

My approach is to use a mostly organic philosophy, which works for me, fitting my budget and time constraints. I work organically on my allotment, I don't use chemical pesticides or weed killers, preferring to use natural methods instead. If there was a serious outbreak of pests, then I would consider the use of chemicals if organic methods failed. I don't buy organic plants or seeds, but I grow my plants organically and then save the seeds to plant the following year. I recycle and re-use as much as I can and opt to use plastic that I can use year after year, so I buy hard seed trays rather than flimsy ones which don't last for long.

Growing organically is a great philosophy, but when you've got four kids, a full-time job and an allotment covered in weeds, the temptation to use chemicals is strong. Most chemical weed killers will now biodegrade in the soil, but they are still chemicals. I have heard of many allotment owners who have treated their plots with chemicals and then been unable to grow anything for months afterwards.

Ultimately, you need to work your allotment in a way that your conscience is happy with, whatever that might be. I don't recommend getting into a debate with any other plot holder about organic growing methods as it usually results in conflict as everyone has their own opinion on the matter. Decide how you are going to work your plot and stick to that.

Allotment Health And Safety

Health and safety on an allotment is common sense, but you need to make sure that your plot is safe for anyone that is walking past it. If you have children, then you need to be especially careful to ensure your plot is child safe. For example, on one allotment site I visited, I saw an enterprising plot holder had built a fence out of pallets, which was a great idea. Unfortunately, they had removed some pieces of woods and left nails sticking out facing the path. Anyone walking down the path too close to the fence would catch themselves on the nails.

Make sure you are not creating trip hazards on your site as you could damage yourself on them very easily while carrying something. My current allotment had parts of it covered in black plastic, and it was only after I almost fell that I realised the previous plot holder had put the plastic over bricks and pieces of wood! Avoid leaving tools on the ground as they are easy to trip over too. Never leave knives out, always close them up or put them away after use. Be careful of your fingers when using knives or secateurs as it hurts a lot when you try to cut the end of your finger off with your secateurs (yes, I've done that too).

Use toughened glass in your greenhouse as normal glass will break very easily and hurt you a lot if you accidentally put your hand through it. And before you ask, there are regular cases of people who have tripped and fallen into their greenhouse glass or otherwise hurt themselves on it.

I would recommend wearing safety boots at your allotment as it is very easy to drop something on your toes or accidentally stab your feet with your fork, which I did today coincidentally! I have a pair of cheap, steel toe capped boots for my allotment as I have dropped heavy items several times on my feet before I learned. People regularly post pictures of their injuries in Facebook groups and often these could have been avoided by wearing a decent pair of shoes. While wearing sandals or crocs may be nice in the summer, they provide no protection against stray nails, your garden fork, nettles or a wide variety of other hazards.

Allotment owners commonly use manure on their soil. Although it is generally safe and okay to use, it is excrement and can carry diseases such as ringworm. When working with manure, always wear gloves, take care to protect your eyes and always thoroughly wash your hands when you have finished. Do not put your hands in your mouth or near your eyes or nose when you have been handling manure just to be on the safe side. I have a pump action bottle of anti-bacterial gel on my plot that can be used on dry hands. This is used when I have been working with manure and always used before I eat anything.

Apply some common sense when working on your allotment and take good care of yourself. You do not want to injure yourself and then be unable to work your plot, so be very careful as they are potentially quite dangerous places! Every year, hundreds of allotment owners injure themselves, ranging from bruises or minor cuts to serious injuries and broken bones. Take good care of yourself when on your plot so you don't become another statistic!

Allotment Security

Security on allotments is a serious problem as many vandals see them as an easy target. People often leave tools and valuable equipment in their sheds, which are often either not locked or are very easy to break on. Security starts with the site, having a secure main gate and usually a surrounding fence that is hard to climb. However, security is the responsibility of each plot holder.

It is your job to ensure the gate is kept shut and locked. If you find it open when you arrive on site, shut and lock it and report it to the allotment management as that is a major security breach. Always shut and lock the gates when you enter or leave the site. If you have communal buildings that you use, lock them when you finish using them.

Padlocks, oddly enough, can encourage thieves as they think there is something valuable inside.

But security also comes down to your personal items on your plot. Do not leave tools laying around on your plot; always put them away when you leave the site. Do not leave anything valuable in your shed, even if it is locked. At the end of the day, it's a flimsy wooden door in most cases secured with a single padlock which wouldn't make a potential thief blink twice. The only items I leave at my allotment are items that, if they were stolen, I wouldn't be too upset about. Nothing valuable is left there as you are, sadly, not only facing external thieves, but sometimes other plot holders decide to 'borrow' items you have left on your plot.

You can get shed alarms, decent padlocks and special insurance for items left at the allotment, but at the end of a day, a determined thief will get in anyway. Often, having a padlock on your shed is advertising that there is something of value in there, so you just cannot win! A shed is a flimsy structure and even padlocked is easy to get into. I advise everyone to store valuables at home or on other secure storage on site and take out insurance for anything particularly valuable, though remember to take into account any excess payable on the policy.

If you post videos or pictures publicly, make sure that you do not identify the allotment site that you are working on so that you do not inadvertently show criminals valuable items on your site and tell them where to find them! There have been several break ins that happened after a plot holder posted YouTube videos of them using a rotavator which they showed was stored in their shed.

Should you encounter a break in, then you must immediately inform the allotment management who will then inform the police? It is important that you do not touch or move anything as it is a crime scene and the police may want to look for evidence, though unless there is CCTV evidence or blood, they are unlikely to do much. Sadly, the chances of catching the perpetrators are minimal, but they will at least try. If valuable items have been taken, then post on local Facebook groups and keep an eye on local selling sites as thieves will often try to get rid of items on there. If you do leave valuable items such as rotavators on your plot, take pictures of them and make sure they can be uniquely identified so that should the worst happen, you can prove anything recovered is yours. It may be worth taking out special insurance for any valuable items you are leaving there, just in case the worst does happen.

If break ins are a regular problem, look at buying trail cameras for your site. These are battery operated cameras used to take pictures of animals in the wild, so they start recording when they detect movement. These can get pictures of the thieves which is valuable evidence for the police. These are not expensive, but they will help you catch anyone who is breaking into your site.

Clearing The Rubbish

Established allotments can often have all sorts of potential hazards on them, left by previous owners and dating back decades! It is rare to get a greenfield site that is beautiful and clean, so usually you are left clearing the previous tenant's rubbish.

Depending on the state of the allotment, you can often negotiate a discount on the first year's rent, sometimes getting it for free if the allotment is in a really bad state. However, this does depend on the committee or council and is not a given. Some sites are happy a neglected plot is being taken over, so will offer you this whereas others give you no leeway at all.

Your new allotment could contain a wide variety of rubbish and debris left by the previous owner. The worst is old carpet, half buried in soil and weeds, but there is often some potentially hazardous waste left on allotments. When clearing the greenhouse on my current plot, I found bags and boxes of blue rice. It was only after asking another plot holder that I found out it was rat poison, so needed handling carefully. Unfortunately, you have no idea what the previous plot holder has left you, so be careful when sorting through what you have inherited as there could be all sorts of unpleasant surprises waiting for you.

Some rubbish carefully stored in the shed.

There is often broken glass on an allotment, usually left over from broken greenhouse panes. These need to be carefully removed and disposed of as it is quite easy to inadvertently cut yourself while clearing weeds or digging. I would recommend cutting high weeds down so you can see what is on your allotment. I have found metal pipes buried by weeds and raised beds, all of which I have tripped over whilst walking around a weedy allotment.

Potentially the most hazardous waste you will find on an allotment is asbestos. Prior to the 1970's, asbestos sheeting was popular as a roofing material and often used in walls of garages and sheds. As allotments recycle old material and often have items decades old left on it, you can find buildings made with asbestos panels or even broken pieces of asbestos left on the plot.

Asbestos sheets are not harmfully providing they are whole and not damaged. Once they are damaged or broken, the fibres can become airborne where they become potentially hazardous. There are extremely strict handling regulations for asbestos and even stricter rules for disposal.

If you find asbestos on your allotment, then your first port of call is the allotment management, whether this is the council or the committee. They will be able to advise you on how to proceed. The council are likely to send a disposal team out to get rid of it, but on privately managed sites it is at their discretion. The committee may or may not pay for disposal or ask you to do so. If you are unhappy about the presence of asbestos on your plot, then you can ask to move plot, but you may have to wait until one is free. I would recommend checking a plot for asbestos before accepting it and if you can see any, discuss disposal then and there.

Clearing away rubbish from an allotment can be a time consuming job. It is made even harder if you do not drive and cannot get to the council tip. Some rubbish can be burnt, depending on your site rules, but much of it needs disposing of properly.

Some allotment sites regularly have skips delivered which you can use, otherwise disposing of the rubbish is a problem. If you cannot take it to the council recycling center, then I recommend piling it all up until you have cleared the plot and then hiring a man with a van to take the rubbish away. You can find someone on your local Facebook selling page that will do this for you at a reasonable price.

Clearing the rubbish from an allotment can take a lot of time. On my current plot, I have made somewhere between 30-40 runs to the local recycling center in a very large car, and do not have much more to get rid of now. Unfortunately, when you inherit an allotment, you inherit the bad with the good, so while you may get a greenhouse, shed, wheelbarrow and tools, you also get all the previous plot holders accumulated rubbish.

Designate an area of your allotment the 'rubbish tip'. Put down some weed membrane so the rubbish does not get into the soil, then pile up the rubbish in this area. Be quite brutal sorting it all out as there are likely a lot of items that you may want to use in the future but, in all likelihood, are never going to get around to using. Offer re-usable items to other plot holders as they can make use of things left on your plot. Half my greenhouse was filled with dry logs that the previous plot holder had kept for his log burner at home. A couple of plot holders have log burners in their sheds, so I offered them the logs and they came and took them away. Quite a lot of the odds and ends on my plot that I was never going to use have been used by other plot holders. It has been a great way to get the 'rubbish' off my plot but also a great way to meet other plot holders and build a positive relationship with them.

Just some of the rubbish found on my plot when I took it over.

Often you do not realise what is on your plot until you start working it, but if it is in a really bad state, then talk to the allotment management. They may be able to help you clear it or offer you a discount on your rent for the first year while you clear it. This is one of the 'joys' of owning an allotment and one of those things that you are unlikely to avoid on an established site.

Overcoming Weeds – The Perennial Problem

Weeds are going to be one of the biggest problems you will face on your allotment. No matter how hard you try, you will never get rid of them and will always need to pull them up. They grow anywhere and everywhere, even in the tiniest patch of soil and will continually crop up through the year. According to gardening folklore, "One year's seed is seven year's weed" meaning that weed seeds can last up to seven years in the ground! This translates as you are playing a long game and will be tackling weeds for years! However, according to research, some weeds can stay viable in the soil for up to twenty years!

Perennial weeds are much harder to get rid of as they entrench themselves in the ground and many such as dock, dandelion and comfrey are more than happy to grow back from the tiniest piece of root left in the ground. To make it even more frustrating, comfrey roots are very fragile and will snap as you try to remove them, making it almost impossible to eradicate this plant with significant excavation work!

It might be hard work, but the results are really worth it.

Bindweed, couch grass, mare's tale, nettles, and wild blackberries are an even bigger problem because they grow by sending out runners under the ground which them pop up all over the place. Autumn fruiting raspberries fall into the same category in my opinion as they grow in the same way and are very invasive. All members of the mint family are similarly invasive and should never be planted directly in the ground because they will take over your plot.

You are going to spend a lot of time weeding, even if you plant through weed membrane, weeds will still appear in clumps of soil blown onto the plastic or around the base of your plants. My opinion on weeding is perhaps slightly controversial in that I think it is okay to have a few weeds! I am not going to spend hours every day obsessing over every, tiny little weed and trying to remove them all. If I did that, I would never get anything else done! I remove weeds from between my plants carefully, so my plants are not competing for resources, but generally, I clear them as and when I need to, which is not too often due to a cunning technique!

My best friend at the allotment is my hoe. For me, it is the most essential tool I have because I use it two or three times a week on open soil to knock the heads off the weeds. The weeds then die and never get a chance to establish themselves, with the roots dying in the soil and the leaves composting themselves. I often get asked how I keep my plot so tidy, and the secret is the hoe. I will, very carefully, use it around my plants, but when it comes to weeds that are too close to my plants, they are removed by hand. This works well for pretty much every weed except bindweed and mare's tail, even working against young docks and dandelions.

An unattended allotment, ready for someone to take it on.

Any areas of your allotment that you are not working on should be covered with a high quality weed membrane. Do not use the flimsy fabric membrane as this, although cheap, does little to prevent weeds. Buy a good quality weed membrane because you will get years of use out of it and it works! Weeding, like digging, is one of my pet hates, so I make sure any area that is not actively growing is covered to stop the weeds coming through. This works fantastically, and I seem to spend a lot less time than my allotment neighbours weeding my plot. Sadly, both mare's tail and bindweed will continue to grow under this but is relatively easy to remove when you uncover the ground.

If you keep on top of the weeds, then the weeds will not get on top of your plot. A few minutes spent weeding on every visit will save an awful lot of work in the long term. Take a few minutes every visit to remove weeds from around your plants, particularly garlic and onions which hate competition, and to hoe any open ground. This keeps the weeds under control and makes your allotment much more manageable.

Common Weeds and How to Tackle Them

There are many weeds found on an allotment and most of these are easy to remove and cause very little problems other than making your neat rows of vegetables look untidy. However, there are some that are much more of a problem.

Keeping on top of the weeds is an important part of owning an allotment. Regular hoeing and using mulch or other weed suppressants will help to keep the weeds under control. Avoid the use of herbicides unless absolutely necessary as some of the stronger ones will stop anything growing for a year or more and cause a lot of harm to the environment. They can also blow onto neighbouring plots and damage other people's plants too.

These are some of the most commonly found, hard to get rid of weeds together with some tips and advice on how to deal with them. For more information about a wider range of weeds and their uses, including how they can be eaten, see my book, "A Gardener's Guide To Weeds".

Horse Tail

Often referred to as mare's tail, this is commonly found on allotments and the bad news is that it is almost impossible to get rid of. Having outlived the dinosaurs, being over 300 million years old, it has mastered surviving just about anything. It is resistant to almost all chemicals and grows deep, winding roots that are you can never manage to dig all of them up. It grows back from any pieces of root left in the ground, making it extremely resistant to your attempts to get rid of it. The plant continues to grow even when covered with black plastic or cardboard.

Horse tail spreads by spores, released in early to mid-spring. Removing early growth will help to get rid of this plant. It commonly makes its way onto allotments in manure where the spores or pieces of root lurk, waiting for their time to grow.

Unfortunately, getting rid of this plant is not going to happen overnight. The only way to get rid of it is to pull it up, together with as much root as possible whenever you see any on your plot. As the plant relies on photosynthesis for energy, sooner or later (though in this case much later), the plant dies when it cannot produce enough energy to continue growing. It is a two to four-year project to get horse tail under control, but it can be done.

Horsetail, the bane of my life.

Although there are weedkillers that will kill this plant, they are generally extremely toxic and can prevent any other plants (including your vegetables) growing in the same area for a year or two. Often, they require injecting into the plant and the effective chemicals are amongst the most toxic on the market. If you have horse tail on your plot, do not rotavate the ground as it will cut the roots up, spread them every and cause the plant to grow even more vigorously.

As horse tail is a very invasive plant it is not recommended to add it to your compost pile unless you are running a hot compost bin. Interestingly, horse tail does have a herbal use, being high in silica, and the above ground growth can be used to make a silica rich liquid feed using the same method as for nettle tea.

Bindweed

Although the flowers of bindweed are very pretty, this is an invasive weed that grows from long, underground roots that spread far and wide. It is often found growing in hedgerows and its large, white flowers are a well-known sight.

The downside of bindweed is that it will strangle your crops. It grows very quickly and climbs up your vegetables, crowding them out so they struggle to get enough light.

This weed will continue to grow under cover, though it does not produce leaves or flowers, just more root. It does respond to weedkiller, but as the roots are so long, it can be difficult for the chemicals to kill the entire plant.

The best way to deal with this weed is to dig out all of the root every time you see it. Bindweed will grow back from any piece of root left in the soil, so be patient and dig out as much of it as you can.

Bindweed has pretty flowers but is very hard to get rid of.

Dock

Another common weed, traditionally used to treat nettle stings, this is often seen on allotments. It grows quite tall and produces seed heads in the summer, which the wind will blow all over the place.

Dock produces a long tap root that will grow two or three feet long. Once established, it is extremely hard to get rid of as the main tap root branches out. If the root breaks, a new plant will grow back from it, so you have to get all of the root out at once. This plant is best dealt with by treating it as soon as you see it.

If you are unable to dig dock out before it seeds, cut the top of the plant off and dispose of the seed heads before they can spread.

As dock is a very invasive plant it is not recommended to add the roots to your compost pile unless you are running a hot compost bin.

Dock has deep roots and is hard to dig up when established.

Dandelion

While dandelion is an annoying, perennial weed, it is also an incredibly valuable plant. The young leaves can be eaten in a salad, the root is used as a coffee substitute and to make beer and the flowers are a vital, early source of food for the local bee population.

These will pop up all over your allotment and, like dock, grow with a long tap root that can grow one or two feet long. It is best to hoe or pull up this weed while the plant is young as it will grow back from any piece of root left in the soil.

Dandelions - invasive but vital food source for bees.

Dandelions can be killed with a weed burner or by putting salt in the middle of the plant where the root is, though be careful you do not poison the soil with too much salt.

As dandelion is a very invasive plant it is not recommended to add the roots to your compost pile unless you are running a hot compost bin.

Buttercup

This is a very annoying weed that creeps across the ground and ends up making your vegetable garden look very until, but in reality, it is just a single weed.

Although the roots are not deep, they are tough to get out as the plant hangs on tightly to the soil. Dig out the entire root and compost this plant.

Buttercup - pretty flowers, but covers a lot of ground.

Brambles

These grow from underground runners and commonly creep in from outside of the allotments and quickly establish themselves. You may appreciate the blackberries, but wild brambles are covered in thorns and produce tiny fruit, so it is much better to plant a thornless, cultivated variety that produces larger, tastier fruit.

The roots go quite deep and are hard to remove, with new shoots being sent up from roots left in the ground. Your best bet is to dig out as much as you can and then pull up any new shoots that appear.

Bramble - hard to get rid of and very thorny.

The young, green growth can be composted, but the older, brown growth and the roots should be burnt or otherwise disposed of.

Nettles

We are all familiar with nettles and they are a common sight on allotments, growing in neglected areas. The leaves are very high in iron and can be used to make a healthy tea you can drink or used to make beer. Young leaves can be eaten like spinach (hot water/cooking gets rid of the sting in case you were wondering) and the leaves can also be used to make an excellent plant food.

Nettles spread via an underground web of roots which are quite difficult to get rid of as they are quite pervasive.

Dig up as much of the root as you can, then compost the green growth and dispose of the roots. Nettles are an important plant for insects and wildlife, with many gardeners growing some in a corner of their garden. If you decide to cultivate nettles, remove the seeds before they can spread to keep this plant constrained to one area.

Nettles, great for wildlife, but spread rapidly.

Couch Grass

Another common problem for gardener's, couch grass appears like normal grass on the surface, but spreads via a network of underground roots. It will grow back from any piece of root left in the ground, so it is important you remove all of the roots, which is a tiresome, back-breaking job.

Because this weed is so invasive, you should dispose of it rather than compost it. A hot compost bin will break down the roots.

Giant Hogweed

Not commonly seen on an allotment, this is another weed you have to be very careful of. It grows very tall and looks similar to parsnip or carrot when flowering. However, the sap or even brushing against this plant can cause an extremely allergic reaction resulting in large blisters on the skin.

If you find this on your allotment, report it immediately to the council/allotment committee who will advise you on how to treat it.

Giant hogweed - a very dangerous plant.

If you are going to dig this up, make sure you wear protective clothing and remove all of the roots. It is best bagged up and disposed of or burnt.

Japanese Knotweed

This is another very dangerous weed that sometimes appears on allotments. It is virtually impossible to get rid of once established. If you find this on your plot or in your garden, then you must inform the council/allotment committee immediately and take the recommended action. It does not respond to weedkiller and cannot be taken to council tips. If it is growing in your garden at home, then it can affect your ability to sell your home as it many lenders will not give a mortgage on a property with Japanese Knotweed growing in it.

Comfrey

This weed is a common sight on allotments as many people cultivate it for the popular plant feed, comfrey tea. It is a beautiful plant that is much loved by bees, but it is incredibly invasive. The roots grow long and deep but are also very brittle. If the roots break in the soil when you are trying to remove it, which they invariably do, then new plants will grow from these pieces or root. I have dug out comfrey plants with three feet long roots, so try to tackle this weed as soon as you see it.

It is not very responsive to weedkiller and the roots should never be composted. The leaves and stalks can be composted safely.

Comfrey has long, deep roots that are hard to get out.

If you want to grow comfrey for comfrey tea, then buy a non-invasive cultivar such as Bocking 14 which does not spread.

Using a Weed Burner

Weed burners are very useful at an allotment, though they are not a cure-all solution for weeds. A wand weed burner or a hand-held device (like a Crème brûlée torch) is very helpful, but you need to be careful as many things on your allotment are flammable! Raised beds, sheds, weed membrane, dried leaves, wood chip can all be set alight very easily with a weed burner if you are not careful.

The best way to use one is for dealing with weeds in hard to get to locations where you cannot weed them by hand. I have both a wand and a hand-held weed burner which I regularly use. They are great for removing weeds that are on paving stones or coming up from under raised beds, my shed or greenhouse. Where a dandelion or dock as escaped your attention and established itself, they are great for burning out the middle of the root and killing the weed off so it cannot grow back.

However, for weeds on open ground or near flammable materials, they are not so good. The smaller, hand-held weed burners are also very useful for sealing the edges of plastic weed membrane to prevent it from fraying.

Home-Made Weedkiller Recipes

Although you can buy weedkiller in the stores, this tends to be full of chemicals and very bad not only for the environment, but potentially for your health too. It is possible to make some herbicides at home that are natural and will kill off weeds. Be aware that these are non-selective and will kill any plants they come in contact with, including your vegetable plants. Always apply these on a dry day when there is no wind so the weedkiller does not blow on to other plants or neighbouring plots. Be careful when using these around the edges of raised beds as they can harm plants growing in the beds. Use a pump action sprayer so you can get the best coverage of the plants and hold it close to the plants you are spraying to direct it as best you can.

Vinegar

Vinegar is a great weedkiller, but is non-selective, so will damage anything it touches. It is not good on perennial weeds as it does not kill tap roots but will burn the foliage. It is effective against other weeds. Ensure you buy vinegar that is at least 5% acetic acid as weaker vinegars are not good weedkillers.

As vinegar is acidic, it can adjust the pH level of your soil if used in excess and stop plants from growing properly in the future. It is a good weedkiller to use on gravel or paving where you are not planning on growing anything.

Add vinegar to a spray and spray liberally on the leaves and stem of the weeds you want to kill.

Salt

Salt is a very effective weedkiller, but it can cause a lot of damage to the ground. In medieval times, traitors had their land salted to prevent anything from growing there for many years. Be careful using salt on areas you are planning on growing plants in and do not use on lawns. Salt is best on paving and gravel where you have no plans to grow anything.

Dilute three parts salt with one-part water and stir well. Leave for ten minutes to ensure the salt is fully dissolved and then spray the weeds. For dandelions that are growing in places where you cannot get the root out, remove the leaves and put a large pinch of salt in the middle of the tap root. This will cause the root to die and stop the dandelion from growing back.

Newspaper/Cardboard

This is a weed suppressant rather than weedkiller and will smother weaker weeds. It is not effective against weeds such as comfrey, bindweed or horse tail. Lay several sheets of newspaper or a couple of layers of cardboard, depending on how thick it is and weigh it down to stop it blowing away (you can use a thick layer of mulch). The paper will rot down and kill the weeds by starving them of sunlight. It will also prevent many weeds from germinating by keeping the light off them.

When you are clearing an allotment, this is a great way to keep the weeds down on areas that you have worked. It prevents the weeds from coming back and you having to repeatedly dig the same area.

Vinegar and Dish Soap

Mix the two of these together and it is a very effective weedkiller. Add a tablespoon of vegetable oil or liquid dish soap (Fairy or Ecover), mix well and spray on your plants.

If you want a really effective weedkiller, add a cup of salt, though be aware that this will affect the soil and can stop some sensitive plants from growing.

Saving Water On Your Plot

You may be surprised to know that not all allotment sites have access to water. There are some which have taps distributed across the site connected to the domestic water supply, but others have no water at all, so you need to learn to save all the water you can to keep your plants alive during the hotter months.

If you do not have access to water on your site, then you need to become very good at saving and collecting water otherwise you are stuck bringing it from home to your plot, which can be really difficult to bring enough to water all of your plants. Even if you do have access to water, good water management makes sense as it reduces the amount of watering you have to do and preserves a precious resource that your allotment society pays for.

One way to reduce your water requirements is to help your plants establish a strong, deep root system. If larger plants have a shallow root system, it means that they are reliant on surface water, which disappears quickest during hot weather. It also means that they are more susceptible to wind damage as they do not have a strong root system to support their weight. Encourage your plants to drive their roots deeper while they are establishing themselves by watering sparingly early in their lives. Water too much, and the plants will not need to develop a deep root system to get water and so they will end up with a weak root system. Water less, and the plants will still survive, but will drive the roots deeper to look for water. This works great for larger plants or those with deep roots, but this does not work well for shallow rooted plants like onions and strawberries as their root systems will never grow that deep.

Direct Watering

Another good way to preserve water is to put a length of 2" pipe in the ground at the roots of larger plants such as pumpkins or trees. Pour water into the pipe and it will be taken directly to the plant's roots and minimise wastage. Sounds easy, I know, but you will be surprised how few people do this. Make sure you do this early on in the plant's life so that you do not damage the root system when you sink the pipe into the ground.

When watering your plants, instead of using a rose on your watering can, remove it so you are watering with a stream of water. With younger plants you should not do this as you can damage the seedlings, but this works well with plants that are bigger. Water your plants without using the rose and aim the water directly at the base of the plant, pausing regularly if necessary, to allow the ground to soak up the water. This is a great way to minimise run off and waste so that more of the water goes to the roots of your plants.

Mulching

Once your plants have grown large enough, mulch around the base of the plants with four to six inches of well-rotted manure or compost. Do not use fresh manure as this is still composting and will burn your plants as it continues to break down and produce heat. This helps to keep moisture in the soil and reduces evaporation so that your plants need less water. Keep the mulch topped up and then dig it in or leave it on the surface over winter.

Water Butts

These are used for collecting rainwater. They can either collect water from the guttering on your shed or greenhouse or you can leave them in the open to collect rainwater direct. Either raise them up on bricks and put a tap on it, or just dip your watering can into it to get the water out. You can use pipes so that when one water butt is full, the water is transported by a pipe to another one so the first does not overflow.

Keep your water butts covered as this helps to reduce evaporation but, more importantly, stops wildlife falling into them which then pollutes the water. Some water butts come with covers or you can make one out a piece of wood or plastic.

Although you can buy water butts, you can make them from plastic barrels or tanks which you can often get for free from companies that have used whatever they contained. Just be careful if you use one of these that they did not contain any harmful chemicals. It can be very difficult to remove the chemical residue which, depending on what the barrels originally containers, could be toxic and harm your plants. If you are not sure what was in the barrels, then you are best not using them to avoid any potential chemical contamination.

The water butt filling up.

You can often find used water butts on sites such as Gumtree, eBay and Freecycle where they are available for a fraction of their new cost. Sometimes, local councils will run promotions for cheap compost bins or water butts to help reduce waste and conserve water. If these happen, it is worth buying some as they offer excellent value for money.

Weed Membrane

Weed membrane can be used as a mulch for your plants to keep moisture in and reduce evaporation. If you are really concerned about the heat or weeds, then you can cut small holes in the membrane and plant through it, which keeps the weeds down very well. Some people will apply a two or three-inch layer of well-rotted compost and then put the weed membrane on top of it as this feeds your plants and helps to keep moisture in.

Preserving water is very important and the more independent you can make your plants of you, then the less work you will have to do to water them. However, on the hottest days, you will have to water your plants to stop them wilting and drying out. Many plants will drop flowers, fruit and leaves if they dry out in an attempt to survive the drought, so if you want to see a harvest, you really need to keep them well watered.

Raised Beds vs. Growing In The Ground

This is another contentious point among allotment holders and the cause of many a heated debate, but once more, there is no right or wrong answer, it depends entirely on you and what you prefer.

Growing in the ground has a number of benefits, including:

- No cost for materials
- Can plant what you want, where you want
- No need for extra soil or compost to fill the beds
- Quick way to start planting
- No building involved

The disadvantages of growing in the ground include:

- Can be hard to locate beds
- Easy for people (i.e. children) to accidentally walk on plants
- Can be difficult to grow in if the soil is in poor condition, heavy clay or gets waterlogged
- Cannot easily amend an area of soil for plants with specific growing needs
- Crop rotation can be a little inaccurate

The advantages of growing in raised beds include:

- Easy crop management
- No chance of walking on your plants
- Simplifies crop rotation and planning
- Can adjust the soil in each bed so it is ideal for the plants
- Allows you to grow vegetables even if your soil is in poor condition
- Ideal for people with disabilities
- Easy to work as no-dig beds, thereby minimising the amount of digging you need to do
- Allows for denser planting due to soil quality, providing greater yields
- Fewer weeds due to using clean compost and denser planting
- Easy to cover selected beds with fleece or netting to protect vegetables
- Can cover individual beds easily when not in use to prevent weeds from growing

The disadvantages of raised beds include:

- Cost of materials and compost
- Time taken to build the beds (though this is minimised by using pallet collars)
- Not really suitable for trailing vines such as pumpkins, butternut squashes and watermelons or potatoes

Originally, I grew directly in the soil because I thought it was easier. I spent hours digging my plot, struggling with a clay soil and having my children trample my seedlings. Then I moved site and inherited raised beds and it changed my life! Suddenly I could easily get around my beds without damaging any of my plants, planning had got much easier and I was not spending hours digging over the soil.

Raised beds in place with paths between them.

Then when I moved site again, I immediately set about building raised beds as it is so much easier for me to garden. Now, I fill unused beds with manure in the autumn and cover them. When spring comes and everyone is hard at work digging their plot over, I uncover the beds, remove any weeds that have popped up and start planting! It looks lovely and neat and I have well defined paths between the beds. This year I have had huge crops of lettuce, cucumber, radish, beetroot and carrots out of them because I was able to plant more densely than normal. It is so easy to plan what I am planting where and to rotate my crops.

Whether you turn your plot entirely over to raised beds, or just have a few to grow salad vegetables in is entirely up to you. You can start working your plot without raised beds and then put them in as and when you can, or you can stick to growing directly in the soil, which suits many people. I would recommend putting in a few raised beds and comparing the difference between the two to see which you prefer. If you do not have a lot of time and are worried about keeping your plot under control, then I would definitely recommend raised beds. The great thing about them is that if you do not have the time to plant them, you can leave them covered and they still look neat when it comes to plot inspection time!

I will admit to being a raised bed evangelist, but I encourage you to try them and see which growing method you prefer. If you have children, another advantage of raised beds is you can easily assign your children an area where they can plant whatever they want and grow stuff themselves.

Like so much in allotment gardening, there is no right or wrong answer and it is a personal preference. Some people prefer raised beds while other people feel they are a waste of space with all those paths. At the end of the day, work in the way that suits you and your lifestyle. What works for me is not necessarily the best for you, but I always recommend trying new things to see whether they are better or worse than the current way of doing things!

Planting direct in the ground in rows.

The Importance Of A Shed

A shed is a very important piece of equipment at your allotment and I do feel that everyone should have one, though not all allotment sites permit them, and some have restrictions on size. Your shed is your home from home when you are working your plot and is more than just a place to shelter from the rain or store your tools. For many people, a shed becomes an escape from their home with people installing small stoves and wood burners so they can cook lunch and enjoy a cup of tea. I have even seen sheds with armchairs in so the owner can sit back and relax after tending their plants.

Finally, the inside of the shed is clear.

How big a shed you have on your plot will depend on what you inherit, what is permitted and what you can afford. Sheds are not cheap to buy new, but can be picked up cheap enough second hand, though you have to be prepared to dismantle, move and repair it before reassembling it on your plot. You will need to build a proper base for it, using concrete or paving slabs, rather than just putting it on soil, plus you need to fix it to the ground securely, so it does not blow away. And yes, before you ask, I have seen sheds blow away in gales. I do not think the owner was very impressed because the contents of their shed were scattered across several plots and the shed itself did significant damage to a lot of plants before the perimeter fence stopped it.

Keep your shed as well organised as you can. It is very easy to just throw everything in it and before you know it, you cannot get a foot in the door as it is filled with rubbish. Having spent two days clearing the shed at my current plot, I now keep it very tidy. Everything has its place and I have nails and hooks all over the shed to hang tools on. Sadly, the shed is not big enough for a wood-burning stove or any home comforts, but I am planning on replacing it sometime with a larger one.

Sheds are also good for storing onions, garlic, potatoes and other vegetables in over winter, but again, they need to be dry and secure for this to work. A shed in poor repair will let too much moisture in or even rodents who will make short work of your harvest.

Every year, your shed needs to be maintained, so check it over for leaks. Pay particular attention to around the floor and the roof, making repairs where necessary. Regularly painting your shed, if it is wood, with a good quality wood preservative, will help to prolong its life. Yes, it is extra work, but a shed is a serious investment and very useful, so you want to ensure it lasts as long as possible.

It is possible, if you are good with your hands, to build a shed out of discarded wood or other reclaimed items. This is not for everyone, but it is a good way to save money if you are good with tools and have the time. I've seen people build sheds out of pallets and discarded doors taken from a skip and they work well!

When you take on a plot, it may already have a shed. Depending on the site rules, you may have to pay the previous owner for the shed. While this is not too common, it does happen, particularly if the previous owner bought the shed new. However, as most sheds have been there for a long time, usually they are just passed on to the next owner.

Some sheds are built from odds and ends.

If you do not have a shed and would like to have one, then you can invest the money in buying new, or you can buy one second hand from eBay, Gumtree or occasionally for free from FreeCycle. These will vary in condition from good quality to dilapidated wreck that the owners cannot be bothered to dismantle and take to the tip. Shop around and you can find some really good bargains. The best time of year to buy a used shed is usually springtime when people are starting to work on their gardens and realise the shed is in the way. A lot of people move to a new house at this time of year and move into a new property that has a shed in that does not fit with their vision for their new garden. You will be expected to dismantle and remove the shed yourself, so bring a friend and hire a van. Take a selection of tools as there is a good chance the shed is nailed together rather than screwed, so you will have to be careful not to cause any damage when dismantling it. Take lots of pictures and label the sections (use chalk as sticky labels tend to fall off) as this will help you when you come to put it back together again.

Put a padlock on your shed and lock the door after every visit. This will deter the casual thief or pilfering plot holder, but there is nothing you can do to stop the determined thief who has broken into the site. Do not store anything valuable in your shed such as expensive tools or equipment, e.g. petrol strimmers, rotavators and so on. I used to have an old filing cabinet in an old shed where I kept all my small tools and anything else that I could fit in it. This could be separately locked and reduced the opportunities for things to be removed from my shed. Some allotment sites will have secure storage for expensive equipment, but even that can get broken into. On one site, enterprising thieves cut through the side of a metal shipping container to get at the tools kept inside. I would recommend taking home expensive equipment or taking out separate insurance if you are going to keep it on site.

A shed is a valuable part of an allotment for storing tools and produce, plus it is handy for sheltering from the rain. If you can introduce a few luxuries to it, then it becomes a nice place to rest when you are spending the day on your plot. It is great to be able to heat up some food or make a cup of tea to warm you up on a cold winter's day, but if your shed is only big enough to store things in, then that's fine too.

Building Paths

You have to get around your allotment and you have a choice whether to build a formal path network, which means defined growing areas, or have informal paths between where you are growing things at that time. Which you choose is entirely up to you, though if you are using raised beds then you will have defined paths around and between the beds. If you are growing in the ground then you are less likely to have these paths marked out, though you may have gaps between vegetables for you to walk down. When growing in the ground, the paths tend to move every year as beds shift around the plot.

This is another personal decision and it is up to you and how you plan to manage your allotment.

Paving slabs on the left between plots and wood chip paths between beds.

Paths provide a defined and clearly marked area for you to walk on and run your wheelbarrow down. It tells visitors and children exactly where they can walk as we all know you stay on the path! If your paths are just patches of ground between rows of vegetables, then it can be very hard to determine where these paths are, particularly while your seeds are germinating or your plants are young.

I like to have paths on my allotment because it appeals to my sense of order. I know where I am growing, and I know where I am walking and never the twain shall meet! The paths can be managed so they do not become infested with weeds, which often happens when you leave informal paths between vegetable rows.

Paths can be made from pretty much anything, from block paving bricks to paving slabs or even left as grass. Paths need to be something that is durable and at least vaguely level, i.e. without large holes in where you are likely to break an ankle. Good quality, plastic weed membrane makes for an excellent path as it is low maintenance and lasts for years. You can use wood chip as a path with a weed membrane underneath it if you want it to look really neat.

The downside of wood chip is that it rots and after a few years, turns into a form of compost and plants will start growing in it. This is when it needs removing and you realise just how much wood chip you have to remove. I did inherit wood chip paths on one plot, and they had been down for several years and were infested with weeds. I started to clear the paths to replace them and realised that three or four inches of wood chip amounts to a massive amount of waste material which I had nowhere to put. It was also a significant job to wheelbarrow dozens and dozens of loads of wood chip from one end of the site to the other. The paths got left as they were until I left the site, and I did not change more than a few metres of wood chip. It was a lot of work!

Keep your paths clear of weeds, whether you weed them if they are fixed, or use a hoe if they are informal. Because paths are not a productive area of your allotment where you are actively growing things, they tend to get neglected because it is more important that you weed between your vegetables. However, weeds can quickly get established on your path, particularly if you have fixed paths, and then they become very difficult to remove. Like anywhere else, it is much easier to remove the weeds when they are small, than struggle when they are larger. It's tempting to use chemicals on your path to kill the weeds, but I would not recommend this approach. It is far too easy for the chemicals to blow from the path on to your plants and kill your plants too, plus any residue will be taken up by the roots of your plants. Pulling weeds up by hand as soon as they appear will make sure that you keep them under control.

Whether you decide to build a structured path system or not is entirely up to you. Both methods work perfectly well and are equally productive. It comes down to personal preference at the end of the day. I know many plot holders who have paths and many who do not. One person I know just lays scaffolding boards on the soil where he wants the paths to be that year. It is something for you to decide when you are planning your allotment based on who is going to come to your plot and how you prefer to work it. If you are new to allotmenting, then try a year without paths, see how you feel about it and then after that year decide whether that is the best solution for you. Once you have worked your plot for a year or two you will have a better idea how you are going to use it, so will be in a better place to decide if you need to put in paths.

Greenhouses, Polytunnels and Coldframes

You may well have inherited a greenhouse, coldframe or polytunnel when you took on your plot which could be in good, poor condition or even derelict. These are very useful to have as they help you extend the growing season and grow tender plants such as tomatoes, aubergines or peppers.

Greenhouses are often made from old windows and doors.

A greenhouse is usually a metal structure, though some have a wooden frame, with glass in the windows. The idea is that the greenhouse stays much warmer than the outside, heating up significantly in the summer months, and protecting plants from the elements and cold. Greenhouse windows will either be made out of polycarbonate (plastic) or special horticultural, toughened glass. You should never use regular glass in a greenhouse as it is very dangerous should a pane break. Learn more about growing in a greenhouse in my book "Greenhouse Gardening for Beginners".

A polytunnel has a metal frame which is covered with a thick plastic sheet. These are a cheaper, shorter-lived version of a greenhouse, but still an excellent way to grow tender plants on your allotment. The plastic covers have a finite life as they usually degrade in sunlight, but you can usually purchase replacements relatively cheaply, depending on the size. Polytunnels are very susceptible to wind damage and are regularly torn to shreds by high winds, so need to be secured to the ground and the frame. Many people will remove the plastic covers in autumn, once their plants have finished, to prevent damage during winter storms. Every year you will see people sharing pictures online of their polytunnels in trees after high winds.

Coldframes are much smaller structures that are often portable, though they used to be built with short brick walls and glass lids. These are not generally used for growing vegetables all year round, though can be a good place to grow lettuce in winter. These are usually used to start seeds off and protect seedlings until they are ready to be planted out. You can buy plastic or glass ones from most garden centers.

Bought new, greenhouses are very expensive. Polytunnels are much cheaper, but have a shorter lifespan, and coldframes are cheaper still, but much smaller. You can usually find greenhouses for sale or free on eBay, Gumtree and FreeCycle, particularly in the springtime when people are tidying up their gardens. You will rarely find polytunnels or coldframes for sale second hand.

If you are buying a second-hand greenhouse, then you will be expected to dismantle and remove it yourself, so bring a friend and a van. Dismantle it as little as possible as they are nightmare to put together again once they have been completely taken apart. If you can leave it as four sides and two roof panels, it will be much easier to put back together. Make sure you have a good pair of gloves as you can cut your hands on the glass or metal. You will need a selection of spanners and screwdrivers to dismantle it, plus a hacksaw and a can of WD-40 for those hard to remove bolts. Be prepared to buy more glass clips, bolts and window rubbers as some will break or be lost. The window rubbers may be perished anyway and need replacing. When putting your greenhouse up on your site, make sure you have a good base in place that you can secure your new greenhouse to; they will blow away and get damaged in high winds if not fixed down securely.

A small polytunnel on an allotment.

All of these are very useful for your allotment, though you are likely to have a greenhouse or a polytunnel, not both. You may have one or more coldframes, as they allow you to move seedlings out of your greenhouse and still protect them from the cold. Don't worry if you don't have any of these to start with, they are not essential, though very, very useful! You will find plants like tomatoes, aubergine and peppers ripen better when grown in these than when grown outside.

Allotment Management And Events

Working on an allotment is just the start. Some people decide they want to give back to the allotment site and do more than just run a plot. They want to get involved in running the site and making it a great place for everyone else. This may, or may not, be something you want to do and if you do not want to get involved, then that is fine, not everyone does. This chapter is aimed at the people who do want to get involved in running their allotment site and to provide them with the information they need to get involved and manage their site. Remember that while not all sites will have a management committee, almost all will have a group of people involved in the smooth running of the site.

How much you get involved is entirely up to you. You could get involved with the committee and the running of the site or you could just get involved in work parties maintaining communal areas. My site has communal chickens, a communal orchard and an allotment shop, all of which plot holders can get involved in if they want.

Allotment Officials

A self-managed allotment will have a committee with a wide variety of roles available. The commitment and work will vary from site to site, but with a good committee, the workload is shared out so no one person gets overloaded.

Although most committees have named titles and specific roles for those people, many allotment committees have positions for 'committee members'. These people do not have the responsibility of a role and their task is purely to help out on the site and contribute to the running of the site and the decision making process.

Most allotments are more than happy for people to join the committee, though make sure your plot is worked, neat and up to the site standards first as if there are site inspections, committee members often get judged a little harder than regular members!

Some of the common roles on an allotment site committee include:

- Chairperson – this person is responsible for organising the committee and events, running committee meetings and generally is in charge of everything. Often the chairperson shows new people around the site and allocates plots.
- Secretary – this role sends all communications to allotment holders and externally. They are responsible for taking minutes at committee meetings and ensuring they are circulated to all members.
- Treasurer – this person is responsible for the site's money. They maintain the bank balance, produce accounts, take the rent from plot holders, make payments and make fund raising applications. This is a very responsible role and usually the treasurer reports regularly to the committee on the state of the finances.

Depending on the committee, there can be a vice-chairperson and many other roles. My allotment site has an official beekeeper who is in charge of the communal bees and an officer in charge of chickens, who organises and looks after the communal chickens. There could be all sorts of roles based on what your allotment site does. Some may have an Event Manager, responsible for organising events, Site Inspectors, responsible for inspecting plots to ensure they meet the site standards, a Competition Secretary, responsible for organising allotment competitions and more. There are some that have Community Liaison Officers and Fund Raisers too. These days there can also be a Social Media Secretary responsible for running the site's Facebook page or Twitter account!

If your allotment does not have a committee, then it may have people whose job is to liaise with the council. This role usually involves communicating concerns and problems from the allotment to the relevant council team and ensuring that required work is done.

Being on an allotment committee can be a thankless task sometimes, but it does allow you to become involved in running your allotment site. As a committee member you can contribute to the direction the site is taking and work to improve the site for all plot holders. Committee members are very important to the future of allotment sites and to ensure they are well kept and well used.

Organising Work Days

Work days are communal days where many people from the site come to work on the site rather than their individual plots. These are hard to organise as people are often busy and you will find the same few people turning up all the time. However, they are essential to keeping a good looking site and stopping the communal areas becoming overgrown.

Providing two to four weeks' notice of a work day tends to work best. Planning too far in advance usually means people forget and too short notice means people have plans and cannot attend.

Organising an event at the same time as a work day, such as a communal barbeque or pot luck lunch, can help with attendance. Unfortunately, the biggest issue is often the weather as if a work day corresponds with a rainy day, people do not want to come and get wet and if it is too sunny, people want to spend time with their family!

Determine a plan of action for your work day and ensure it is something that is achievable in the time available. Depending on the amount of people available, you may work on several different areas as one area could become a bit over-crowded.

Ensure that all the materials and tools required for the work day are available when you are due to start. If people are hanging around with nothing to do, then they are less likely to turn up in the future. Have one person responsible for assigning people to tasks and take into account people's abilities. If specific tools or machinery is required, then either hire it or ask people to bring them along to the work day. To save any potential problems, people are best to only use tools they own rather than those owned by other people.

Works days are a great way to socialise at your allotment and get to know fellow plot holders. Even if you are not on the committee, these are worth attending so you meet other people and help keep your allotment site looking great.

Running Open Days

Open days are less common these days, but are an opportunity for an allotment site to open its gates and show the local community what they do. Often these are combined with competitions, a barbeque and plant sales as a fund raiser for the allotment site.

These can be very rewarding as a good way to engage with the local community, raise awareness of the allotments and build local links.

Obviously when you are running one of these, you have to take into account security, so valuables need to be put away out of sight. While you may think this is not trusting your local community, it is sensible to do so as not to encourage any potential problems in the future.

Exactly what you do on an open day is up to you, and it is something for the committee to discuss and organise. It could be used as a fund raiser for the allotment society, an opportunity to promote the site and get tenants for empty plots or to encourage interaction between the allotment society and community.

The length of time the open day runs for will vary, though they are usually run at weekends when more people are around. They will usually last for anything

from a couple of hours up to six to eight hours, depending on what is being organised. One allotment site has a yearly open day that runs from 12:00 until late as they have bars, bands, vegetable exhibitions and more. Initially though, your event may be shorter. It depends on what you are planning on doing!

While these can be hard work, with a dedicated team organising it, an open day can be really good fun. If your allotment society does not already run an open day, it may be worth talking to the committee about starting one to help build a good relationship with the local community.

Setting up Tool Shares/Community Tools

Some allotment societies will have tool shares or communal shares. Often these are more expensive tools such as rotavators, mowers or strimmers, rather than tools you are expected to own such as spades and forks.

How these run vary from site to site, but it usually involves the tool being stored in a secure facility and signed out to the person wanted to borrow it. Some sites charge a deposit for hiring which is returned when the tool is returned undamaged.

While these are a good idea, they rely on someone being available to hand over the tool at the time the borrower wants to use it and the borrower returning the tool undamaged. For something like a strimmer where the strimmer wire is used up during use and petrol is required to run it, a small charge could be made to cover these costs.

The tools need to be checked by whoever is running the tool share after each use to ensure no damage has been done. Our allotment site has a communal petrol strimmer, but it is often returned damaged where the user has not known how to properly use the choke or adjust the wire.

Not everyone can afford to buy a strimmer or rotavator, certainly when they may only be used a couple of times a year. Having these available to borrow or hire on the allotment is a big attraction and can be very helpful to the plot holders. These tools may also be used by volunteers to maintain the communal areas.

The cost of a good quality petrol strimmer and mower is not excessive and if you charge a small hire fee or for the cost of petrol, then the items can be relatively cost free to run.

General Site Maintenance

Allotments have communal areas, whether these are buildings, paths, roads or grassy areas. These, quite rightly, have to be maintained and the responsibility usually falls on the management committee, though if the local council are involved, they may provide some assistance. Exactly what help the council offer will depend on the site and how it is managed. On council run areas they may maintain communal areas, but on self-managed sites they may only maintain perimeter trees.

Site maintenance is important and usually it will be done by a handful of people; the same people that do most things. If you have time, get involved in this as it is a great way to build relationships with other plot holders and it shows some community spirit, which is always appreciated.

At the very least, you can keep the communal areas around your plot tidy. One of my allotment neighbours has put flagstones down as the path between plots, which is something I plan to emulate on the other side of my plot. They are not laid professionally, but they are mostly level and make the path passable in wet weather.

Other communal areas such as roads will also need maintaining. Often these are quite literally dirt tracks which get damaged in wet weather with cars driving on them. This results in large ruts and a raised ridge in the middle of the road which can damage the underside of a car. These can be repaired by a work party where feasible, or external contractors can be brought in to take care of the job.

Whether or not you get involved in maintaining the communal areas is up to you and depends on your time. Many allotment holders are retired and have the time to work on these whereas younger plot holders who work full time and have young families may find it harder to dedicate the time to do anything more than maintain their plot. If you have the time, get involved, but at the very least, do what you can to make sure the communal areas near your plot look fantastic.

Allotment Competitions

Some allotment sites will hold annual competitions, whether these are vegetable shows or awards for best kept plot, best newcomer or biggest pumpkin will depend on the site. These can be fun to get involved in and a great way to join in the community, though if you are starting out, entering the vegetable competitions can be difficult.

If your allotment does hold these competitions, then talk to your committee and find out more about them so you are aware of the entrance criteria. Depending on where you live, there may also be village, town or even county competitions; many of the big, annual county fairs hold fiercely competitive vegetable competitions. Ask around on your allotment site and someone will be able to tell you what competitions there are in your local area.

The classes in a vegetable show will vary from show to show. Not every show has classes for giant vegetables, though there are specific giant vegetable shows across the country. The aim of most vegetable exhibitions is to grow vegetables that confirm to a defined size and appearance, presented in the show approved way. These are defined to test the growing skills of the exhibitor, with the hardest thing often being getting the vegetables ripe and perfect in time for the show.

Shows have a point system that is used by the judges and this is usually available for review prior to the show so you know how vegetables will be judged. Many shows follow the guidelines published by the RHS in their book, 'The Horticultural Society's Show Handbook'. The best way to understand this though is to attend a few shows and look at the exhibits, though be careful taking photographs as they are not always permitted!

Many vegetable shows not only exhibit fruits and vegetables but can also have categories for crafts, baking, jam making and more. They can be a very educational experience and all the categories are hotly contested; growers have bred their own cultivars and have secret fertiliser recipes which they will not give away.

Each vegetable will have its own criteria for judging. They need to be clean, free from pest damage, evenly sized and shaped as well as the leaves neatly trimmed and the whole thing nicely displayed. Adhering to the presentation rules will help you score more points as many people lose competitions due to poor presentation.

Vegetables are usually displayed on large, white paper plates; the show organisers can tell you what they expect here. Each play will be accompanied by an exhibitor's card which shows the variety of the vegetable. It will also contain the name and number of the exhibitor, though these must be hidden from the judge.

Most vegetables are eligible for exhibiting, though there are certain cultivars that you can buy which have specifically been bred for the exhibition table. Over time, you will breed your own varieties and guard their seeds jealously, but these varieties are always a good starting point for the new exhibitor. New exhibition cultivars are released every year, so keep an eye on the seed catalogues for the latest releases.

- Broad Bean – Imperial Green Longpod, Exhibition Longpod

- Dwarf French Bean – any flat podded variety such as The Prince or Masterpiece
- Runner Bean – Liberty, Enorma
- Beetroot (round) – Boltardy, Pablo F1
- Cabbage – Any F1 hybrid that matures at the time of the show
- Carrot (long) – St Valery or New Red Intermediate
- Cauliflower – Any F1 hybrid with white curds that matures at show time
- Celery – Evening Star, Morning Star or Mammoth
- Cucumber – Any F1 hybrid or King George
- Leek – Mammoth Blanche, Mammoth Pot
- Onion (Large) – Ailsa Craig, The Kelsae
- Onion (Small) – Sturon, Turbo, Centurion
- Parsnip – Any F1 hybrid
- Pea – Show Perfection, Alderman
- Potato (white) – Nadine, Winston
- Potato (coloured) – Kestrel, Maxine
- Tomato – Any F1 hybrid

Most of these are available as seeds from reputable suppliers and some can be bought as pre-grown plants. If you look through the seed catalogues, you will see many more exhibition varieties. Once you understand the requirements for the show, then you will be better placed to choose the right varieties.

What judges look for in the exhibition will depend on the show, all of which publish guidelines well in advance of the show. To give you an idea of what is expected, here are some commonly exhibited vegetables and some judging criteria.

- Beetroot – 3 standard bunches, each containing between 3 and 5 roots. The beetroot should be uniform in size, free from cracks, smooth, without any rough spots and have no worm damage. Typically, a size of 1½" to 2½" is required with an even, dark red colour. Tops are usually cut at between 1" to 1½" above the shoulder of the root and the main tap root left intact.
- Savoy Cabbage – 3 marketable heads, trimmed, firm and free from damage, decay or discolouration.
- Bunched Carrots – 3 bunches of 6 to 8 roots of

between ¾" and 1½" in diameter. The roots all need to be the same length and diameter, smooth and bright orange in colour. The tops need to be a good colour and have no damage. Typically, carrots with cut tops are a different class.

- Cauliflower – 3 marketable heads of uniform size with tight, white buds and no protruding leaves. Each head should be between 4 and 6 inches wide with the leaves trimmed neatly to the top of the head. Yellowed curds or any damaged leaves are considered a negative.
- Cucumber – 3 to 6 marketable fruits of between 7" and 8" long and 1½" to 2¼" inches in diameter. The fruit need to be dark green in colour, straight and have rounded ends. The stem is cut ¼" from the shoulder of the fruit which should be evenly coloured and free from damage.
- Lettuce (head) – 3 marketable heads of uniform size, colour and maturity. The heads must be firm to hard with two intact wrapper leaves and trimmed to ¼" of the bottom leaves.
- Onions – 4 to 6 bulbs of uniform shape, size and colour with a diameter of between 2" and 4". Tops are cut cleanly to ½" from the shoulder and roots completely removed.
- Peppers – 6 marketable fruits of uniform size, shape and colour. All fruits should have the same number of lobes and the stem cut level with the fruits shoulder.
- Tomatoes (Cherry) – 20 fruits of uniform shape, size and colour with fresh, green stems, though stems can be removed. Fruits should be free from cracks and blemishes.

You can see from these few examples that the judging criteria is very strict. If your display does not conform to the requirements, then you can expect to lose points or be disqualified.

Growing vegetables to exhibit is good fun to do. It is highly competitive and can be very stressful ensuring that vegetables are ripe at the perfect time. However, it is a very sociable experience and there is a big community built up around these exhibitions. Growers will guard their secrets jealously, but they are generally friendly and sociable.

Coping With An Average British Year

The weather through the year will vary depending on where in the country you are located. While there are general weather patterns, they are changing as any long-term allotment owner will tell you and there are greater variations in the weather now. For many areas, a late frost or snow can be expected into May or even June, which was virtually unheard of twenty years ago. Coping with the weather is one of the hardest things to do as an allotment holder and a major contributor to people giving up their plot. Learning to go with the flow and keep going regardless of the weather is important if you are going to succeed with your allotment.

Winter

The rain in winter will usually replenish the moisture levels in your soil, though in recent years there has been so much rain that it has turned many allotments into rice paddies! The temperatures will hopefully drop below freezing, which will kill off many pests and diseases and is good for your garlic. If there has been excessive rain, you can end up with nutrients being washed out of the soil, so be prepared to feed the soil well the following year. The weather and dark nights usually limits what you can do at your plot and usually it is just simple maintenance such as weeding between winter vegetables, pruning some fruit trees and working on the structure of your allotment ready for spring. In winter, it is a case of going to your allotment in between the bad weather.

There are onions and garlic under that!

Spring

This is always a busy time as you are starting your seeds off indoors before planting them out in late spring, carefully watching the weather ready to fleece your delicate seedlings in case of a surprise late frost. You will be very active at the allotment at this time as the weeds will also be springing up as the weather warms. For many of us, this is a time of high winds and lots of rain, so make sure all your guttering and drainpipes are clear so you can collect as much water as possible before summer.

Summer

Summer can be anything from a damp squib to a scorching heat wave and you need to be prepared for both! When it is hot and dry, you need to spend a lot of time watering your plants. When it is wet, you need to keep a close eye on your plants as some can struggle to grow and mature. It can be hard work keeping your plants alive, but when it comes to harvesting you will realise it is worth it.

Autumn

Nowadays, autumns tend to be warmer and many plants are still growing, with tomatoes ripening outdoors as late as October in some areas. As the days get shorter and the weather cools, many plants will bolt or go to seed. You are hoping for plenty of dry days so that you can harvest your produce and store it; wet produce does not store well and has more chance of rotting. You are planting overwinter vegetables and mulching/covering any areas of ground that won't be planted in. If you dig your allotment, now is the time to turn it, just hope it isn't too wet so it is too hard to do.

What To Do First

We've talked a lot about what to do with a new allotment, and now I want to summarise it all into a simple action plan that you can follow. This will help you get the most done with the least effort when on your plot and get your allotment productive quickly. Often you are under pressure from the site management to get your plot cultivated, so knowing how to get started can help reduce your stress and make taking on a new allotment more exciting. Just remember that you do not need to do everything in a week and to take your time to do it right.

1. Visit your plot and assess what you have – look at structures, boundaries, sun location and work out what plants are already there
2. Measure your plot so you can draw up a plan
3. Familiarise yourself with the site rules so you don't inadvertently break any
4. Draw a plan of your plot and mark out existing structures, drawing in permanent beds before marking out the rest of the growing area
5. Build some compost bins or designate an area that will permanently be for compost
6. Strim or cut weeds down to ground level and either compost or dispose of them
7. Cover the ground with good quality weed membrane or tarpaulin
8. Dig an area, following your plan, keeping unused areas covered so the weeds don't come back
9. Plant areas when ready
10. Any areas you aren't planting, mulch with manure or compost and then cover to keep the weeds down
11. Enjoy

This simple process makes it sound easy, but there's a lot of work in each step! I'd recommend visiting your plot with a plan so that you know what you are doing when you are there. I have found that starting with a quick weed every visit helps to keep them under control

plus it allows you to check the health of your plants. This stops weeds from taking over and transforms weeding from a chore you avoid doing to something that is fun and pretty quick. Once this quick weed is done, you get on with your plan of action, doing the jobs you have allocated for that day, ignoring anything else unless it urgently requires attention. This focused approach will help you to get a lot done very quickly, you'll be surprised how quickly you can transform an overgrown plot when you visit with a targeted plan.

An allotment ready for someone to work on it.

Of course, like anything with an allotment, this plan is fluid and subject to change. But this section should give you a good idea of how to get started and what to do first, so you aren't overwhelmed by an overgrown allotment. It can be very daunting, particularly if you are new to gardening, to set foot for the first time on your plot and realise the weeds are taller than you. Following this simple action plan and targeting your work will help you quickly get the plot under control, so you can get on with the fun stuff like planting and eating what you grow!

Chapter 3 – Creating Your Own Compost

Composting is an essential part of owning an allotment. Most people will throw their weeds into a pile and hope for the best, but there is a science behind it. Composting takes the waste material from your allotment and your kitchen and turns it into a highly beneficial soil additive to use on your plants.

Every allotment has a compost pile of some sort, run to varying degrees of success. In a typical year, your compost pile will shrink to about a third of its size and produce a lovely compost that can be used as a mulch or to condition your soil. When you build your compost bins, I can guarantee, that no matter how big you build them, you will always find more than enough to fill them! As well as composting waste from your allotment, composting kitchen waste provides valuable micronutrients, such as calcium from eggshells, that your plants will appreciate.

A couple of my home-made compost bins

So why compost at your allotment?

- Waste Reduction – somewhere between a quarter and half of all waste is either garden or food waste. This is typically put in landfills where it generates methane as it rots and contributes to global warming.
- Fewer Tip Visits – driving to the tip takes up time and fuel, so if you compost your allotment waste it means you don't have to put it in your car and drive it to the tip! From experiencing, putting garden waste in your car usually ends up full of slugs or spiders.
- Saves Water – compost, applied as a mulch or soil conditioner, helps the soil to retain water. A couple of inches of compost applied as a mulch in a hot summer will help prevent water evaporation, meaning your plants do not suffer as much in the heat as well as keeping the

weeds down. Digging in compost conditions the soil and helps it retain moisture better without become waterlogged.

- Saves Money – by making your own compost you are reducing the amount of compost you have to buy and saving all the resources associated with purchasing compost. Unless you are composting large amounts, you may struggle to produce enough compost to meet your needs year after year, but you will certainly be able to save some money and know you are using high quality compost.
- Destroys Weeds and Pathogens – running a hot compost pile at a temperature of 40C/104F for a couple of weeks will not only kill pathogens, but also kill perennial weed roots such as dandelion, dock and mare's tail. These perennial weeds are usually burnt or removed from your allotment as they do not break down in conventional, cool compost heaps.
- Improves Soil Structure – compost is great to improve your soil structure. Whether your soil is sandy or heavy clay, compost helps the soil become more friable, retaining moisture and nutrients much better.
- Replenishes Nutrients – your compost will contain essential nutrients for your soil, including micronutrients that are often lacking from commercial fertilisers. Compost is a natural slow release fertiliser, releasing about a quarter of its nitrogen in the first year, and then less in subsequent years. As you tend to apply compost annually, you are constantly and naturally replenishing the nutrients in the soil.
- Reduces Pest Problems – according to research, soil treated with compost results in strong plants that have fewer pest problems. Regularly top dressing your allotment with compost will help produce stronger plants and prevent soil based pests and diseases from running rampant.

Creating your own compost is an important part of running an allotment and this chapter is going to teach you both the science and the practicalities of composting.

The Composing Process

The composting process happens because of micro-organisms such as bacteria, fungi and enzymes. You need to provide them with the ideal living environment so they can do their job and break down the waste material into something you can use. When well-attended and turned regularly, a compost heap can break down in as little as three to four months. Usually, when left to their own devices, a compost heap will take a year or more to break down so it is useable.

A well run compost heap needs four things:

- Carbon – material rich in carbon provides energy so that the micro-organisms can thrive. These are usually found from dry leaves, straw and shredded paper.
- Nitrogen – materials high in nitrogen provide food for the micro-organisms so they can multiply. Nitrogen comes from materials such as manure, blood and bone meal, seaweed, weeds, grass clipping and kitchen scraps.
- Water – the composting micro-organisms are living creatures that require water. Too much and they will drown; too little and they become dehydrated and die. Your compost needs to be as damp as a well wrung sponge. Sprinkle your compost heap regularly while it is composting and cover when it is not in use to prevent moisture loss.
- Oxygen – like other living creatures, these micro-organisms require oxygen to survive. Over time, as the material in a compost heap rots, it begins to compact and oxygen levels are reduced. Turning your compost aerates the mix and provides much needed oxygen to the composting micro-organisms so they can break down the waste materials. If your compost heap appears to have stopped working, a common problem in autumn and winter, throw in a bucket of manure and then turn your compost heap. The manure introduces beneficial micro-organisms back into the mix and turning it provides oxygen so they can thrive and work.

When Is Compost Ready to Use?

Compost is ready for use on your allotment when it is dark brown, has a strong, earthy smell and has become crumbly. If it is powdery, rotten or mouldy, then it hasn't composted properly and needs reworking. You shouldn't be able to see any of the original materials in your compost, apart from larger, woody pieces. Finished compost is at the same temperature as its surroundings and should not steam.

Once your compost has finished, dig it out and pile it in another location for a couple of weeks to be sure that the composting process is finished. Using compost that hasn't finished can harm your plants as the composting bacteria will compete with nitrogen, taking it away from your plants so they become stunted with yellow leaves. Hot compost can end up burning seedlings and even stopping seeds from germinating.

The composting process is very simple when you understand what you need to do. A lot of people will keep a bag of dry leaves or straw on their allotment to use as the brown materials on their compost pile. You will have a lot, and I mean A LOT, of green materials, but the brown is essential to stop your allotment from getting too wet. It doesn't take long to get the hang of composting and it will quickly become second nature. The fresh compost will be very helpful for you and beneficial for your plants.

Compost rotting down nicely.

What You Can And Cannot Compost

Now you understand the composting process, you need to understand what you can and cannot compost. There will be lots of things on your allotment and perhaps even from your kitchen that you may be tempted to use, so this section will tell you exactly what you can put on your compost heap.

A home-made compost bin.

Although you need a good balance of green and brown materials for efficient composting, it doesn't always work that way. Many times you end up with a huge pile of green waste that you cannot just pile up and wait until you have enough brown waste to compost it all. You have to use your best judgement here. Throw all the green waste on, add some brown and turn it regularly, adding more brown material as and when you can. Regularly turning of the compost will help a lot when you have too much of one type of material.

So, what should and should not be used on a compost heap?

- Pet Waste – cat and dog waste should never be compost as it contains potentially fatal toxins such as Toxoplasmosis. Rabbit, chicken and guinea pig waste can be used and will usually contain brown material in the form of straw.

- Leaves – whether you gather them from home or on your plot, these are excellent brown materials for your compost. They are best shredded before being used as they can take a while to break down. Avoid using leaves from the black walnut tree as they contain toxins designed to inhibit the growth of other plants. Also avoid using leaves from eucalyptus trees. You can fill black plastic bin bags with leaves for them to break down or to keep near your compost heaps to add as brown material. Be careful collecting leaves from public areas as you do not know what toxins they contain. If you do collect leaves, wear protective gloves to protect yourself from anything harmful buried in the leaves.

- Pine Needles – these break down very slowly and are acidic in nature, so should be used sparingly. Creating an acidic compost heap high in pine needles is useful if you have acid soil loving plants such as blueberries, but for general purpose compost, you shouldn't use too much. Shredded Christmas trees should also not be composted because they will make the compost too acidic for many plants.

- Grass Clippings – if you cut your lawn, compost the grass cuttings as they are very high in nitrogen. However, they do have a tendency to clump together and starve the beneficial micro-organisms of oxygen. Therefore, mix grass clippings with plenty of brown material and turn more often for a couple of weeks. If you have used any lawn products in the last couple of weeks, check the safety of them before composting your grass clippings as you don't want the chemicals to transfer into the soil at your allotment and potentially harm your plants.

- Kitchen Waste – a great source of compostable material, though transporting them to your allotment can be the tricky part. Any vegetable peelings or waste fruit and vegetables are perfect for composting. Egg shells can be composted, though crush them first as they are slow to decompose. Teabags can also be composted, but concerns have been raised that some contain plastic which you will be introducing to your soil, so check first. Do not compost meat, dairy, bread or cooked food as these will attract pests such as rats into your compost pile. When you introduce kitchen waste into your compost, ensure you cover it with brown waste to prevent it from smelling and flies finding it.

- Wood Ash – anyone who has a log burner can compost the wood ash as it is high in potassium and a good alkaline material. To avoid upsetting the pH level of your compost, add no more than two gallons to a three-foot cube of compost. Do not compost coal ashes as these have high levels of sulphur which is damaging to your vegetables. Charcoal briquettes do not break down, so should not be used.

- Weeds – great for the compost, so throw them all on! If you are anything like the rest of us, you'll have plenty of these to compost. Avoid adding roots of perennial weeds such as comfrey, dock, bindweed, mare's tail, nettle and dandelion as these can be difficult to break down and will grow back from even a small piece of root. Remove flowers from weeds before composting as the flowers can continue to mature and produce seeds which you will then spread on your allotment when you use the compost.

- Waste Vegetable Matter – any of your vegetables that are damaged or not up for use can be composted. The tops off vegetables such as carrots and parsnips can be composted rather than brought home. Avoid composting the thick stalks of sweetcorn or brassicas as they are very slow to decompose. Potatoes should not be added to compost heaps as they can spread diseases but more commonly grow in the compost pile before they have broken down fully.

- Manure – great for your compost pile, though ensure you use manure from vegetarian animals such as horses, sheep, ducks, pigs, chickens, cows or pigeons. Manure from carnivorous animals can contain dangerous pathogens and should not be used. Be careful with fresh manure as it can be very hot as it is composting which can kill the composting micro-organisms you have been carefully nurturing. Instead, leave the manure in a separate pile for a few weeks to cool before adding to your compost heaps.

- Seaweed – jam packed full of nutrients; this is ideal for your compost pile. Ensure you wash them thoroughly before adding to your compost pile to remove salt from the sea otherwise the salt can harm your plants.

There are lots of things you can compost and before you add anything, ask yourself if it is natural and will it break down. If it will, throw it on, otherwise don't compost it. Think about how long it will take to break down. The stems from your raspberry canes, cut back in spring could be composted, but would take far too long to break down so are better burnt or otherwise disposed of. Garden soil can be put on your compost heap. Remember to balance the green and brown materials to ensure an efficient compost heap. Turn it regularly to aerate it and keep the composting process going.

Building A Compost Heap

One of the early projects you are likely to undertake on your allotment is to build your own compost bin. These can be built from anything, old doors, wire mesh or anything else you can find, though many people will use wooden pallets which can often be found for free. If you are fortunate, your allotment will already have a compost pile, but you may want to build multiple bins so you can have more than one compost heap running or can easily turn your compost from one bin to another.

Pallets are very easy to build a compost heap from and it won't take more than an hour or two at most. Try to choose pallets that are in good condition, without any damage or nails sticking out. Most are pressure treated, but you can use a wood preservative to help them last longer. Avoid pallets made from plywood or chipboard as these have a very short lifespan outside.

Pallets are often not light and can have splinters or nails protruding from them, so be careful when you are carrying them around. A single compost bin will require three pallets plus, if you can, a fourth to use as a door to prevent the compost falling out. For each additional bay, you will need an additional two pallets, three if you want a door.

Also required is some coated garden wire, used to tie together the pallets in the corners, some nails and some stakes for the corners for extra support, particularly useful in windy areas. Also, you will need some wire cutters, a hammer, some gloves and a couple of hours of decent weather.

This is how to build a pallet compost bin, repeat it for as many bins as you need. I recommend a minimum of two and ideally three. With three, you have plenty of space to turn your compost, which helps it break down quicker, and plenty of space for all the weeds; you'll be surprised how much you can compost every year!

1. Clear the site where your compost list will be located. Level the area and remove any perennial weeds. There is no need to cover the ground as you want worms to migrate out of the soil into your compost.
2. Arrange three pallets to form a box. Whether the slats face in or out is up to you, it does not make a huge difference. If your site is windy, dig a trench a few inches deep at the base of the pallets and sink the pallets into the ground.

3. Use wire to tie the corners together securely. Nails can be used as well or instead to provide additional support.

4. For additional support, drive stakes into the corners of the pallets.
5. A fourth pallet can be used as a door. Tie it on one side of the box so it acts as hinges. I leave this off initially, and then put it in place once the bin is mostly full and then load it up from the top.

6. Build the second and third bins next to the first, using one less pallet as you are using the original bin as one of the walls.

7. Some pallets have a spacing between the slats. Generally, this is ok as it aids air circulation around your compost. However, if you feel it is too far, staple weed membrane or black plastic to the pallets. Remember to be careful with your fork when turning your compost otherwise you will damage it.

This is a cheap and easy way to build a compost bin and gives you plenty of space for your weeds. Turning it regularly will help it break down faster and produce good quality compost that you can use on your plants. Remember to bring compostable material from home to put on your compost pile. Kitchen waste can provide some valuable micronutrients for your plants.

Compost Tea

Compost tea is a very rich, liquid fertiliser that is considered one of the best liquid fertilisers you can use. Together with worm casings and comfrey tea, these are often the 'secret sauces' used by championship vegetable growers. This is very easy to make; all you need is some finished compost!

Get a shovel of your well-rotted compost. If your heap is still active, dig down to the bottom and you should find enough to make a five-gallon batch of tea. You can use store bought compost if you have none ready on your allotment.

This compost tea naturally forms in your compost bin, but usually it drains away into the soil. However, rather than attempt to collect this, it is just as easy to make your own compost tea.

Get a large bucket, one that will hold at least five gallons of water. Then either put the compost directly in the bucket, which means you will need to strain the finished product, or you can put the compost in a burlap bag so you don't need to strain the tea. Steep the compost in the water for three to four days, stirring occasionally. Ensure it is covered to stop flies and keep pests away.

Once it has finished, the liquid is kept and the compost is put back onto your compost pile. The tea should be used within a few days as the beneficial bacteria and other micro-organisms in the tea will suffocate over time as they are suspended in water and not exposed to the air.

Young or delicate plants should use a dilution of 10 to 20 parts water to 1 part compost tea, depending on how delicate the plant is. It is then used as a foliar spray and sprayed onto the leaves of your plants or added to your watering can and watered direct to the roots. Established plants can take neat compost tea, though seedlings and younger plants need this tea diluting before use. If you are making a foliar spray, then add a dash of vegetable oil so the tea will stick to the leaves.

Compost tea is very nutrient dense and easily absorbed by your plants. Sprayed onto the leaves, it helps to keep the plant healthy as well as nourish it. Foliar sprays are best used in the morning to allow plenty of time for the leaves to dry out.

This is a very easy to make liquid feed that is highly nutritious for your plants. It costs nothing to make and is great for the environment plus, there is no waste!

Comfrey Tea

Comfrey grows in the wild, usually along rivers and streams with a very distinct appearance. It can be grown on allotments, though grow it in containers or buy a non-invasive cultivar otherwise it will take over your allotment. The roots are thick, deep and very brittle and it will grow back from even the smallest piece of root and if you cover it with plastic!

Comfrey flowers.

Comfrey tea is smelly, so this is best done away from areas people frequent. You will need a large plastic bucket with a lid and a bowl. This mixture does not need to be left in the sun and can be tucked out of the way somewhere on your allotment.

Drill three holes 6 to 10mm in the bottom of the bucket in a triangle around the middle. Put the bucket on bricks, high enough that the bowl fits underneath it.

Shred the comfrey leaves and stems and fill the bucket with them. Put a brick or something similar on top of the leaves to weigh them down. Do not add water and cover the bin so water cannot get in.

Over the next three/four weeks, the leaves start to rot and a dark brown liquid will drip out of the bucket and be caught in your bowl, which is comfrey tea.

Use it like compost tea, diluting it at a ratio of 20:1 with water before use as it is very strong. Comfrey tea is very good for strawberries, tomatoes and cucumbers.

Nettle Tea

This is made from common stinging nettles. Make sure you don't get any seeds or roots when you are harvesting the nettles. Fill a bucket with nettles, weigh them down with a brick and then cover the nettles with water. Cover the bucket and leave for four weeks before straining off the liquid. The rotted leaves can be added to your compost bin.

Nettle tea is very high in nitrogen, so is great to use when plants are setting leaves or for leafy crops such as lettuce and spinach. Dilute at a ratio of five parts water to one-part nettle tea.

Worm Farming

Vermiculture, or worm farming, is an excellent way to recycle your kitchen scraps. A specific type of worm digests waste material and turns it into a high quality compost that is much sought after by championship growers. The resulting compost is very high in nutrients and can be applied directly to plants or turned into a liquid feed compost tea.

This is a completely natural, organic process where worms break down waste and turn it into soil. This happens all the time on your allotment as the worms work tirelessly underground. You are harnessing their ability and controlling their food source so that the resulting worm castings are highly nutritious for your plants.

The worms used in vermiculture are known as red wigglers and are a specific type of worm. You cannot just go digging up any old earthworm as they won't work properly. These special worms can be bought online and are not expensive. Alternatively, you may find them in bags or piles of well-rotted manure, the red worms are the red wigglers you need to produce worm farming. The red wigglers or red worms used in vermiculture are Eisenia foetida and Lumbricus rubellus, though depending on where you live in the world, other species may be available. Make sure you get the right worms as it will ensure the composting process goes smoothly.

A wormery is very easy to set up. Most people will buy a pre-made one as it is simple to get started and requires very little work. You can make your own out of lidded plastic boxes. As well as a womery, you will need damp strips of newspaper and some food for the worms to convert into castings.

Kitchen waste is best. Any fresh food such as fruit and vegetables will do, though avoid dairy, meat and oils as these attract pests and take much longer to break down. Do not add any cooked foods as these will attract flies and avoid citrus fruits as it can make the resulting compost too acidic. Using a good variety of food will mean a better quality, better balanced compost.

When your worms have food, damp newspaper and are in the dark, they will thrive. The newspaper helps to create the damp environment worms thrive in and air pockets, which allows them to breathe.

If you are making your own worm farm, then pick a decent sized, shallow container with a lid. Red worms like to live in the top six inches of soil, so you don't want a box that is too deep. It should also be an opaque container as worms do not like light and will not go near the edges of clear container. A 24x18x8" dark plastic box is ideal for a worm farm.

Before using any box, it needs to be thoroughly cleaned and rinsed so that there is no soap or residue left on the box which could harm the worms. The lid needs to be loose enough fitting to allow air to get into the container so the worms can breathe.

Pack the container with damp strips of newspaper so it is full, but not packed so tight that there are no air pockets for the worms. Scatter some food scraps around the container, burying some under the surface of the newspaper. Finally, add the worms, put the lid on and put the womery in a quiet location where the worms won't be disturbed.

Add more food scraps every few days as the ones in there are eaten. Initially, until the worm population has built up, it may take a while for the food scraps to be eaten. Do not add too much food as it will rot rather than get processed by the worms. Mist the newspaper regularly so it is damp, but not wet, to maintain a good habitat for the worms.

In anywhere from three to five months, you will notice that there is less newspaper and more compost in your womery. When there is little newspaper bedding left, then it is time for you to harvest the compost and provide the worms with a fresh environment to start working on.

Worms, like any other animal, do not like living in their waste materials, so when the womery has too high a content of castings, the worm's health will struggle. Before you harvest the castings, stop adding fresh kitchen scraps for about two weeks so the worms work to finish breaking down what is in the worm bin.

One method of harvesting the castings is to push the castings over to one half of the bin and then fill the other half with fresh newspaper and kitchen scraps. The worms will then migrate over a week or two to the new side, leaving the castings behind which you can easily remove. Don't worry if you get any worms in the castings as they can be released into the soil or put back into the worm bin. You can speed up the migration process by leaving the side of the bin with the castings in exposed to the light. The worms will migrate to the fresh side to get away from the light.

Once you have harvested the castings, remove any non-decomposed material and either put it on your compost heap or put it back into the worm bin.

A worm farm can be used all year round and over time the worm population will naturally increase. The excess worms can be released into the wild, given to other allotment holders or used to create additional worm bins. Be aware that worms do not like freezing weather and if the temperature drops, you should move your worm bin into a greenhouse or shed to protect them from the cold. Wrapping the wormery in bubble wrap can also help to keep them warm.

The worms live for about a year, but don't worry when they die off, they will have produced offspring and their remains will be composted in the soil.

Worm castings can be mixed with potting soil, used as a top dressing or made into a compost tea.

Worm farming is quite a fun project and if you are serious about giving your plants the best food, then this is one of the best composts you can use. There is much more information in my book on worm farming.

Chapter 4 – Working Your Allotment

Your allotment is going to require work and, at least initially, quite a lot of work. However, you can set your allotment up to be low maintenance, but even then, you will still have to do some work. Juggling an allotment, a family and a job can be quite a challenge; there is a reason most neat allotments belong to retirees!

Working your allotment involves many different tasks including:

- Maintaining structures
- Digging and maintaining the soil
- Pruning bushes and trees
- Starting seedlings
- Planting out plants
- Protecting plants from pests
- Watering
- Tending your plants

And of course, the best task of all … harvesting everything and eating it! In my opinion, some of the hardest work comes when you have a glut of vegetables that you are trying to preserve! Imagine having sixty or seventy pounds of carrots that you have to clean, peel, blanch and then freeze!

In this chapter you will learn about working your allotment, so you understand everything from dealing with pests and problems on your allotment, to choosing seeds, feeding your plants and more.

We will discuss many of the other things you can do on your allotment, such as keeping bees or chickens. You will also learn how to prevent the build-up of diseases and pests in your soil through crop rotation, a practice that is thousands of years old. One of my favourite subjects that you will learn is companion planting. This is a natural way to help keep your plants healthy and reduce your reliance on chemicals. This is also based on ancient methods that are being researched by modern day scientists and implemented by farmers across the world to reduce their need to use chemical sprays.

Once you get started on your allotment, you will soon realise that you don't have enough space. I know virtually no allotment owners that wish they had less space. In fact, almost to a person they want more space as there never seems to be enough room for everything you want to grow! You will learn some great techniques for maximising the productivity of your allotment so that you can grow more in less space.

There is a lot involved in working an allotment and it's more than just putting plants in the soil. You need to learn to amend your soil, maintain good soil health and keep your plants healthy. You will constantly battle pests, diseases and the weather, but as you gain experience, you will understand what to look for and how to minimise the risks. If your area suffers from potato blight you plant first earlies which are harvested before blight strikes. If you live in an area with particularly strong winds, you surround your allotment with espalier trained trees to act as wind breaks.

When you take on an allotment, you won't have this knowledge, but you can understand what pests and problems are prevalent on your site by talking to other plot holders. Those that have been there for years will be a wealth of information on what to watch out for. This alone will help reduce your workload and losses.

When I took on my new plot, I got chatting to my plot neighbours, as you do. From them I learned that everyone on the site has problems growing leeks due to allium leaf miners. These pests decimated everyone's leek crop one year in the past, and since then, everyone has had to net their leeks to protect them against this pest. As I was planning on planting leeks, this information was vital because I'd have lost most of my crop if I hadn't learned this from them.

Understanding your local environment will help to reduce your work and make owning your allotment a bit easier. Enjoy this chapter and don't be put off as an allotment isn't as much work as you might think, particularly if you set it up to be low maintenance, which I'd recommend if you work and/or have a family. Always think about how you can reduce the amount of work you need to do as it makes it much easier to maintain your allotment and concentrate on the 'fun' parts of allotmenteering!

Allotment Pests And How To Deal With Them

Pests are always going to be a problem at the allotment. Whether this is slugs and snails, which we all suffer from, squirrels, rats, cats or foxes will depend on where you live, but learning about the commonly found pests and the steps to take to stop them damaging your plants will help make your allotment journey more enjoyable. It is devastating to come down to your plot the day after you've planted out something to find it gone.

This section will help you understand some of the more common pests you are will encounter and how to take steps to reduce their impact on your crops.

Aphids

These are usually a problem on new growth and will be found on many different plants from broad beans to blackcurrants. They can easily be picked off by hand or sprayed off the plants with water, though serious infestations will require the use of sprays to treat them. You will often notice ants around farming the aphids as they feed from the secretions of these pests. For trees you can put grease bands around the trunk which stop the ants getting to the aphids as they will fight off any pests that try to feed on their flock. Growing plants that encourage aphid predators such as hoverflies and lady birds will help keep the population at bay. Sacrificial crops can be grown to attract the aphids away from your main crop, but these don't always work. Check the new growth on your plants when watering and weeding and remove the aphids by hand before they can establish themselves.

Ants farming aphids.

Ants

Generally, these are not a problem as they don't cause any damage or harm. They will farm aphids, which can be a problem, but are generally okay to be left alone. The only ants to consider getting rid of are red ants as they sting, which can be a problem if you have children or are allergic to the sting. Black ants are best left alone.

If you find them in a bed, then dig the bed over and they will move elsewhere because their nest has been disturbed.

Butterflies and Caterpillars

A real problem for many plants, particularly brassicas. Although you can pick caterpillars off by hand and 'dispose' of them, most people are a bit squeamish of this, plus some people are allergic to the hairs on some caterpillars and come out in a rash. The best defense against caterpillars is to stop the butterflies landing on your plants to lay eggs. Use a very tight weave mesh such as scaffolding netting which has a very fine mesh which will let light and rain in, but stop those pesky pests. You can build a cage, or you can use lengths of plastic piping with either end in the soil to form a hoop around your plants and then drape the netting over the pipes. This has the advantage of being mobile and you can easily move it around from year to year. Keep the netting on from the moment you put the plants in the ground until you have finished harvesting them because this will also protect your plants from pigeons. Some butterflies will still get in, usually when you lift the netting to weed, but this will minimise the damage they do to your plants. You can often get used scaffolding netting for free from a scaffolding company or purchase it online relatively cheaply. Whatever netting you use, it has to be a very tight weave to prevent the butterflies from getting in. You can even use old net curtains, so long as they are clean enough to let the light get to your plants.

Cats

These aren't necessarily destructive, but they can leave little 'presents' in your nicely dug beds, but then so can foxes and other wildlife too. Sadly, their waste can contain worms and toxins which can transfer to you if you handle it. It is not so much of a problem unless you have children visiting your plot who may accidentally pick it up. There isn't a lot you can do to stop cats coming to your plot, but if you are concerned that they are making a mess in your beds then putting plastic forks with the prongs upwards can deter them, as can leaving prickly brambles around your plot. Mostly, if you scare them off when you are down there, they'll go find somewhere else to do their business.

Foxes

Generally, only a problem if you are keeping chickens as they love poultry as a snack. Make sure your chickens are put to bed every night and their run and coop are securely fenced off, roofed and that the fox cannot dig under, into the chicken area.

Pigeons

These love anything you've just planted and will decimate seedlings. I planted over fifty brassica plants one afternoon and came back the next morning to find that pigeons had ripped them to shreds and destroyed the plants. Protect young plants from pigeons by putting them in a portable plastic polytunnel or covering them with netting. The netting doesn't have to be as tight weave as that used to protect against caterpillars, but it needs to be tight enough that the pigeons can't get through. However, if you are protecting any member of the brassica family, you will want a tight weave mesh because you have to protect them not only from pigeons, but also from butterflies laying eggs. Cover your plants as soon as you put them in the ground to avoid any damage and keep them covered until they are established and no longer of interest to the pigeons.

Rodents

Generally, a nuisance, these will dig up and eat seeds, eat your sweetcorn off the plant and generally make a mess of the place. If you have a rodent problem, then you can use traps, there are humane ones available, or you can disturb their nests and they will, in most cases, leave home. Watch out for them nesting under sheds or in piles of debris on your allotment. If you encounter rats on your plot, then you may need to speak to the site management who will usually work with you to resolve the problem. Rats are considered worse than mice as they are more destructive and can carry diseases. Most allotment sites, and in particular, those that keep chickens, will already have rat traps on site to keep the population under control.

The slug - bane of many gardeners.

Slugs and Snails

These will very quickly become your worst enemy. They are voracious feeders, cunning in their ability to hide and seemingly able to get to virtually any plant no matter how you protect it. Slugs and snails will decimate seedlings overnight and are one of the biggest headaches you will face on your allotment.

Controlling them is actually very difficult. There isn't a lot you can do to prevent them as most of the traditional solutions such as crushed eggshells, copper tape and so on do little other than mildly inconvenience them. If you want to see evidence of this, search online and you'll find tests people have done showing these pests aren't stopped. Oddly enough, the one barrier that proved very effective was spiky bramble branches which both slugs and snails refused to cross, presumably because the thorns were too painful. Put some of these at the base of your plants and you may have a fighting chance of keeping them off!

However, there are other things you can do which will help prevent these pests. Firstly, these pests need somewhere to hide during the heat of the day and to avoid predators. Keeping your plot free of plant debris and other rubbish that they can hide in will help keep their population under control. Encourage beneficial predators onto your site such as frogs, toads, and hedgehogs, which dine on slugs by building habitats for them such as a small pond. Either early in the morning, around dawn, or at dusk, visit your plot and remove the slugs and snails by hand, then dispose of them. Beer traps work very well in catching these pests, but they need regular emptying otherwise they start to stink. Sink a plastic container into the ground, leaving about an inch of it above the ground to stop other insects falling into it (namely beneficial beetles). Fill it three quarters full with beer, don't waste the good stuff on these pests, they aren't connoisseurs, and leave it. Place these around the at risk plants and they will catch some, but not all, of the slugs and snails.

There are many other potential pests that you will encounter, but these are the common ones that affect most of your plants. Taking the steps suggested above will help minimise the effect these pests have on your plants. Vigilance is by far the best option, keep a close eye on your plants and take steps immediately that you encounter a pest or problem to stop it spreading and affecting too many plants. Some simple precautions, such as netting your young plants, and keeping your plot free from debris will go a long way to keeping the pest population under control.

Home-Made Pest Sprays

Many store-bought sprays are bad for the environment and for your plants. Some of them are labelled as food safe, meaning you can use them on vegetables, but these tend to be a little bit more expensive and still generally contain chemicals that some people do not like to use.

It is surprisingly easy to make your own insecticides at home which are very effective and cheap! Remember that, like all sprays, these do not differentiate between beneficial insects and pests. Personally, I tend to pick beneficial insects, such as ladybirds, off plants before spraying them with any of these as I do not want to harm these creatures.

In the section you will learn a number of different recipes for home-made insecticides. Most of these are generally not toxic to the soil or the environment but remember to use them carefully as they will harm beneficial insects. Always use these on a still day where there is no wind and be careful not to spray on bees as some of them can cause them harm.

Many of these sprays use dish soap or washing up liquid as a key ingredient as it helps to kill the insect. Be careful using popular brands of washing up liquid as many of them contain chemicals which can actually be harmful to your plants. With the constant push by the manufacturers to make better products, the ingredients lists are changing regularly. The best washing up liquid to use is a natural, environmentally friendly product such as the Ecover brand. Dr. Bronners castile soap is another mild soap which is suitable for use in home-made pest sprays. Whichever you choose to use, find one that has tallow in it as this is one of the main components which is effective against the insects.

Simple Oil Spray

This is a very simple insecticide to make. Mix 1 cup of vegetable oil with a tablespoon of washing up liquid (dish soap). Dilute two teaspoons of this with a quart of water, shake well and spray directly on to plants. The oil coats the insects which suffocates them as it blocks the pores they breathe through. Use an eco-friendly washing up liquid so that this breaks down in the soil and leaves no chemical residue.

Simple Soap Spray

This is similar to the previous insecticide though just mixes 1½ teaspoons of washing up liquid with one quart of water. Spray directly on insects, either in the morning or evening rather than during the hottest part of the day.

Neem Oil

Neem oil is extracted from the seeds of the neem tree and is a natural insecticide that is very effective. It disrupts the lifecycle of insects whether they are an egg, larvae or adult, and so is a superb resource for the organic gardening. It is biodegradable, non-toxic and effective against a wide variety of pests. Neem oil also acts as a natural fungicide and can be used to treat fungal infections such as powdery mildew. The bottle will come with instructions for use, though mixing two

teaspoons of neem oil with one teaspoon of eco-friendly washing up liquid in a quart of water is a good start. Neem oil can be used preventatively by spraying leaves before they are infested with pests.

Diatomaceous Earth

This is a natural substance created from sedimentary rock formed by diatoms (fossilised algae) and is very abundant, making up as much as 26% of the earth's crust by weight. It has many uses and is an effective, natural insecticide that works through its abrasiveness and its ability to absorb liquid, which dries out insects, causing them to die. Dust the ground around your plants or spread it on the leaves, depending on where the pests are. Diatomaceous earth is effective against both slugs and snails. As it is dried, it must be applied during dry weather and reapplied after it has rained.

Garlic Spray

Garlic not only keeps vampires away, but also acts as a natural insecticide, affecting a wide variety of insects. Whether it kills the insects or just repels them no one is quite sure about, but it is effective and easy to get your hands on. Puree two bulbs (not cloves) in a blender with a little bit of water. Transfer into a container with a quart of water and leave to sit overnight. Strain the liquid into a jar, adding ½ cup of vegetable oil (helps the mixture to stick to the insects) and one teaspoon of washing up liquid. Dilute one cup of this mixture with one quart of water and spray infested plants.

Chilli Spray

This spray is similar to garlic spray in that it is a natural and powerful insect repellent. Make this from fresh chillies if you have them to hand or from dried chilli powder, in which case, use the hottest you have available.

Mix together a tablespoon of chilli powder in a litre of water and several drops of mild liquid soap.

If you are using fresh chilli peppers, then blend a cup of water with two or three chillies. Put this into a saucepan with a litre of water and bring to the boil. Leave to cool, strain and put in a sprayer with a few drops of liquid soap. Be careful with this liquid as it is a form of pepper spray, similar to that used by the police, so handle with care and do not touch your eyes or anything sensitive if you have this on your hands. Use hot chillies to make a powerful liquid that will kill off the pests.

Tomato Leaf Spray

This is an interesting spray that is surprisingly effective according to its users. Tomato plants are a member of the nightshade family, related to deadly nightshade which most of us have heard of. Tomato leaves contain alkaloids known as 'tomatine' which are deadly to many insects, including aphids. Cut up two cups of fresh tomato leaves (remove them from the bottom of the plant rather than higher up) and steep overnight in a litre of water. Strain and then spray directly on to infected plants.

Potential Allotment Problems

Owning an allotment is a fun and enjoyable process but occasionally you will encounter problems. Knowing what these problems are and how best to tackle them will help to make your time on your plot more enjoyable and relaxing, though there is always going to be the unexpected designed to catch you out. The best way to avoid problems with your plants is to keep the ground free from debris, space your plants well, always water at the base of the plant and to feed them regularly. Healthy plants are less likely to struggle, but not all problems are plant related!

Here are some of the common problems you may face and some tips and advice on how to deal with them.

Disease Attack

With any luck, you will avoid many of the nastier diseases out there on your allotment, but you are likely to suffer from some common diseases such as:

- White rot on your onions
- Rust on leeks, garlic and onions
- Potato blight
- Powdery mildew on squashes
- Tomato blight
- Club root on brassicas

Reduce the risk of disease by rotating your crops every year and practising good plant hygiene, i.e., removing debris from under the plant. Crop rotation prevents diseases from building up in the soil and if you don't replant the same crop there for four years, leaves plenty of time for the disease to die out in the soil. Unfortunately, many of these diseases are blown on to your allotment by the wind and there is little you can do to avoid them. If they are a problem every year, and you can find this out by talking to other plot holders, then buy disease resistant varieties of plants as this will help them to fruit before succumbing to the disease.

Some potato varieties have blight resistance, and these are worth growing if you want a main crop variety. As blight often strikes towards the end of June or July, you can usually avoid it by planting first early potato varieties which are harvested and stored before blight takes effect. Potatoes and tomatoes are from the same family and will cross-infect each other with blight, so do not plant them near each other. You can help delay or even avoid tomato blight by growing them in a polytunnel or greenhouse, though you can still bring blight spores inside on your clothing or shoes.

Infected with blight

Club root will occur if you grow any of the brassica family such as cauliflower, kale, cabbage, Brussels sprouts, or broccoli in the same area for multiple years. You may be fortunate and miss it for a year or two, but for the sake of rotating your crops you do not want to risk your plants.

Powdery mildew is very common on squash plants such as pumpkins and butternut squash. It occurs when the leaves and stems are damp or wet overnight, so is particularly prevalent during warm, wet summers. Gardeners often cause this by watering the leaves of the plants, particularly in the evening time when many of us visit. The risk of powdery mildew can be reduced significantly by watering your squash plants directly at the base of the plant. Sink a pipe or upturned plastic bottle into the ground by the roots to make it easier for you to direct water to the roots.

Powdery mildew visible on the leaves

Unless you are very unlucky, you should not encounter many other diseases, though if you have fruit trees on your plot then there is a chance your apple or pear trees may get a disease. Following the advice in this section will help you to avoid the common diseases, but if there are diseases on your allotment site, look for disease resistant plant varieties in online seed catalogues and grow those.

Germination Problems

Sometimes you will have issues with your seeds not germinating. We discussed this in depth earlier in the book when we talked about how to grow from seed.

If your seeds do fail, then don't panic. Depending on how late it is in the season, you may be able to start a second set. If it is too late or you are not confident you can get them to germinate, then look at ordering a different variety as plug plants or buying larger plants from your local garden centre or DIY store. You may not be able to find the same varieties, but you will at least be able to find similar plants that you can use to fill the space. Then try to work out what went wrong and why germination failed so you can do better next year.

Neighbour Problems

Hopefully, this is something you will never encounter as, generally, allotments are harmonious places where people all get along, providing they follow the rules and respect their neighbours.

However, sometimes you will have neighbour issues, whether it is them constantly offering unwanted advice, accidentally spraying your plants with weed killer or cutting down an overgrown bush or tree on your allotment. These are difficult situations to deal with and can be uncomfortable. I heard of a new plot holder recently who cut down the blackberry bushes that were acting as a fence between their plots that the other plot holder had been tending for many years and made prize winning jam from. The same person also damaged their neighbours polytunnel at the same time, leaving the resident plot holder wondering if it was worth carrying on. I regularly hear of plot neighbours who have used weed killer on their plot, forgotten to take into account it was a windy day and killed half of their neighbours' vegetables.

Many neighbour disputes can be prevented by being considerate and thinking first. Don't use weed killer on windy days and when you do use it (if you do), then apply as closely as you can do the weeds you are trying to kill. Don't cut anything down between plots without first talking to your neighbour as it could be there for a reason, to provide shade for their plot, to act as a windbreak, or any other reason. Do not let your dog or children stray on to your neighbours' plots and generally

keep an eye out for them and be helpful where you can.

Your first action should be to talk to your neighbour about the problem and try to resolve it. Not all people are comfortable doing this, in which case you should approach the site management and ask for their help resolving the issue. How much help you get will depend on the site management and it will vary, but hopefully you will get the problem resolved. If it is just that you don't get on with your neighbour you can try visiting your plot at different times when they aren't there or making sure you work at the furthest point from their plot when they are there, but avoidance doesn't always solve the problem.

Hopefully between yourself and the allotment management you will be able to resolve the problem harmoniously. Sadly, this is not always possible. In the worst cases, people have felt they have had to move plots, move sites, or even give up their plot completely. Hopefully, this will not be the case for you and that you will not have any issues with your allotment neighbours. In all the years I've had an allotment, I've been fortunate in that the biggest problem I've had with a plot neighbour was that they were really chatty and I'd never get any work done when they were there. In fact, I have been the problem neighbour on at least one occasion when work commitments meant I was unable to get to my allotment for several weeks and arrived to find a polite note asking me to cut back some blackberries that had gone wild and were growing over my neighbour's plot. Of course, I cut them back straight away and when I finally saw them some weeks late, apologised for letting them get out of control. Generally, problems can be resolved, but sometimes they are more difficult to put right, particularly when a neighbour has damaged your property.

Pest Infestation

Pests are another problem you will encounter on your allotment, though which ones you meet will depend on what you are growing and where in the country or world you live. There are plenty of pests out there more than willing to eat your crops for you, but you are unlikely to encounter most of them. These are some of the most common pests you are going to encounter.

- Allium Leaf Miner
- Aphids
- Carrot Fly
- Caterpillars
- Slugs and Snails
- Wasps

Good allotment hygiene will help deter many pests

as will companion planting, specifically, planting sacrificial plants and plants that attract predatory insects to your allotment. Dill, calendula, coriander, marjoram, parsley, fennel, cosmos, chives and mint all attract ladybirds who will feast on a wide range of pests. The same flowers also attract hoverflies and some of the predatory wasps which can help keep your allotment clear of these voracious pests.

Checking your plot at sundown is the best way to remove slugs and snails, though leaving them nowhere to hide during the day is a great way of deterring them from coming on to your plot in the first place. Wasps are not so much of a problem as more of a nuisance. The occasional wasp you can ignore, but a nest is potentially dangerous, particularly if you have children on the plot or are allergic to their stings. Your local beekeeper can help get rid of a wasp's nest, or you can buy powders or sprays that will kill them. However, if there are bees on your allotment site you need to talk to the beekeepers there first before using any chemicals as they can get into the beehives and harm the beneficial bees.

Being vigilant and taking action as soon as spot a pest problem will help to stop it spreading and becoming a serious infestation. You can make or buy organic sprays that will kill some pests, or in serious cases, you can use chemical sprays. Just be aware that these sprays do not differentiate between beneficial and harmful pests and will kill them all indiscriminately. If you can take action early on, then usually you can stop them from spreading.

Watering Problems

Most of the year you should have no problems watering your plants and they should be fine with the rain. When they are seedlings and freshly planted, they will need watering more frequently until they have established themselves and have grown a deeper root system.

The hard part comes during extended hot, dry weather when you have to regularly water your plants just to keep them alive. As most allotment sites do not permit the use of hoses, you are left carrying watering cans from the nearest tap or water butt to your plants. It is at this time you realise just how far away the tap is and how little water a water butt actually contains!

I would recommend buying two watering cans as big as you can comfortably carry when full. If you struggle to carry them when full, put them in your wheelbarrow and push them to where you need them. Make each journey with the two cans and water as many plants as you can as thoroughly as they need. Apply a good mulch around the base of your plants, which will help to retain moisture and reduce the need for watering.

Watering at the base of the plants, i.e. where the stem meets the ground, helps to retain moisture as the water goes directly to the roots. If you water on the leaves, then water can pool on the leaves or it runs off the leaves and doesn't get to the plants roots where it is needed. This results in you using a lot more water that you need to for each of your plants and the ground the water runs off to quickly becomes infested with weeds.

If your site does not have access to water, then you will need to collect your own, which means multiple water butts on every gutter and collecting rainwater whenever you can. In hot, dry spells, even this is unlikely to be enough. If this is the case, then you will need to take every water conserving technique you can and bring water with you from home, which can be difficult if you do not drive.

If your plants are well established and mulched, then they will need a lot less water than those that are not and so are more likely to survive hot, dry summers. Watering problems are something you are going to encounter but keep an eye on the weather forecast and prepare for it as best you can.

Pipe for watering direct to the root and wood chip mulch

Weather Problems

Weather problems are part and parcel of owning an allotment and you will encounter them almost every year. As the climate seems much more variable now than it was in the past, it is not uncommon to have late frosts, snows or even temperate Decembers where many plants will continue to grow outside.

Sadly, weather problems, like water problems, are a significant contributor to people giving up their allotment, but if you are prepared, then you can minimise the effect they have on you. There are always going to be surprise storms, heavy rain or late frosts, but over the years you will get used to the weather patterns where you are and understand when these are going to happen. I've found that listening to some of the old timers who are at the allotments all day, every day, gives you an insight into the weather as they are usually right in their predictions!

Wind

This is a very destructive type of weather and over recent years, the UK has been regularly hit by severe stores with winds in excess of 60mph. High winds will damage polytunnels, greenhouses and sheds as well as tall plants. In the last severe wind storm, my runner beans were blown over and the eight-foot bamboo canes used to make the structure they climbed up snapped by the winds!

Runner beans blown over by the winds.

Make sure all structures on your plot are securely fixed to the ground so that they cannot blow away. Ensure they are in good repair as high winds can blow roofs off sheds if they are not attached properly! For greenhouses and polytunnels it is usually best to close all windows, doors and ventilation flaps as this will help protect them from damage. If you are in an exposed site that regularly suffers from high winds, then try positioning your structures in the most sheltered spot possible or even planting trees or fruit canes close to the greenhouse to act as a wind break.

There is little you can do to prevent damage to your plants, though larger plants such as sunflowers can be staked, but even that will not always protect them from damage. If you do stake plants, put the stakes in the ground at an angle, rather than upright as that will help prevent the wind from toppling the stake too. You may

visit your plot the next morning to find the sunflower and the cane toppled over! If your plants are blown over, check for root damage and see if you can stand it back up again and firm the soil down around it to keep it secure. You may need to put in some supports to help keep the plant upright until it has finished fruiting. One of the biggest frustrations is the wind blowing the fruit from your trees and you realise that your entire crop of apples is now on the floor. Depending on how late it is in the season, you may be able to save some of them and cook with them, but early in the season and they are good for nothing except compost.

Rain

Rain is generally welcome on an allotment, but extended periods of heavy rain can be an issue. It can prevent you from visiting your plot so that the weeds can get established, but this can be minimised by covering unused areas of ground to inhibit weed growth. If you have clay soil, then heavy rain is generally very unwelcome because it will soak your soil, turning it into a quagmire and often kill any plants that you are growing in it because their roots become waterlogged. Growing in raised beds helps to reduce this problem, but you can work to amend your soil, though it will take several years for the soil to stop getting waterlogged.

If your soil regularly gets waterlogged, look at digging drainage ditches along the side of your plot to help the water run-off. Raised beds are a good idea as this can lift your plants above the water level.

Any plastic structures should be checked to ensure water isn't pooling on the plastic and the water removed. Too much water pooling on a polytunnel or small plastic tunnel over plants can cause the tunnel to bow and break. Check your shed and greenhouse for leaks and make any require repairs as soon as you can.

Collect as much rain as you can in water butts as this will be very helpful in the summer months, but there is little you can do apart from the above to stop the rain affecting your plot.

Snow

Snow may be a problem for some people, but for others it is rarely seen. So long as snow comes at the right time of year, it doesn't cause any problems as the only plants in the ground don't mind being covered with snow for short periods of time. It is only when they spend a couple of week or more under snow that they start to get upset. Garlic and overwinter onions are both generally quite happy under snow, though they do not like it if they are under it for too long.

Snow fall can damage some plants and structures.

You can protect your plants by using plastic half hoops pushed into the ground to support fleece or tight weave netting over them. This helps to keep them warm and stop them being buried in snow. In areas where there is significant snow fall, this can be a good way to protect your plants when snow is on the ground. Remember to visit regularly to brush the snow off the fleece so it does not get weighed down and rest on your plants.

Apart from fleecing or moving delicate plants indoors or into the greenhouse, there is little you can do to protect from snow. Keep your eye on the weather and always be prepared to protect delicate plants as best you can.

Frost
Frost can be a major problem for an allotment owner. A surprise early frost can damage plants before fruit has fully ripened and is ready for harvest. A late frost can kill your seedlings and young plants, sometimes leaving it too late for you to start again. In this case, you may have to resort to buying pre-grown plants from a local store. Plants such as squashes which have hollow stems are decimated by a late frost and the fruit of the butternut squash is harmed by frost and then doesn't store well.

Depending on where you live, the last frost could be as late as May and it's not be unheard of for parts of the UK to be covered in snow in early June!

Listen out for the weather forecast to determine how cold it is going to get. Check online daily or install a weather app on your phone. If it looks like it is going to get close to freezing, go and fleece your delicate plants as it is better to be safe than sorry. Horticultural fleece can be rolled or folded and stored when not in use and then taken out when there is a risk of frost. Fleece will protect your plants from a light frost but may struggle to protect them properly from a heavy frost. Some people leave their plants covered with fleece until there is no risk at all of frost. This is worth doing if you cannot get to your allotment quickly in an evening to cover your plants.

Drape the fleece over your plants or use hoops and bamboo stakes to make a cage to support the fleece. Make sure you weigh down the edges with something to prevent them from lifting in the wind and the fleece blowing away, leaving your plants exposed.

Frost is part of the natural cycle of the year, but with the current disturbed weather patterns we are experiencing, surprise late or early frosts have become more common and catch many allotment owners out. By keeping a close eye on the weather and speaking to other plot holders you will be aware of when there is a risk of frost and can take steps to protect your plants. I've found many of the older generation of allotment holders have some strange connection with the weather and can 'feel it in their bones' when there is a frost. Often, they are right in their predictions and it is worth taking precautions at the slightest risk to avoid damage to your plants.

Buying Seeds And Plants

A commonly asked question by new allotment owners is where to buy their seeds and plants from. There are a wide range of suppliers, both on and offline, and this section will help guide you to the best places to buy your plants, seedlings and seeds from so that you get a good germination rate and healthy plants.

Just a few of my seeds!

Where you buy them from will depend on your budget and the time available to you. Many discount stores sell seeds, often very cheaply, that are just as good as those you buy from more expensive stores, though you tend to get fewer seeds in a packet and the selection of varieties is limited. Seeing as often you have more seeds than you have space, this isn't necessarily a bad thing. Supermarkets and garden centers all sell seeds, any of which are perfectly good.

Online becomes a bit more of a minefield, particularly if you buy from eBay as you are never quite sure what you are getting plus there are fake seeds for sale, such as those for the Photoshopped blue strawberries. The reputable online suppliers such as Thomson and Morgan, Suttons, DT Brown, Mr Fothergill's, Kings Seeds and so on, are all very good places to buy your seeds from and there will be lots and lots of varieties available. These are also good places to buy plug plants, bare root trees and bare root fruit canes, though I'd be wary about buying larger plants by mail order because of the issues with transporting them and the potential for damage.

Plug plants are great to buy from online suppliers and are usually well packaged so they are protected from the postal service. As soon as these arrive, open them up and at least put them in water or water them if they have soil on until you are ready to plant them. They will not do well if they are left in their packaging and ignored. Get these planted as soon as you can after they arrive so they can get established and start growing. Being disturbed and put in the post is quite a shock to these plants and they need planting out quickly, so they don't suffer and weaken.

Established plants are best bought from plant nurseries or garden centers rather than online as often the transportation process causes stress and damage to the plants. Although the plants may be more expensive, they are not going to be damaged in transit and you can choose plants in good condition. Look for strong plants that are free from damage. Any with yellowing leaves or any spots or unusual marks on their leaves are best avoided as they are either low in nutrients or have a disease. Plants that have become leggy are best avoided as they are going to be weak and may struggle to support fruit later on. Squat, bushy plants with strong stems are the best option. Try to avoid any that are flowering or fruiting as they have been started too early and are unlikely to grow much larger or produce too much more fruit when you put them in the ground. However, if you are late planting, these are a great short cut.

At the end of the day, you buy seeds from anywhere that is convenient for you. If I'm in the supermarket and see some seeds I want to try, I'll buy them! I've signed up for seed catalogues from all the major suppliers (do this on their websites) and whenever they arrive, I read them and order seeds that I want to try. In most cases, you are going to get good quality, viable seeds that will grow. Issues only come, in my experience, from smaller suppliers who often get seeds mixed up or send older seeds that are less likely to germinate.

How To Grow From Seeds

People seem to think that growing plants from seeds is some sort of dark art, yet it is shockingly easy; Mother Nature has been doing it for millions of years without any gadgets and gizmos. There is generally some failure when germinating seeds, but there are some things you can do to improve the germination rate and the number of plants that mature to adults.

The key to getting seeds to germinate are:

- Good Quality Seeds – always buy good quality seeds as these are much more likely to have a high germination rate. Either keep your own or buy from a reputable supplier. Personally, I am always dubious about buying seeds from eBay as you are never entirely sure what you are getting and there are a lot of cases of people getting the wrong seeds. Saying that, there are plenty of people who swear by some of the suppliers on eBay. Personally, I prefer to buy from stores or from the bigger online seed suppliers because I know I am going to get seeds with a high germination rate. I also know that if I buy a packet of seeds and few or none germinate, they are much more likely to give me my money back.

- In-Date Seeds – seeds do have a use by date and after this, the germination rate falls. Although seeds can be stored for a long time in the right conditions, a packet on a shelf isn't the right conditions, so it is important that you regularly replace your seeds with new ones. Older seeds can still germinate, but you will find that as they get older and older, they become less viable and fewer will germinate when planted. I tend to keep my seeds for two or three years and then I replace them with new ones. As you usually get far more seeds than you can use in a packet, I generally swap some of the leftover seeds with friends or family for their leftover seed too. Parsnips are notoriously difficult to germinate and the germination rate plummets after the seeds are a year old.

- Provide Them with Enough Light – once a seed germinates, they need light and often people start seeds on shady windowsills where they quickly become leggy and unhealthy because they do not have enough light. I start mine off indoors under LED grow lamps on top of the fridge (to try and keep the cats off them) and then, once they have germinated and are big enough to transplant, they get moved to plastic greenhouses in the garden where they get plenty of light. Leggy seeds are not going to mature properly and will be unhealthy plants.

- Do Not Overwater – overwatering seeds is going to cause them to rot in the compost. Seed compost should be kept damp, but not moist. Be careful not to overwater and use a small watering can with a rose or a water sprayer so that your seeds get just enough water.

- Give Them The Right Conditions – this is one of the most commonly made mistakes people make with seeds. They plant a hot chilli pepper seed in compost and expect a plant which is used to the tropical conditions of South America to germinate and thrive on a shady windowsill in the North West of the UK. It's not going to happen! Think about where the plant originated from and then give it the conditions it needs to germinate, usually the seed packet will tell you this information. Generally, plants from warmer climates require a temperature above a certain level for their seeds to germinate. However, go above a certain temperature and the germination rate will drop. A heated propagator is a great way to keep the seed temperature consistent and improve your germination rate.

- Good Quality Compost – always use the best quality seed compost you can afford. This should be loose, without any chunks in and free draining. You will get a far higher germination rate in a good quality compost than in a poor compost which either holds too much moisture, or not enough. Since moving to a more expensive and better seed compost, my germination rate has improved dramatically and now is usually between 90-100%.

- Pearlite or Vermiculite – these are relatively cheap and are used to retain moisture. They absorb water and then slowly release it back into the soil. Either of these are a great addition to see compost to help make it a little looser but still help it retain moisture. Mixing this in at a ratio of one-part vermiculite to three or four parts compost will make for an even better seed compost.

Planting a seed is very easy indeed. If you are starting off larger vegetables such as chilli plants, tomatoes, squashes, brassicas and so on, then start the seed in a single pot as there is less transplanting involved. The more you have to transplant a seedling, the more chance there is of it being damaged, so ideally you want to move it as little as possible. Start these plants off in a three-inch plastic pot. Although you can buy peat pots for seedlings, I have found these to be a poor choice as they either dry out too quickly or get too wet and start to go mouldy, so I would avoid them.

Plant the seed according to the instructions on the packet and then cover loosely with compost. Water in and put somewhere for it to germinate. If you are planting squash seeds, then plant them on their side as they do have a right way up. Generally, the leaves come from the pointy end and the roots from the rounded end and if they are not planted the right way up or on their sides, they start to grow upside down before dying!

If you are growing plants such as beetroot, radish, lettuce and other plants which are smaller and you plant lots of seeds at once, these can be grown in plastic seed trays. You can get clear plastic lids for these which create a mini greenhouse which helps germination. Some plants, such as carrots, hate being transplanted and are usually sown directly into the soil.

Scatter the seeds across the top of the compost or plant individual seeds at spaced intervals, cover with a loose layer of compost according to the instructions on the packet and then water in.

The advantage of growing from seed rather than buying plants is that it is a lot cheaper, you will get hundreds of seeds for the price of a single seedling in some cases. You also have access to many more varieties in seed form than in seedling form. Nurseries will grow the few most popular varieties to sell as seedlings, usually boring varieties without a lot of taste because they transport well and are hardy as seedlings. Seeds give you the opportunity to grow more unusual and better tasting varieties of vegetables that you would not find as seedlings. You can find more unusual plants at specialist plant nurseries or very large garden centres, those these usually attract a premium price. Go through any seed catalogue and you will see a multitude of varieties of every vegetable you can grow. I always like to choose one that I am familiar with and then try a new variety, usually a heirloom variety as generally these are better tasting than F1 varieties plus you can keep the seeds. If you live in an area that is commonly afflicted by a particular plant disease, then you can look for seeds that have resistance to that disease. It many cases these are not varieties that you can save the seeds from, but it does mean you have a chance to grow plants that would not otherwise survive. Remember though, that disease resistance means the plants are resistant, not immune, to the disease and they may still succumb to it.

All in all, growing from seed is a great idea, but if your seeds fail to germinate or get eaten by pests, buy some seedlings. These are also great for filling gaps if you have not grown enough seeds. Some people make a big fuss that you have to start your plants off from seed. That is great if you have the time and space, but for many people, that isn't practical. In a busy year when I've not had time to start my seedlings off, I will buy a collection of plug plants online (ready grown seedlings, smaller than those from garden centres, but ready to go in the ground) and plant them. They are a huge time saver if you need to get something in the ground quick, and when you are starting out, you often do not have the time to grow from seed and clear your allotment.

The Difference Between F1 Hybrid And Heirloom Seeds

When you are buying seeds, you will see some seeds called F1 seeds. F1 stands for 'filial 1' which translates to 'first children'. Other seeds may be labelled as 'heirloom' or even 'hybrid'. So what on earth do these mean and which are best?

Heirloom seeds come from wild plants which have been bred by humans over hundreds and, in some cases, thousands, of years. People have taken plants with desirable characteristics and deliberately cross pollinated them with other plants to bring out those characteristics, though many are actually just open pollinated and nature is left to run its course. Many heirloom seed varieties are very old, though they often do not have the disease or pest resistance that other seeds may have. This is because it takes a long time to breed heirloom seeds because you have to wait for generation after generation of plant, saving seeds and crossbreeding.

Heirloom seeds are very popular with gardeners because they tend to have a much fuller and nicer flavour than other varieties. Modern breeding programs often sacrifice taste for reliability, yield and transportability. As you don't have to transport your harvest, you can grow plants based on taste, which are generally very nutritious for you too.

Another advantage of heirloom seed is that they are open pollinated, meaning you can save the seeds from your plants and use them year after year. This allows you to develop varieties that are native to your area and can help you save money from having to buy seeds for your favourite plants every year. These will produce plants that are true to type, unlike hybrid seeds which are not. By growing heirloom seeds you can, over time, develop strains that perform well in your soil in your climate and have a resistance to pests and diseases that are common on your allotment site.

Hybrid seeds are cross-pollinated by hand and are designed to produce high yields and usually to ripen all at once. Hybrid seeds are aimed at commercial growers so are designed to produce high yields of vegetables that can easily be transported. Commercially grown tomatoes, for example, are often picked before they are ripe and then ripened with ethylene gas while being transported. The difference between a store bought, F1 variety, and an heirloom variety is truly amazing. Some shops are now stocking some heirloom varieties which have a fantastic taste, but because of their shorter shelf life, they are much more expensive to purchase.

Hybrid seeds usually bear the label 'F1' and come from plants that have been hand pollinated to ensure the seeds have the positive traits of both parents. This allows for the development of plants that have resistance to pests and diseases plus you end up with fruit that is very uniform in its flavour and appearance with a much higher yield. This is good for a commercial grower, but it is not so important for the home grower.

The problem with F1 seeds is that the resulting plants are often sterile and the seeds do not grow true, meaning the second generation plant is unlikely to have the traits of the first generation plant. For the allotment owner, this means it is not worth saving the seeds of F1 plants.

F1 seeds are great if there is a known problem where you grow with pests and diseases and you need a resistant strain. However, if you want to grow plants that have great tasting fruit and that you can keep the seeds from, which many allotment owners do, then F1 seeds are not suitable.

Usually, F1 seeds are more expensive to buy than heirloom seeds because of the work that has gone into producing them. Although hybrids have their place and their uses, for most allotment owners, the focus is on taste rather than on yield or conformity. Myself, along with many allotment owners I speak to, prefer heirloom seeds because the flavour is so much more 'real' than the F1 varieties. Heirloom seeds usually do not ripen all at once, meaning you have a longer harvest time and more chance to use your produce without having a glut which can be difficult to process.

Which you buy will be up to you and depend on your needs. If you need disease or pest resistance, then buy F1 seeds. If you do not, then buy whichever seeds are available in your price range for the varieties you want to grow. If you want to save seeds to grow the follow year, then you must buy a heirloom variety as the F1 varieties are not suitable for replanting.

There is no right or wrong answer here, though please do experiment with heirloom varieties as you will find the flavours very enjoyable. If you want to test this, grow an F1 variety together with a heirloom variety and compare the taste of the two. You may well be surprised; I know I was the first time I grew heirloom tomatoes!

Growing In Containers On Your Allotment

Although you can grow almost anything in the ground at your allotment, there are some benefits to using containers for some plants. Here we are not discussing growing in your greenhouse, but out on your plot.

Invasive plants such as mint and lemon balm should always be grown in containers because they will spread out and take over your plot. I would also recommend putting autumn fruiting raspberries in containers for the same reason because they too are very invasive, growing by runners that are sent out underground. All of these plants will quickly start to pop up in your vegetable beds and it won't be long before you are busy pulling up unwanted mint plants or raspberries.

Potatoes grown in potato bags.

Trees can also be grown in large pots because it helps to keep them compact and stops them sucking up nutrients from the ground. Unless you buy very dwarf varieties, most trees will quickly grow very large and send roots out all over your plot, which then takes moisture and nutrients away from your other plants. However, trees grown in pots will never grow to their full potential or produce a high yield, plus they will struggle with drying out and fruit drop in hot weather.

Any plants which are susceptible to the cold should also be grown in containers because they can be moved into a greenhouse or taken home when the weather turns cold to protect them. I grow my chilli plants in containers, leaving them outside when it is hot and sunny and moving them into the greenhouse as the weather starts to cool. This usually allows me to get a good crop from them far more reliably than if I was growing them in the ground and worrying about fleecing them.

Potatoes are another vegetable that I think should be grown in containers. When you plant potatoes in the ground and dig them up, you will always leave one or two little potatoes in the ground, no matter how hard you try to dig them all up. The following year, these will start to grow, usually in the middle of other vegetables and are then hard to remove without disturbing your new vegetables. Growing them in containers (special potato bags are available) means you don't have this problem and it is very easy to harvest your crop; you just empty the bag on to the ground and sift through to find the potatoes. The spent compost is then used as a mulch or soil amendment. The downside is that you cannot plant as many potatoes as you could in the soil and you need a fair bit of compost for each bag. However, unless you have somewhere to store your potatoes, it isn't worth growing huge amounts of them. The other upside of growing them in containers is that you can avoid some soil borne diseases and pests such as wire worm, though they will still be susceptible to blight.

Plants that have very specific soil requirements such as blueberries, which need an acidic soil, also work well in containers because you can easily amend the soil so it is ideal for the plant.

Although you have lots of ground space to grow plants in, growing in containers on your allotment can be very useful and an efficient use of space. It allows you to grow plants in areas where the soil isn't usable (either due to pollution or rubbish or because you haven't had time to clear it) and move plants around your plot to benefit from sun, shade, or protection from the elements. When growing in containers, you must remember to water them much more often than ground grown plants. You will have to water them even when it is raining because they do not have access to ground water and surprisingly little rainwater actually gets into most containers, particularly when the plants are mature and their leaves act like an umbrella.

The strategic use of containers is a great way to help make the most of your plot, maximise your use of space and grow efficiently. While some people will shout heresy at the thought of using containers on an allotment, they are a very useful way to grow invasive or sensitive plants or anything that needs its size limiting.

Feeding, Fertiliser and Manure

When you are growing plants, they need regular feeding in order to stay healthy, grow and fruit. Healthy plants are better equipped to fight off diseases and survive pests, just like a healthy human is less likely to get ill. Although your plants can get many of the nutrients they need from the soil, they benefit from extra feeding in order to grow stronger and to replace nutrients that they take from the soil. If you do not add extra nutrients to the soil, eventually it will become poor quality and your plants will struggle to grow due to low levels of nutrients.

Fresh manure spread on a bed in autumn.

How often you feed your plants will depend on the plant and its individual needs. Some plants don't like being fed too often, whereas others, such as giant pumpkins and squashes, are greedy plants that literally cannot get enough food! The seed packet will give you instructions on how often your plants need to be fed.

As a rough rule of thumb, feed your plants once a week during the growing season. Newly planted seeds don't need feeding and anything planted in fresh, store bought compost, will not require feeding for two or three weeks as there will be plenty of nutrients in the soil for them. Even if the compost has slow release fertiliser in, you should still feed the plants after a couple of weeks as they need a lot of food to grow and develop properly.

How you feed your plants is entirely up to you. Some people make compost, nettle or comfrey tea and use that, whereas other people use pelleted or liquid fertiliser. I've found that scattering handfuls of pelleted chicken manure on the soil once a month, followed by weekly liquid feeds works very well. Although you can buy general purpose liquid fertilisers, seaweed based ones are particularly good for your plants as they are very high in micro-nutrients. Tomato plants have specific feeds designed for them and it is best to use a tomato feed on tomato plants, rather than a general purpose feed. Dilute liquid feed according to the instructions on the bottle.

The NPK Ratio Explained

It is important that you have a basic understand of the chemistry behind fertilisers so you know what to apply to your allotment at different times in the growing season.

Every packet of fertiliser you buy will have, somewhere on it, an NPK ratio. This is three numbers that indicate the ratio of Nitrogen (N), Phosphorus (P) and Potassium (K). This is usually displayed in a format similar to '5-10-5', which would mean that fertiliser contains 5% nitrogen, 10% phosphorous and 5% potassium. Understanding these elements and how they benefit your plants means you can apply fertiliser that gives your plants exactly what they need at that stage of their lifecycle.

Nitrogen
High nitrogen fertilisers are used to encourage leafy growth and are applied early in a plant's life, before they have started to set fruit. High nitrogen levels are great for leafy vegetables such as spinach and lettuces but should not be given to plants that are fruiting as it will make the plant concentrate on producing leaves, not fruit.

Phosphorus
Phosphorus helps your plants to develop a strong root system and to produce flowers. You should switch to a high phosphorus fertiliser when you want your plants to start producing flowers and slow down producing foliage.

Potassium
Potassium encourages fruit to set, so once your plants start to flower, switch to a fertiliser with higher levels of potassium to encourage the production of more fruit.

Micro-Nutrients
All fertilisers contain micro-nutrients such as iron, calcium, manganese, magnesium and more. These are important for the healthy development of plants and if your soil is deficient in any of these, then your plants can suffer. Most fertilisers contain varying trace elements in them, but the levels can differ significantly between fertilisers. Home-made compost will usually have higher levels of micro-nutrients, but it is worth using a seaweed based feed once a month on your plants to ensure they have sufficient levels of micro-nutrients. Seaweed feeds tend to be very high in essential micro-nutrients and using one occasionally can help prevent these from being depleted from the soil.

You can buy general purposes fertilisers which have average NPK ratios that are good to use all year round with very little detrimental effect on your plants. If you are growing for exhibitions or growing giant vegetables, then you will need to use fertilisers with the right NPK ratios to ensure the plants get the nutrients they require for maximum growth. A general purpose tomato food is good to use throughout the life of a tomato plant, providing you follow the instructions on the label. You can also purchase general purpose vegetable feeds or blood, fish and bonemeal feeds, which can be used throughout the year.

Fertilisers are important for your plants as it helps to give them a boost of nutrients, keeps them healthy and makes sure they produce a good yield for you. Even if you condition your soil every year, your plants will still benefit from regular feeding throughout the growing season to ensure they perform well. I always try to use natural fertilisers rather than chemical based ones purely because they are better for the environment and my plants. You can buy fertiliser from the shops or you can make your own compost, comfrey or nettle tea on your allotment which make for a wonderful feed for your plants.

How to Use Manure

Many people use manure on their allotment to amend the soil and as a mulch. This is a really good way of adding nutrients to the soil, raising the soil level and filling raised beds. Manure is often freely available, the only difficulty can come from trying to transport it yourself, though often you can get it delivered for a small charge.

The most commonly used manure is horse manure, but cow manure works well as does chicken and rabbit waste. Fresh manure is still composting and will burn your plants because it is hot, so it should never be applied directly to plants. The best manure to use is well-rotted, which can take up to a year. When manure is ready to apply directly to plants, it will be very crumbly and not have any smell. If it still smells like manure and/or is steaming, then do not put it on your plants as it will harm them!

Filling raised beds with manure for the following year.

Often it is more difficult to get well-rotted manure as few horse owners want to store manure for a year, they want to get rid of it as soon as possible. Although it can be applied to bare soil and left to rot, horse manure in particular is often full of partly digested weed seeds which will germinate if applied to soil. If you can, put fresh manure in your compost pile, cover it, and turn it regularly so it breaks down quickly so it can be used on your plants. Our allotment site gets regular deliveries of fresh manure which I use to fill my raised beds in the autumn. They are then covered and by spring, the manure has rotted down and left a wonderful soil to plant in. I often top this up with some compost or sharp sand to make it a little looser and raise the soil level as it drops when the manure rots.

Some allotment sites will have manure regularly delivered to site that you can use for free. If yours does not, then ask around on site as someone will be able to give you the contact details for a manure supplier. Alternatively, find a local horse stable and ask them as they will be more than willing to get rid of their waste product, though you might have to bag and collect it yourself. It is very useful to apply to your soil, but ensure it is well rotted otherwise you can end up introducing weeds to your allotment, including the dreaded mares tail.

Replenishing Nutrients in Your Soil

At the end of each growing season, your soil will benefit from some extra attention to replenish the nutrients that have been removed from it by your plants throughout the year. This is very important to maintain soil health and ensure that next year's plants have a good growing environment. How you replenish these nutrients is up to you and everyone has a different method of doing it.

Three of the most common and effective ways of improving your soil ready for the next growing season are:

- Green Manure – these are plants that you grow and dig in before they flower which then rot in the soil to break it up and provide nutrients. There are many different types of green manure from vetch to clover and more, check out a seed catalogue for the ideal green manure for your location and planting time. This can be grown any time a bed is left fallow and dug in before you plant.
- Mulch – covering your allotment with a mulch, whether it is manure, mushroom compost or home-made compost and then leaving it will allow it to break down over winter and the

goodness to be taken into the soil. You can then dig it over in spring or plant directly into the mulch if it is suitable.

- Pelleted Chicken Manure – this is relatively cheap to buy from most garden stores and discount, bargain stores. Scatter handfuls of this over the soil and it will break down as it rains, releasing nutrients into the soil.

Which you use is entirely up to you, but you will keep your soil in good condition by treating your soil at least once a year. This encourages worms and other beneficial insects into your soil plus improve the quality of the soil. After several years, even a terrible clay soil will become very friable and good to plant in with the right amendment. It is vital that you replenish the nutrients in the soil every year to prevent it from become exhausted. When this is done, you will get healthier plants, larger yields and fewer problems with diseases.

Soil pH Levels

Understanding the pH level of your soil isn't essential with an allotment, but it can be helpful if you are struggling to grow plants or want to grow plants such as blueberries which require an acid soil. Most allotment owners will have never, and are never going to, test the pH levels of their soil. However, some people like to know and if you find you are struggling to grow certain common plants, it could be down to a soil that is too acidic or too alkaline.

Symptoms such as yellowing leaves can often be blamed on diseases, but in many cases is down to the pH level of the soil being wrong for the plants you are trying to grow. Every plant prefers a different range of acidity, though the more common plants like a similar level and are broadly tolerant of some variation.

Understanding the pH levels will help you ensure your plants have the best possible growing environment. If you are growing plants that are sensitive to acidity levels, then you will want to check the pH levels a couple of times a year to ensure these plants remain healthy.

What is pH?

The pH scale is a measure of how acidic or alkaline something is, ranging from 0 to 14. A pH level of 7 is neutral. The lower the number, the more acidic the soil and the higher the number, the more alkaline it is. Soils will vary from an extremely acid pH 3, to a very alkaline pH 10.

The pH is influenced by a lot of different factors, including what is already in the soil, what composts on the soil every year, how much rainfall there is and more.

Most cultivated plants prefer a slightly acidic soil with a pH of around 6.5, but the majority of plants will grow perfectly well in a pH of around 6 to 7.5. Certain plants like blueberry, azalea and rhododendron prefer a more acidic soil and grow best when the pH is between 4.5 and 5.5.

What Does pH Do?

The acidity of the soil might seem insignificant but can have a major effect on your plants. Depending on the pH level, vital nutrients could become available or unavailable. For example, young leaves developing yellow veins indicates an iron deficiency which often occurs because the soil is not acidic enough for the iron to be in a form that your plants can absorb. A slightly acidic soil is beneficial to plants because it makes most nutrients available.

The downside of wrong soil pH levels is that if it is too low then the plants can become sick. If the soil pH is too low, then manganese becomes available to your plants at toxic levels, as does aluminium, which isn't a plant nutrient. The former can cause brown flecked or dead leaves while the latter can stunt root growth and prevent the plant absorbing vital nutrients. High pH levels result in molybdenum, another plant nutrient, becoming available at toxic levels.

The acidity of the soil also has an influence on the beneficial micro-organisms living in the soil, which are vital for healthy soil and plants. These micro-organisms turn nitrogen into a form that your plants can absorb, and they thrive in a slightly acidic soil, just like earthworms.

Testing Soil pH

You can send off for professional soil analysis, which gives you a very comprehensive report on your soil, but it isn't cheap and takes time for the results to come back.

Alternatively, you can test the soil at home. Soil testing kits and meters can be bought online or from larger garden stores. Follow the instructions in the kit and it will measure the pH level of your soil. Test in several different points around your garden and then average the pH levels. If you are having problems growing plants in a specific area, then test several points in that area and average the results. There can be pockets of acidic or alkaline soil in your vegetable patch.

What the Different pH Levels Mean

A pH level of 7.0 is considered neutral; neither acidic or alkaline. If the pH level is below 7.0 then the soil is acidic and if it is above, then it is alkaline. The pH level has an effect on your plants and the soil quality.

- pH 3.0-5.0 – Very Acidic – The majority of nutrients, including calcium, potassium and magnesium become very soluble at this level of acidity and are easily washed away by watering and rain. Most phosphates are not available to your plants; though acidic loving plants may be able to absorb aluminium phosphate. If your soil is sandy as well as acidic, then it is usually deficient in trace elements and your plants will benefit from regular feeding with a seaweed feed to replenish these elements. When the pH level falls below 4.7, bacteria cannot rot organic matter, meaning waste material does not break down and release nutrients into the soil. Add lime to the soil (see below) to raise the pH levels.

- pH 5.1 – 6.0 – Acidic – Perfect for ericaceous (lime hating) plants which include blueberries, heathers and camellias. If you want to grow other plants, add some lime to raise the pH level.

- pH 6.1 – 7.0 – Slightly Acidic – This is ideal for the majority of plants and they will thrive at this pH level. The major nutrients are easily available to your plants and this level of acidity supports the earthworms and micro-organisms found in your soil. There is no need to amend your soil at this pH level.
- pH 6.1 – 8.0 – Slightly Alkaline – Phosphorus, manganese and iron availability decreases, often leading to lime-induced chlorosis (cured with a chelated iron solution liquid feed). However, at this pH level, clubroot, which affects members of the cabbage family, struggles and is less likely to infect your plants. Add acidifying agents such as iron sulphate or sulphur to reduce the pH level.

Acidifying Soil

Soil is acidified if it is too alkaline or if you are planning on planting ericaceous soil loving plants. Sulphur is most commonly used to acidify soil. Peat is not recommended any more due to the environmental impact from digging up the peat.

Although you can acidify soil at any time of year, it is best done while the soil is warm, from spring to autumn, as sulphur takes longer to work on cold soil. Before adding anything to your soil, check the pH level so you can gauge how much to apply. Follow the labels on whatever you are applying to your soil.

The three most commonly used soil acidifiers are:

- Sulphur – the most frequently used substance. Micro-organisms in the soil convert the sulphur into sulphuric acid, which acidifies the soil. Sulphur dust works faster than chips, though it is more expensive. This is because the micro-organisms need the sulphur to be finely ground to convert it effectively. It can take weeks for this to break down and acidify the soil, though in winter it can take months. This is the cheapest of the three materials and is unlikely to cause any damage to your plants.
- Aluminium Sulphate – commonly used with hydrangeas to make the soil more acidic so the plant produces blue flowers. It is relatively quick to acidify the soil, but it can reduce phosphorus levels in soil when applied in large quantities. Applying too much of this too often can result in a build-up of harmful aluminium in the soil.
- Iron Sulphate – also known as ferrous sulphate, this acidifies the soil and supplies iron but, like the previous material, can reduce the availability of phosphorus when used in large

quantities. This can be alleviated by applying a phosphate fertiliser after acidification.

Clay soils need more sulphur than sandy soils to change the pH level. Soils rich in organic matter will also need more sulphur. If your soil contains free chalk or lime, then it is almost impossible to acidify your soil. Test for free lime/chalk by taking a soil sample and adding vinegar to it. If it fizzes, then your soil contains free calcium carbonate.

Usually, you will acidify the top 6"/15cm of soil, though if your plants have deep roots, then you may need to acidify further down to 12"/30cm or more, which is going to be more expensive and labour intensive.

When acidifying soil, it is better to do a little at a time rather than make your soil too acidic by accident. This is a long-term process as it will take a couple of months after each sulphur application for the results to be accurately known.

Sprinkle sulphur over the soil at the rate specified on the instructions in still, dry weather as the dust will drift. It is recommended to wear a mask, gloves and goggles to protect yourself from the dust, particularly if treating a large area. Rather than just scatter it on the surface, dig it in so that it can be broken down faster and acidify your soil.

Chalky Soils

Alkaline soils are very common throughout the UK and are often referred to as chalky, containing chunks of either limestone or chalk as well as calcium carbonate in the soil itself. Chalky soils are often free-draining, stony and quite shallow, which makes it hard to keep them fertile. You will often see chlorosis (yellowing of the leaves) on your plants in chalky soil as they are not able to properly absorb manganese and iron through their roots. Treat them with a foliar spray, but you may need to look for plants that prefer alkaline conditions.

A chalky soil can be anything from gravelly and stony to clay-like, which is often due to calcium carbonate in the soil. In a chalky soil, clay is a benefit as it helps the soil to retain water. The easy way to test for a chalky soil is to put a couple of teaspoons into a jar and cover it with vinegar. If it froths, then your soil is full of calcium carbonate.

Although chalky soils can be difficult to grow on, the bright side is that they do warm up quickly in spring and are less likely to flood. However, that isn't going to help you much in producing a gorgeous crop of tomatoes!

Chalky soils benefit from lots of organic matter being dug in regularly, at least once a year, if not twice.

Fertilise regularly and mulch where you can to retain moisture. Growing green manure in unused beds will help fix nitrogen in the soil, which your plants will benefit from.

Of course, you can build raised beds and fill them with a better mix of soil. This is a great solution because most vegetables are shallow rooted and if your beds are 8-12" deep, that will be enough for the majority of vegetables. Any deeper rooted plants can then go into the thin chalky soil or you can build taller raised beds if necessary.

With a chalky soil it is not practical to add sulphur to acidify the soil as it would take several years and a lot of money to change the pH level of the soil.

Lime and Liming

Liming reduces the acidity of your soil and increases the pH level. It is usually applied in winter for annual crops, before digging, so that it can be absorbed by the soil and not damage any plants. Applying lime to the soil's surface can take years for it to take effect, so it is important lime is applied before planting and dug in.

Once you have added lime to your soil, leave it at least three months before testing again to get an accurate measurement of the adjusted pH. It takes some time for the lime to be absorbed and to change the acidity of the soil.

Lime is high in calcium carbonate and usually found as 'garden lime' which is just ground limestone. Some stores will sell ground chalk and calcified seaweed which are other types of calcium carbonate.

Dolomite lime is a ground limestone high in both calcium carbonate and magnesium carbonate. It is more commonly used on soils which are low in magnesium.

Calcium hydroxide or hydrates lime is sold for use on building projects but can be used on the garden. It is a quick acting, fine powder and must be handled correctly as it can irritate your eyes and skin. Wear gloves, goggles and a face mask when applying this lime.

Lime sold for use in gardens will usually have a Neutralising Value (NV) displayed on the packaging in the form of a percentage. This indicates how much calcium oxide is contained in the lime. Garden lime typically has an NV of between 50% and 55%, as does ground chalk. Calcified seaweed can have an NV as low as 44% whereas hydrated lime is usually in the region of 70%. The NV level influences how much lime you need; the higher the NV, the less lime is required. The finer the lime powder, the quicker it will work on your soil, so avoid anything that has lumps in as it will take much longer to break down.

When applying lime at a rate of more than 14¾oz per sq yd or 0.5kg per sq m, dig half of it into the soil, then spread the rest on the surface once digging is complete. If applying less than this, dig it all into the soil if you can, otherwise just spread the whole lot on the surface.

Clay soil has what is called a buffering capacity, meaning it resists attempts to change its pH levels. Heavy clay soils need much more lime to change the pH levels than soils with little clay in.

If you are using builders' lime (hydrated lime), then you have to be careful as it can irritate you skin and eyes. Ensure you are wearing suitable protecting clothing.

Lime is also added to the soil before growing brassicas (cauliflower, cabbage, etc.) as it helps to prevent clubroot.

In most cases, you are not going to need to change the pH level of your soil. This is usually only done in exceptional cases where the soil pH is not good for plants. If you do need to add lime to your soil, remember to take appropriate precautions and apply it on a calm day so the wind does not blow it around.

Keeping Chickens On Your Allotment

Some allotments will allow you to keep chickens on your allotment, though not all sites allow it, so ask when you are shown around if this is something you are considering. There is the occasional site that will even allow you to keep pigs, but they are few and far between these days. Check your contract to see whether or not you are allowed to. If you are not, then you can approach the allotment management for special permission, but do not be surprised if it is turned down.

Chickens are a great addition to an allotment.

Keeping chickens is significant investment in both money and time, with you needing to visit ideally twice every day, once to let the chickens out of their coop into their run, and once to put them to bed at night. You are unlikely to be allowed to keep a cockerel (male chicken) as these are very noisy and disturb local residents with their crowing.

To keep chickens, you will need a secure coop and run. The coop is where the chickens will roost at night and, hopefully, lay their eggs. The run is where they spend their day so they are outside and have space to walk around. The size coop and run you buy will need depends on the number of chickens that you are going to keep. A half dozen chickens will usually provide enough eggs for most families.

The coop and run needs to be secure to prevent the chickens from getting out and predators such as foxes and cats from getting in. This typically means that it has to be a secure wooden structure with wire mesh that is dug into the ground to prevent animals from digging underneath it.

Chickens need regular attention and feeding, plus they need checking for mites and diseases. There is quite a lot of equipment you need for them, but they are fun to keep. Although they will eat slugs, I don't recommend letting them run loose on your allotment as they will happily eat your seedlings and quite a few of your vegetables!

The number of eggs your chickens give you will depend on the breed. Some chickens lay daily, some less frequently, but most chickens stop laying in wintertime when it gets too cold for them. One thing you must consider before you start is that most chickens will only lay eggs for four or maybe five years. After this, egg production drops rapidly and stops. The question you have to ask yourself, is what do you do with a bird that will live up to another five years producing no eggs? You can end up with a coop full of chickens that aren't laying eggs. What do you do with these unproductive birds? You can keep them as pets, and not have fresh eggs for a good few years or you can slaughter them and eat them. However, older birds tend to have tougher meat and only be suitable for stews rather than roasting as a Sunday lunch. Not everyone is willing to slaughter their chickens, though you can take them to a butcher if you live in the right area. For me, this is a very important consideration that needs to be made right at the start.

Keeping chickens is good fun and they can be quite sociable birds. Kids will love them, but the time commitments are significant. I would recommend thinking hard about whether you have the time to be there twice a day, every day including Christmas Day, and what you will do with unproductive birds before you start. Some allotment sites will have communal chickens which you can get involved in to see if it is for you.

There is a lot more involved with keeping chickens and if you are interested in the subject, then I recommend you read my book, Keeping Chickens for Beginners, available online and from all good bookstores for an in-depth discussion on the subject.

Keeping Bees On Your Allotment

Some allotment sites will allow you to keep bees, which can be an enjoyable hobby, but like chickens, is a significant investment of time and money. Check your allotment contract for whether or not this is allowed. If you see other people keeping bees on your site, then that will mean it is allowed, but you will probably need permission from the site management and to demonstrate your qualification to keep them.

Bees are good on an allotment if you have time.

If it is, you will need to attend an accredited training course first. This teaches you the techniques for keeping bees. Then you will need to buy the equipment and site the hive(s) on your plot. It is best to surround the hives with a fence that is at least seven feet tall as this encourages the bees to leave your plot that far above the ground and fly over the heads of other plot holders. Remember that there are people who are severely allergic to bee stings, so you do need to be considerate in where you place your bees. Many residential homeowners may object to bees being kept too close to their houses too.

If you are interested in keeping bees, then I recommend you start talking to other beekeepers on your site and find out more about what is involved. While the fresh honey is delicious, there is a lot of work involved in producing it and often the other beekeepers are happy to sell you some of their honey. Even if you decide not to keep bees on your allotment, plant flowers and allow some weeds to flower to provide nectar to support the local bee population. These insects are vital for pollinating your plants so they produce a good yield.

This is another in-depth subject, beyond the scope of this book. You must talk to other beekeepers and research the subject thoroughly before committing.

Creating a Bee Friendly Allotment

Not everyone wants to keep bees on their allotment, or is able to, but you may still want to provide an environment that encourages these insects and gives them a haven. Bees are vital to our survival due to their role as pollinators for commercial crops. In parts of America, bees are in such short supply they are transported around the country to pollinate crops! In the winter months, they are shipped from the north to warmer, southern states like Mississippi where they overwinter. In spring and summer, they are shipped around the country to pollinate crops. Over half of the bee colonies in America are transported to California every year to pollinate the almond crops. To give you an idea of numbers, it is estimated that there are over 2.6 million bee colonies transported around the country for pollination purposes!

Sadly, with our busy lifestyles, the natural environment for bees is dying out. Years ago, wildflowers grew at the side of farmer's fields, yet with today's intensive, chemical laden farming, these flowers are gone. Many households used to have flowers in their gardens which bees could feast on, yet today, fewer houses have flowers with many preferring decking or artificial grass to reduce maintenance requirements.

I live in an urban environment and there is one house (mine) on our street, which numbers about 70 or 80 houses, that has flowers in the garden.

Whether you have an allotment or you are growing vegetables at home, you can create a bee friendly environment and encourage these, and other, insects into your garden. These naturally pollinate vegetables and often feed on pests that damage crops. By encouraging these beneficial insects into our gardens or allotments, we can reduce our requirement for chemicals and safeguard these insects that are vital to our food supply.

Creating a bee friendly environment is surprisingly easy and does not have any impact on your ability to grow fruits and vegetables. It does not reduce your available growing space or cause you any inconvenience at all!

Aim to have plants on your allotment that flower from early spring through to late autumn, while the bees are active and looking for food. Bees particularly require support in early spring when there are few flowers around. That dreaded weed dandelion, is one of their vital sources of food early in the year and many allotment owners will allow dandelions to flower to support the bees and then dead head them afterwards.

Flowering herbs are particularly loved by bees and make for a very delicious honey. Plants such as chives, marjoram and thyme produce lots of flowers and will be covered in bees when they are in bloom. I have a patch of chives that I allow to flower every year and I use the herb in my potato salads and egg mayonnaise sandwiches. There is a marjoram plant that is at least three feet across that the bees go crazy for every year, plus several thyme plants. Other herbs like dill, fennel, angelica and borage are also fantastic for bees and certainly worth planting some of.

As well as herbs, growing flowers among your vegetables is also beneficial as they help to attract predatory insects. Marigolds are great to plant at the base of trees and near your greenhouse as they help protect your plants from harmful pests. Nasturtiums are a great trap crop to grow to catch aphids, but the flowers are enjoyed by bees.

Many of the plants you grow will have flowers that bees appreciate, all of which will help them feed and survive.

One thing to be careful of is the chemicals that you use on your plot. Some of these are harmful to insects. You must remember that an insecticide cannot tell the difference between an insect that you want on your plot, such as a bee, and one that you do not want, such as an aphid or wasp. If you do have wasp's nests, avoid using wasp killer as this can affect bees. It is better to burn out the nest or otherwise remove it, which any on-site beekeepers will help with. It is best to use natural and organic insect treatments where possible as this reduces the impact on beneficial insects. Even spraying a weed killer on your plot can harm insect life. Some of the stronger chemicals kill worms and insects as well as weeds so again, these are worth avoiding unless absolutely necessary.

Build a habitat where solitary bees can nest and live. These are just as important as honeybees and still have an important role as a pollinating insect. This could be a store-bought insect home or one that you make yourself.

An important part of allotment life is working in harmony with the natural environment instead of against it. We are not here to fight nature and battle against it, but to work with it. The most successful allotment owners are those that create an environment that encourages insects and beneficial organisms while providing a high yield of fruits and vegetables.

It does not have to take a lot of extra work, but it is very important if you want to run a successful plot. More and more growers are creating environments that encourage insects as they start to recognise the importance of wildlife for their allotment.

Companion Planting Explained

Companion planting does not involve putting plants close together so they don't get lonely, it is perhaps better called complimentary planting, where plants are sited together so they benefit each other. Some plants, when planted together, either help each other grow stronger, improve the flavour of the fruit or protect one another from diseases or pests. With people being more focused on organic, environmentally friendly gardening, this is a great way to give your plants a helping hand and reduce your reliance on sprays and chemicals. Companion planting is nothing new and has been practiced by farmers for centuries, though modern day scientists are researching companion planting and how it can help farmers use less chemicals on their plants.

This is a very effective way of helping your plants and a great way to keep pests off, it works surprisingly well. Perhaps one of the best known companion planting techniques is that of planting flowers around your fruits and vegetables to encourage pollinating insects to visit. However, there is a lot more than this involved and if you decide to use this method, it will influence what you plant where.

There are lots of different combinations of plants that help each other. One of the most commonly used on the allotment is to protect against carrot fly. Carrot fly hunts by smell and will decimate your carrot crop. They typically fly about 18-24" above the ground and will hunt out your carrot crop, particularly once you start thinning them out. It is, however, quite easy to confuse the poor carrot fly by planting onions, garlic or leek around your carrots. Many people plant two rows of carrots and then surround them on either side with onions or garlic. The smell from the alliums confuses the carrot fly, which struggles to detect and destroy your carrots. This means you get tasty, undamaged carrots and do not need to resort to any sprays to protect your plants.

The following table illustrates some of the good and bad companion plants for your allotment.

	Beneficial	Harmful
Apples	Chives, foxglove, garlic, onions	Grass, potatoes
Apricots	Basil, tansy	Tomatoes, sage
Asparagus	Basil, parsley, tomatoes	

	Beneficial	Harmful
Beans	Cabbage, carrots, cauliflower, cucumber, lettuce, parsley, peas, spinach	Fennel, garlic kohl rabi, onions, sunflowers
Beans (broad)	Dill, potatoes, sweetcorn	
Beans (dwarf)	Beetroot, brassicas, carrots, cucumbers, dill, lettuce, potatoes, radish, spinach, strawberry, sweetcorn	Fennel, garlic, kohl rabi, onions sunflowers
Beetroot	Cabbage, dwarf beans, kohl rabi, lettuce, onions	Climbing beans
Brussels sprouts	Beetroot, celery, cucumber, dill, dwarf beans, marigold, nasturtium, onions, rhubarb, sage	Strawberries
Broccoli	Beetroot, celery, cucumber, dill, dwarf beans, marigold, nasturtium, onions, oregano, rhubarb, sage	Strawberries
Cabbage	Beans, beetroot, celery, dill, mint, nasturtiums, onions, oregano,	Garlic, strawberries, tomatoes

	Beneficial	Harmful
	potatoes, rosemary, sage, thyme	
Capsicum (sweet peppers)	Basil, carrots, dwarf beans, marjoram, parsley	Fennel, kohl rabi, tomatoes
Carrots	Chives, leeks, lettuce, onions, peas, radish, sage	
Cauliflower	Beans, celery, nasturtiums	
Celery	Beans, cabbage, cauliflowers, leeks, tomatoes	
Chillies	Basil, oregano, parsley, rosemary	
Chives	Apples, carrots, parsley, tomatoes	
Courgette	Nasturtiums	
Cucumbers	Beans, celery, lettuce, nasturtiums, potatoes (earlies), savoy cabbage, sunflowers, sweetcorn	
Garlic	Basil, carrots	
Kohl Rabi	Beetroot, onions	Beans, fennel, tomatoes
Leeks	Carrots, celery	
Lettuce	Beetroot, cabbage, carrots, marigolds, onions, radish, strawberries	Celery, parsley

	Beneficial	Harmful
Mint	Cabbages	
Onions	Beetroot, carrot, kohl rabi, lettuce	Beans, peas
Parsley	Asparagus, chives, roses, tomatoes	Potatoes
Parsnips	Beans, garlic, peas, peppers, potatoes, radish	Carrots, celery
Peas	Carrots, potatoes, radish, turnips	Garlic, onions, shallots
Potatoes	beans, cabbage, peas, sweetcorn	Apples, cherries, cucumber, pumpkins, raspberries, rosemary, sunflowers, tomatoes
Pumpkins	Sweetcorn	Potatoes
Radishes	Lettuce, nasturtium, peas	Hyssop
Raspberries	Tansy	Blackberries, potatoes
Sage	Cabbages, carrots, strawberries	Basil
Spinach	Broad beans, cabbage, cauliflower, celery, peas, strawberries	
Strawberries	Borage, lettuce, sage, spinach	Brassicas, garlic, tomatoes
Sweetcorn	Broad beans, cucumber, potatoes, squashes	

	Beneficial	Harmful
Tomatoes	Asparagus, basil, carrots, celery, chives, garlic, parsley, sweetcorn	Apricot, fennel, kohl rabi, potatoes, rosemary, strawberries
Turnips	Beans, carrots, chives, nasturtiums, peas, spinach	Potatoes, tomatoes

It is definitely worth trying companion planting because it does work. Many allotment owners use it as it is a natural, and easy way to protect your plants against diseases and pests. It is very simple to do and effective. If you are planning on being an organic allotment owner, then this is definitely something you will need to use. To find out more about companion planting and how it can help you at your allotment, please check out my book, Companion Planting, available online and in all good bookstores.

Crop Rotation Explained

Crop rotation is an important part of owning an allotment and is practised by virtually all vegetable gardeners and farmers. It is the practise of not growing vegetables in the same location for two or more successive years. The idea behind this is that it stops pests or diseases from building up in the soil and allows the soil to recover from the plants that have been growing in it.

Different plants require different nutrients, so growing one type of plant in the same area year after year, depletes the micronutrients in the soil, leaving it deficient. By rotating crops, you allow these micronutrients the chance to build back up again.

Note that crop rotation only applies to annual vegetables such as cabbages, radishes, etc. and does not apply to perennial vegetables such as rhubarb, asparagus, strawberries, etc. which are grown in one location and left there.

Crop rotation is usually performed over three or four years, depending on the amount of space you have and what you are growing. Raised beds make it much easier to plan crop rotation because you know exactly where you grew your plants last year, but even if you grow direct in the soil, you still rotate crops.

There is a lot of debate about crop rotation, with some gardeners saying it is hogwash and others convinced it is vital. On an industrial scale, it is absolutely vital, but on a smaller scale it is still important and helpful. Grow cauliflowers or cabbages in the same bed for several years and you are likely to encounter clubroot. Grow carrots in the same bed for more than a year and your crop will be decimated by carrot fly the following year.

On an allotment, crop rotation does not create any extra work and can help reduce work by keeping your soil healthy and pest/disease free.

Every year keep a written record of what you have planted and where it is. This will help you plan your crop rotation. I used to think I would remember what was planted where, but it is surprisingly easy to forget. It is one reason I use raised beds; it is very easy to track what has been planted where, contain the soil and plan for crop rotation.

Not all plants need to be rotated. Perennial crops such as asparagus, rhubarb and strawberries are never rotated because once they have established themselves, they stay in one place for many years. If you were to dig them up every year, you would never harvest a crop. Some people will move their strawberry patch every 3-5 years when the plants are spent, but a lot of people just replace the plants with fresh ones.

Plants such as French or runner beans, salad crops such as lettuce or radish and sweet corn can be grown anywhere and do not need rotating every year. Most people do rotate them just out of good practise, particularly as the roots of the bean plants help to fix nitrogen into the soil.

Other crops such as pumpkins, potatoes, tomatoes, carrots and more, all need regular rotation to prevent pests and diseases building up in the soil.

Plan your crop rotation at the end of a growing season, while what was planted where is still fresh in your mind. This gives you the winter months to plan, prepare beds and get ready for the new planting scheme.

Some of the key benefits of crop rotation include:

- Improved soil fertility – crop rotation prevents a single type of vegetable from exhausting the soil's nutrients. As each vegetable has a slightly different requirement from the soil, this means that they do not suck the soil dry, helping you to keep a healthy, nutritious soil that is good for all of your plants.
- Weed control – Squash plants are great at covering the soil, which will suppress the weeds and stop them from taking over.
- Pest/disease control – soil borne pests and diseases tend to target specific families of plants. By only growing a plant in an area every three or four years, you stop the pests/diseases from building up to harmful levels. It is used to prevent diseases such as white rot, found in onions, and clubroot, found in brassica plants.

Crop rotation can be as simple or as complex as you want to make it, and I will freely admit, I like to keep it simple! Your plants are divided into five different groups:

1. Brassicas – include Brussels sprouts, cabbage, cauliflower, chard, kale, kohl rabi, oriental greens, radish, swede and turnips.
2. Legumes – broad beans and peas (note that French and runner beans are planted anywhere as they don't have issues with soil borne pests and diseases.
3. Alliums – these are all members of the onion family including garlic, leek, onion and shallot.
4. Potato and tomatoes – although both aubergines and peppers belong to the same family, they suffer from fewer problems so may be grown anywhere unless you are gardening in an area that suffers from blight. If this is the case, include them in your crop

rotation plant.

5. Root crops – including beetroot, carrot, celeriac, celery, fennel, parsley and parsnip.

For a simple example, imagine you have five beds, each bed only containing vegetables from one of the above crops. Each year, you move the vegetables along one bed so that, for example, the bed that contain legumes this year will have brassicas in next year.

Here is an example with three beds:

	Bed 1	Potatoes
Year 1	Bed 2	Legumes, onions and root crops
	Bed 3	Brassicas
	Bed 1	Legumes, onions and root crops
Year 2	Bed 2	Brassicas
	Bed 3	Potatoes
	Bed 1	Brassicas
Year 3	Bed 2	Potatoes
	Bed 3	Legumes, onions and root crops

This simple crop rotation plan is easy to execute. The same principles though, apply to a four-year crop rotation plan, no matter how many beds you have. Typically, smaller gardens work best on a three-year rotation plan whereas larger gardens work better on four-year plans.

Crop rotation combines well with companion planting as a vital tool in natural, organic gardening to help keep pests and diseases to a minimum. A well thought out and rigorously exercised crop rotation plan helps to reduce your reliance on chemicals.

Although in a garden or allotment you are growing on a smaller scale than a farmer, crop rotation is still good practice. You often can get away with growing the same crop in the same area for several years without a problem, but from year two onwards, you will notice a decline in quality as pests and diseases build up in the soil and vital nutrients are exhausted. Crop rotation helps keep your soil healthy and helps you grow vegetables in a more natural way with less need for chemicals.

Making The Most Of Your Space

Your space on an allotment is limited and unless you are going to take on a second plot, if that is permitted on your site, you are going to end up running out of space. I know few allotment owners who wish for less space … most dream of a several acres of land for them to grow in!

However, do not despair because you can produce a surprising amount of fruit and vegetables from an allotment by the use of succession planting, interplanting and vertical gardening. These allow you to maximise the use of your space so you can grow more plants in the same space. There are also other techniques you can use which help you make the most of the space available to you. Through these techniques you can dramatically increase the productivity of your allotment and grow more than enough fresh produce for your family.

Interplanting

This is a great technique, also known as intercropping, where you plant a slow growing crop together with a quick growing crop. By the time the slow growing crop has got big enough to be bothered by the second crop, the rapid growing crop is ready to harvest! A great example of this is to alternate radish and carrot seeds in rows. The radishes grow very rapidly compared to the carrots and will sprout in a few days. Carrots, by comparison take a lot longer to germinate, so the radishes mark out the carrot rows so you don't forget where they are and accidentally pull them up thinking they are weeds, and trust me, that happens more often than you think! This marks the rows out very nicely so that you know exactly where your carrots are.

Anything that grows slowly can be planted with a faster growing crop so that you can make the most of your space. Lettuces and spinach grow relatively quickly so can be planted with slower growing crops like onions or parsnips. Sweetcorn takes quite a while to grow and the space below it can be used for smaller, rapidly growing plants too.

Some large plants that take time to fill out are cabbage, cauliflower and Brussels sprouts. These take up a lot of space and the ground around them can be used to plant rapid growing vegetables such as beetroot, rocket, spinach or lettuces. These will act as a living mulch and help to keep the weeds down and stop water loss.

Any of the dwarf bean varieties or bush beans are rapid growing and can be planted in spaces around tomato and pepper plants. The really good thing about these beans is that when they are finished cropping, you cut the stem off at the root leaving it in the ground. The roots fix nitrogen in the soil, which your tomato and pepper plants need to help them grow better.

Some of the faster growing plants to consider for intercropping include:

- Bush beans
- Beetroot
- Lettuce
- Mizuna
- Radish
- Rocket
- Spinach
- Spring onions

Some of the slower growing plants which you can plant faster growing plants among include:

- Broccoli
- Brussels sprouts
- Cabbage
- Cauliflower
- Kale
- Sweetcorn
- Tomatoes

There is a lot that you can do here to really maximise the use of your space so you get two or even three crops out of the ground. One of my favourites is in early summer, a few weeks before harvesting onions and garlic, plant beetroot and carrots in between the rows. The onions and garlic will have been harvested well before the carrots and beetroot become big enough to worry about the competition. The other benefit of this is that the smell of onions and garlic puts off carrot fly!

In late summer or early autumn, when you are a few weeks away from harvesting summer vegetables, plant autumn or winter vegetables such as broccoli, cabbage, kale and cauliflower. This overlap, which is really succession planting, helps maximise your use of space.

Using interplanting does not negate crop rotation. As you are planting small quantities of a vegetable, e.g. a few cloves of garlic among your carrots, the pathogens are rarely present in a large enough quantity to become harmful.

Intercropping is an excellent way to make the most of your allotment and, when combined with the other techniques detailed below, will allow you to produce a lot of vegetables from your plot.

Raised Beds – Dense Planting

If you are using raised beds on your allotment and you have good quality compost in them, then you can plant more densely that is recommended on your seed packet. This is an off shoot of the square foot gardening theory, where instead of planting in square foot grids, you plant your entire bed with a single vegetable, but more densely than normal. Because the soil is in such good condition, you can get away with this and the plants will thrive. An additional benefit of this technique is that you have few weeds in the bed because your vegetables crowd them out. Those that do grow are usually weak and leggy, so easily removed.

If you are planting more densely than normal, then be careful combining it with intercropping because there is a risk that you could damage seedlings by removing mature plants.

Square Foot Gardening

This is an interesting technique which is worth experimenting with, but is best, in my opinion, for small areas. If you have an allotment then it is not really worth doing as you don't need to restrict your space as much, but you can certainly apply the techniques to raised beds to plant more densely as detailed above.

The principle behind this is simple. By having high quality compost in your raised beds, you can plant more densely. You divide each raised bed into a grid, with each square of the grid being one foot by one foot. A single type of plant is grown in each of the squares. Using this technique, you plant sixteen onions, radishes or carrots in a single square foot or eight beetroot, spinach or bush beans, or four leaf lettuces.

This type of gardening is very productive, but I do feel that it is more applicable to people growing at home with a small area available to them. I prefer to take the planting guidelines for this method and apply them to a whole bed so I get the quantity of vegetables I want in a single bed rather than having multiple vegetables per bed.

A bed set up for square foot gardening.

Succession Planting

In succession planting, you plant vegetables in the same area one after another, i.e. in succession. Unlike interplanting where you grow two different types of vegetable in one area, here you grow a single type in each area and then plant a second type when the first has been harvested. Any succession will work, providing both vegetables have enough time to mature before the end of the growing season. You can cheat a little and plant the new crop anything from a week to a month before the old crop is harvested providing harvesting the ripe vegetables will not disturb the younger plants.

When I grow potatoes in the ground, I usually plant swedes and turnips in the same place once I have dug them up. When I harvest my carrots in the autumn, I put onions and garlic in the beds because they grow over winter and help to drive off carrot fly. There are lots of opportunities with succession planting and it is a great way to get the most out of your allotment.

Alternatively, succession planting means to plant the same type of vegetable in the same area at 7-14 day intervals so that you do not get overwhelmed with ripe vegetables and have a longer cropping season. For example, if your bed will hold four rows of vegetables, you plant one row now, then, depending on how rapidly the plant matures, you plant the second row 7-14 days later, the third row a further 7-14 days later and the final row a further 7-14 days later. Instead of all four rows being ready at once, you have a longer harvesting period of vegetables, so you are not struggling to use or store the ripe ones.

Vertical Gardening

This is another technique which allows you to let your imagination run wild as you invent creative ways to grow more vegetables on the same ground space. Vertical gardening is the practice of growing plants vertically rather than horizontally on the ground. I regularly grow lettuce in drainpipes driven into the ground. Holes are drilled in the pipe; it is filled with soil and then the lettuces are grown in the holes. This means that in a six-foot piece of drainpipe which takes up no more than square foot of ground, I can grow 30 lettuces plus a tumbling tomato plant in the top of the pipe!

A lettuce planted.

This is a whole subject in itself with lots of potential and possibilities, but it is a great way for you to really make the most of the space at your allotment. I have three ten-foot pieces of gutter piping attached to stakes in the ground spaced about a foot between them. These are on the boundary of my allotment in some dead space where I wouldn't have been able to grow anything. My strawberry plants grow quite happily in these, though they do need extra watering in summer as they dry out fairly quickly, and I have over thirty plants growing in this small area that couldn't otherwise be used.

There are lots of different things you can do and I would recommend that you look into this and unleash your creativity to come up with some ideas on how you can grow vertically on your allotment. It is an excellent way to increase your yields without increasing your space requirements. I really recommend it.

Maintaining Your Allotment

An allotment is a long-term, ongoing project. Some people say you never really finish an allotment as there is continuously more work to do. After a period of time, you will get to the stage where the structural work, i.e. building beds and structures, is completed and you can concentrate on the maintenance work of planting, tending the soil and weeding.

When designing your allotment, you need to think about the time that you have available to work on it. If you do not have a lot of time, then you need to set your allotment up so it requires as little ongoing work as possible. Some people, myself included, hate digging, so we use raised beds and a no-dig approach to reduce the amount of work required. We will talk about low maintenance allotments in a few pages.

Maintaining your allotment requires several tasks:

- Weeding – this is vital as weeds grow much faster than your vegetables and can quickly crowd out your plants. It is important to keep them under control. Cover areas of your allotment that are not being worked to prevent the weeds from taking over. Use a good quality weed membrane and weigh or peg it down so it does not blow away. Invest in a good hoe and use it two or three times on any bare soil. Perennial weeds such as dandelion, dock and mare's tail need digging out by hand. Weed in between vegetables with a hand hoe or by hand, being very careful not to damage your plants. A quick weed every time you visit your allotment stops this job becoming overwhelming.

- Watering – young plants need regular watering until they are established. Deep rooted plants require less watering than shallow rooted plants. Use mulch and other techniques to help retain moisture and reduce the amount of watering you have to do. Drive pipes into the ground by larger plants so you can water direct to the roots. Remember to water at the base of the plant rather than on the leaves to ensure water gets to the roots rather than runs off. Most sites will require you to use a watering can, so you want to do as much as you can to reduce the amount of watering so you do not have to carry so many cans of water around.

- Feeding – no matter how much you prepare the soil, your plants will still require feeding to grow to their full potential, with some being greedier than others. Condition your soil with manure or compost when not growing and feed your plants regularly during the growing season. Use store bought mixtures (seaweed based mixtures are extremely good) or make your own feed, as discussed earlier. Pelleted chicken manure is an excellent feed to scatter on the soil or dig in.

- Repairing – raised beds, sheds, greenhouses, paths and everything else all require maintenance. Taking action when you first spot a problem and it usually requires a lot less work than putting it off until later.

- Planting – while not technically maintenance, it certainly is a job to do and one of the most fun parts as far as I am concerned. Plant out early in the morning, trying to avoid planting out in the heat of the day. Ensure sufficient space is left between plants as dense planting can often encourage fungal diseases. Follow the directions on the seed packets for the correct time of year, but adjust this depending on how far north you are.

- Harvesting – another fun part of owning an allotment, only beaten by the eating part! Harvest regularly to keep the vegetables fruiting. Many vegetables if left too long become tough or not as nice. Runner beans are best harvested when young as they become tougher when they grow too long. Beetroot is best harvested when it is around the size of a tennis ball as when it grows much bigger, it can become woody. Many herbs and leafy vegetables become bitter or chewy when they become too mature. By regularly picking your vegetables, you encourage the plants to keep on producing.

How much of all this you need to do will depend on how you have set your allotment up. To me, the less of the 'boring' work like digging and weeding you have to do, the more time you have to enjoy your allotment. However, there are some people out there who love to dig, and if that is you, then that is absolutely fine. Everyone runs their allotment in a different way and however you want to run your allotment is the right way for you!

Planning a Low Maintenance Allotment

Many of us live busy lives and while we love the idea of growing our own fruits and vegetables, we don't have hours to spend on an allotment gardening. Too many people give up their allotments far too quickly because they find they are a lot of work and hard to keep up with. Let's face it, if you are working full time and/or looking after children, it can be very hard to have enough time to maintain your allotment to the satisfaction of the allotment inspection team. Warning notices on plot cultivation or use only cause stress and division, making what should be an enjoyable hobby into a stressful race to get a wild patch of land under control and planted. It is not unknown to be given two weeks to clear and plant an allotment that is waist deep in weeds.

After a lot of work, it is starting to look much neater.

If you are busy, you can still have an allotment and work it successfully, by being efficient, or as my allotment neighbours call it, 'lazy'. It means setting up your allotment so it is low maintenance and you are not having to spend days digging and weeding plus growing plants that do not require constant attention and will grow relatively happily if you neglect them.

Consider what you are going to grow and how you are going to grow it, with maintenance being foremost in your mind. Low maintenance crops include winter squashes, onions, garlic, shallots, carrots, beetroot, lettuce, chard, rhubarb, artichokes (both globe and Jerusalem), potatoes, radishes, runner beans, French beans, bush and dwarf beans, chillies and kale. These will all grow without requiring a lot of attention from you. Weed them a couple of times a week and water

them when dry, but in general they will get on with it and produce an edible harvest at the end of the season even when neglected. Other members of the brassica family such as cabbage and cauliflower require a lot more work because they need netting, checking for caterpillars and will quickly be destroyed by pests if you aren't watching them close enough. Other low maintenance crops which are easy to grow include courgettes, peas, broad beans and sweetcorn. Many herbs are also very easy to grow and chives, marjoram, thyme, mint (make sure it is in pots though), parsley and fennel will happily grow with little attention from you.

Cover unused areas of ground with weed membrane or tarpaulins so that weeds do not grow, which then require more work to deal with. I like raised beds because I can cover and uncover each bed as and when I need it plus unused beds can be filled with fresh manure and left to rot down until the bed is required.

Watering does not have to be difficult either. A good soak once or twice a week is much better for your plants than a regular light sprinkle. It encourages your plants to develop a deeper root system. It is only in the hottest of weather you need to visit more regularly to water, but even then, many of your larger, established plants will be fine as they have a deep root system and more access to moisture. Cut the bottom off a two litre soft drink bottle, remove the cap and push it cap end down into the soil by larger plants such as squashes so the cap end is near the roots. Fill this with water and move on, it saves a lot of time!

Once you have set your allotment up and planned for low maintenance, it will be much easier for you keep on top of it. There is more work up front, but it will allow you to run your allotment without having to invest the hours every day people seem to think are necessary. If you know you are going to struggle for time, design your allotment to be low maintenance from the start. For me, raised beds, covered soil and weed membrane paths makes sure I have little digging to do and weeding is a breeze. I never dig my plot and the raised beds are filled each autumn before being covered. In spring, they are uncovered, given a quick going over with a hand fork to loosen the soil and then planted. It is possible to run an allotment on a few hours a week when it is set up properly and there is no reason you cannot enjoy an allotment when you work or have children.

Amending Your Soil

When you get your new allotment, check out the soil to see what type of soil you have, bearing in mind that this can vary across your plot. One plot I worked had half great soil, then a streak of heavy clay about a quarter of the plot wide, and then normal soil again. Turn a shovel of soil in several places across your plot and then feel the soil with your fingers to see what type it is, whether it is clay, sandy or normal soil.

Soil that is neither too sandy or too much clay is fine for you to grow most plants in, just top it up with manure or compost every year to keep it healthy and full of nutrients.

Your soil may be full of stones too or even debris from whatever was on the site before it was turned into allotments. One allotment site I worked on was used in World War II as a field hospital and had a number of buildings on it. The soil was full not only of stones, but bricks, chunks of concrete and all sorts of debris from human occupation. Between us, we found spoons, belt buckles, marbles and all sorts of things, all of which were donated to the local historical society much to their excitement. You never know what you are going to find until you start digging. It is worth removing any stones larger than about ½" as these can hinder the growth of your plants. Either dispose of these or keep them to put in the bottom of containers or for other use; I keep mine in buckets and then regularly take them to the local tip.

Working With Clay Soil

Clay soil is notoriously difficult to grow in because it gets extremely waterlogged. In heavy rain it can turn into a quagmire that will pull your boots off your feet. In hot, dry weather, it will dry out rapidly and crack, leaving plants struggling to get enough moisture. Few plants will grow successfully in heavy clay soils and it needs amending so that it is better quality. Bear in mind that this is a long-term project that will take several years of effort.

One thing that does work well in clay soil is potatoes. Plant potatoes and this will help to break up the soil.

Every year dig in manure, gravel, or sharp sand, which will also help to break up the soil, though you need to dig down a good couple of spade depths for this to be effective. Straw and green manure can also be dug in as that will rot and break the soil down too.

While you are working to improve the soil, you can either grow in raised beds or mound good quality compost into beds which is then dug into the soil at the end of the growing season. You have to be patient with a clay soil, but after a few years of persistence, the soil will improve, and you can grow anything in the ground.

Working With Sandy Soil

Sandy soil is a lot easier to improve. Because sandy soil is so free draining and loose, many plants struggle to get enough water. Taller plants will have difficulties developing a strong root system and are easily damaged in high winds.

Dig in plenty of compost or manure to a sandy soil and it will very quickly improve. However, one thing that does grow well in sandy soil is carrots, which love a free draining, loose soil.

Some manure to improve the soil.

Making The Most Of Your Allotment With Children

A lot of people take on an allotment with the plan of taking their children to it to help out and learn where their food comes from. It is an excellent education for the children, it gets them out of the house, and it is enjoyable exercise for them while they spend time with you. I regularly take my children to the allotment and they really enjoy their time there, but I have learned over the years what I can, and cannot do, when they are there.

Firstly, children tend to like certain activities at the allotment. They are not going to be interested in building raised beds, wheelbarrowing manure around (after the first time) and many won't even enjoy watering after a couple of goes. Children, generally, enjoy planting, harvesting and occasionally digging. When you are taking your children down, plan your activities so they can do the things they like and they will associate pleasure with being at the allotment. Over time, introduce new activities and get them more involved in other things and they will expand their interests.

I regularly take my daughter to the allotment as she enjoys being there, but she only really likes planting and picking. She helped plant all my carrots, lettuces and onions this year, so I prepared the beds, so they were bare soil, ready to be planted when she wasn't there. Then when she came down, she could plant seeds and write labels, activities she enjoys, and I could focus my attention on her and enjoy quality time together. Incidentally, from this planting I had the best crop ever of both lettuce and carrots!

While you can plan activities for them you should also make sure that your allotment is a safe place for them to be. Always keep your children on your own plot and don't let them stray on to other peoples as this can cause offence. Unfortunately, not everyone likes children, and another plot holder may get annoyed if something gets damaged or taken and they blame it on your child, even if it was not them. It's another unnecessary source of friction. If your child does like to explore, then keep them busy and supervise them closely or fence your plot so they have to stay on your area.

A good way to keep them engaged is to give them their own area of your allotment to manage, often with your help if they are younger. Mark out an area or assign then a raised bed and then let them loose with the seeds! They will love thinking about what to plant and then making the area their own. Interest may wane when it comes to weeding, watering and digging, but you can help them with that so they can enjoy themselves. This does help to stop them planting random plants all over your allotment and helps to keep them engaged as they have their own area. Try to encourage them to plant fast growing plants so they see results quickly, which will keep their interest.

Think about site safety too. Cover or fence off any ponds, remove any dangerous debris or trip hazards and do not leave tools out. If your children are going to use tools, then supervise them closely and show them how to safely use the tools. They may not appreciate the knowledge now, but they will later on, and it is better they are taught to use a fork, spade or hoe safely than they play with the tools and end up injuring themselves.

Children can benefit a lot from an allotment as it is good exercise for them, and it can encourage them to eat more fruit and vegetables. It is a great way to spend quality time with your children and for them to learn to enjoy your allotment.

Running An Environmentally Friendly Allotment

These days, and quite rightly, our focus is on being more environmentally friendly, reducing our carbon footprint and preventing damage to our precious environment. Allotment holders can do their bit here and help save the planet by running an organic, or at least mostly organic, plot and reducing their reliance on potentially harmful chemicals.

Providing a haven for wildlife is also very helpful, though this does not mean leave part of your plot to grow wild, it means building environments where wildlife can flourish that are in keeping with the rest of your allotment. You do not want to attract pests such as rats and mice which are going to damage your allotment, but you want to give bees and other insects a place to live so they can help you out on your allotment.

Use plants that flower early, mid and late season to encourage pollinators and predatory insects on to your allotment for as long as possible. Build log and stone piles for invertebrates, slow worms and toads. Feed the birds to encourage them to eat the insects on your plot, though make sure you cover any crops that they could be attracted to. Build a small pond, which will also encourage wildlife, but make sure that frogs can get in and out of it easily.

You can buy insect houses to nail on walls and fences or put up in trees. These are very helpful and are, at the very least, better than nothing. I have several (bought for me as presents) sites around my allotment, and they are all inhabited by different insects.

An insect home, ready to be put up.

If you have fences on your plot, plant climbing plants such as passion fruit, jasmine or honeysuckle. These provide a home for all sorts of wildlife as well as looking fantastic! I have a very high, ugly green fence at the back of my plot. I am currently training several honeysuckle plants to grow up the fence and into the trees to help birds nest and attract pollinators. Plus, honeysuckle flowers make for a delicious, delicate home-made wine!

A key part of running an environmentally friendly plot is to reduce your use of plastic. Eliminating it completely is extremely difficult and, in reality, not practical. However, you can reduce your reliance on plastic and eliminate your use of single use plastic. Whenever buying anything that is plastic, look for items that will last several years.

Woven plastic weed membrane is an excellent way to keep the weeds down on your plot and something I recommend. This will last for years, providing you buy a good quality membrane. The cheaper membranes breakdown in ultra-violet (UV) light very quickly, so are not good for the environment, your allotment or your wallet!

Seed trays are another common source of plastic on an allotment, with many of these thrown away each year. Buy stronger plastic seed trays and buy the trays that the multi-celled trays fit into to support them. If any do break, then take them home and recycle them.

The same with pots, buying plastic pots is fine, but buy good quality ones that will last for multiple seasons. Terracotta pots, while not plastic, tend to have a relatively short lifespan because they fracture during cold weather if left outside. Resin is a good choice for durability, but they are not recyclable so when damaged or broken, go to landfill.

Large plastic bottles, such as those fizzy drinks come in, can be used as cloches for tender plants where you cut the top off and put the rest of the bottle over the plant. Alternatively, you can poke one or more holes in the lid, fill the bottle with water, up-end it and put it in a container with a plant to drip water the plant (great for when you go on holiday). I use the 500ml drinks bottles in containers to drip water my plants; they are fantastic in my greenhouse where they keep my plants alive on hot days. The larger, gallon or water cooler sized plastic bottles also make for excellent cloches, being suitable for larger plants.

Lay the bottles on their side, tightly fit the lid and cut a rectangle of plastic out of it. Fill it with soil and then hang it on a wall or fence to make a great planter, ideal for shallow rooted plants like lettuce and strawberries. All of these ideas will last for years on your plot and when they have reached the end of their useful life, you can recycle them! Plastic bottles can also be turned into a variety of bird scarers too.

It is possible to make your own pots at home from newspaper. A simple device available online or from some garden centres will turn newspaper into pots. You use them as normal and then plant the pots directly in the ground rather than taking the seedling out of the pot. The newspaper will rot quite quickly in the soil.

An alternative that many people use is the cardboard tubes found inside toilet and kitchen rolls. These are another great bio-degradable pot. They are ideal for planting seeds like sweetcorn that have long tap roots or other plants that do not like their roots being disturbed.

Composting as much of your waste as possible, instead of burning it will help reduce your environmental impact. Wood waste from trees and fruit canes cannot be composted, but you can take it to a local council recycling centre where they shred it before composting it. Fruit canes are relatively easy to shred on your plot, but branches from trees are not easy for you to shred.

Perennial weed roots such as dock, dandelion and mares tail are not suitable for cold composting as they tend to grow before they rot down. You can run a hot compost bed on your plot or take them to the local recycling centre where they will be hot composted. They can be burnt, but they have to be thoroughly dried first otherwise they struggle to burn and can give off a lot of smoke.

Basic Gardening Techniques

There are plenty of different gardening techniques, and most of these you can work out from trial and error or you may already be familiar with these tools. For people who are new to an allotment, this section is going to explain some of basic techniques and how to efficiently use some of the tools on your allotment. It will hopefully help you get started quickly and speed up the learning process of owning an allotment.

Using a Fork

A fork is a very useful tool down at the allotment and one that you will use a lot. Buy a good quality fork rather than a cheap one, particularly if you have a heavy clay or stony soil as the cheap ones will break or bend. A fork is used to lift soil without cutting through it as much as a spade. It is great for digging in manure or compost and excellent for digging up plants and weeds as it can lift the plants without damaging the roots, which a spade would do. There are ladies forks which are smaller and lighter, which are useful if you are shorter. Taller people will prefer a normal fork as there is less bending involved. Forks are not suitable for digging holes because you may struggle to remove the soil, use a spade instead. If your budget cannot stretch to both a fork and a spade, buy a fork because it is a much more versatile tool.

To lift a weed or vegetable plant, put the prongs of the fork on the ground a few inches away from the plant. How far you position it will depend on the size of the roots of the plant you are lifting. Angle the fork so that the prongs will go into the ground either under or near, but not into, the roots. Then put one foot on one side of the fork, left or right foot, it's up to you, and push down until the fork is full in the ground. Then with one hand on the end of the handle and the other part way down, push the fork down towards the ground and lift the prong end up. This should lift the plant. If it doesn't, then straighten the fork and wiggle it around to loosen the soil or remove it and repeat on the opposite side of the plant.

Forks are excellent for lifting potato plants, though make sure you are at least a foot from the main plant as you risk damaging your harvest if you are too close to the stem. Dig around the plant at this distance to lift the soil so you can remove the potatoes. Don't worry if you spear a potato with your fork, just put it to one side and use it that night.

If you are turning soil with a fork and it has large lumps in when you turn it, hit those lumps with the flat of your fork to break them up or stab at them with the prongs. This will help break the lumps up, which can

then be finished by hand or using smaller tools.

Using a Spade

Spades are another useful tool down at the allotment and, once more, buy a good quality one. Buy a ladies or men's spade, depending on how tall you are and your strength. Spades are great for turning soil and shovelling manure, but not so good for removing weeds or digging up vegetables as they will damage the roots. When lifting perennial weeds such as dandelion and dock that grow back from their roots, a spade will chop up the roots and encourage the plant to proliferate.

Spades are used in the same way as forks, though be careful when lifting it from the ground as you can damage your back if you are lifting heavy soil or the spade gets stuck on something and doesn't move as expected.

Your spade can be used to divide plants such as rhubarb when they have grown too big.

Using a Rake

Rakes are used to level the soil and can be used to hit lumps of soil to break them up. As you rake, you will be able to catch the stones in the ground with it and remove them.

A rake is used by putting the tines downwards into the soil, they don't need to go deep into the soil, just on the surface, and then pulling it towards you. Rake over a bed to help remove stones and get it level. You would also rake over any soil where a path or building base will go to level it. For beds though, the soil does not have to be completely level, mostly level will do so that plants are at an even height.

Using a Hoe

A hoe is one of my favourite tools at the allotment and it is your best friend when it comes for keeping weeds down. There are a few different types of hoe, so pick the type that works for you.

Its best use is to cut the heads of young weeds, which are then left to compost into the soil. Use this a few times a week, and your plot will be mostly weed free! To use a hoe, hold the end of the hoe with one hand, knuckles up, and then place the other hand part way down the handle with the knuckles down. The hoe isn't used to dig into the soil, it is run along the soil, just under the surface so it cuts the heads off the weeds. It is usually used in a sharp stabbing motion to remove the heads rather than being dragged long distances through the soil. I find hoeing quite therapeutic, and the best way to keep weeds down on your plot. This is a more important tool than a rake.

Double Digging

This is a technique used to improve aeration and drainage where two layers of soil are loosened and organic matter is added. You will hear this term, but it is not something you need to do unless you have a new allotment, require deep top soil or have a heavy clay soil. In most circumstances, normal digging will be sufficient, though if you are planting a demanding vegetable such as asparagus, it may be worth doing. You do not need to double dig every year, but if you have a clay or poor soil, then double digging every few years will help improve the soil quality.

It is best to double dig in the autumn or winter when the soil is not waterlogged or frozen, but nicely moist. Mark out a straight trench across the area that you are going to double dig. This ensures that you are efficient in your digging and that you dig the entire area. Dig the first trench to a spade's depth and put the soil to one side. Fork over the bottom of the trench to loosen up the soil to a fork's depth. Add well-rotted manure or compost to the bottom of the trench and lightly fork it in.

Measure out a second trench, next to the first and

turn the top layer of soil from this into the first trench, lightly breaking up large clumps. Then repeat the process until you have dug over the entire area. The last trench is filled with the soil removed from the first. Take care to ensure the plot remains level as you are digging it. By spring when it is time to plant, the soil should have settled. If it is still too loose then gently tread it down to compact it slightly. Avoid walking on the dug area over the winter months.

Note that this is hard work and will take a lot of time, but if you want to improve your soil, this is an excellent way of doing it. If your allotment hasn't been worked for a long time or the soil is very compacted, then double digging will improve the quality of it.

Marking Out Straight Rows

If you are planting in rows, one of the challenges you will have is to plant straight rows. For many of us, wonky rows of vegetables make an allotment look great, but we all aspire to regimented rows of neat looking plants.

Firstly, prepare the soil, so dig in your manure, remove stones, weed it, level it and get it ready for marking out. Put a stake into the ground at one end of your allotment, and then line another stake up with it at the other end. Tie a piece of string to each stake and check that it is straight. Then dig a furrow along the string and plant your seeds. You can then move the stakes along your plot at the right spacing for the vegetables you are planting. You can buy or make a measuring line with two sticks and a long length of twine.

A quick word about vegetable spacing. If a seed packet says that plants should be spaced at six inches and you plant them at five or five and a half, you don't need to panic, they will be ok! The spacing on a seed packet is for guidance only and if you have a high quality soil, you can plant much denser than recommended.

Although many people plant in rows, studies have shown that planting in blocks or squares is a much more efficient use of space than planting in rows. Although many people prefer to grow in rows because that is how it's always been done, there is a definite move towards block planting for better use of space at an allotment. Note that sweetcorn should always be planted in blocks for pollination purposes.

Watering Your Plants

You will get very good at watering your plants very quickly as it is something we all have to do unless we are able to install some kind of irrigation system. These often require pumps and as it is rare for an allotment to have electricity (though you can investigate solar power), we usually water by hand.

If you have followed all the tips already provided in

this book, you will be retaining water in the soil which will reduce the frequency of manual watering. As most allotments do not permit the use of hoses, you will have to water using watering cans. Pour the water at the base of your plants, directly to the roots. This reduces run-off and makes sure that your plants get the water you are giving them rather than it disappears off and the weeds benefit from it.

A newly planted apple tree with watering pipe.

In dry areas, plants are sometimes put in a slightly depressed hole compared to the soil around them so that water pools at the base of the plant and does not run-off. In wetter areas though, this just encourages the plant to end up waterlogged.

Try putting 1-2" pipes into the ground by the base of your plants so that you can pour water into the pipe rather than on the soil. This will direct the water at the roots and make watering much more efficient. Instead of pipes, use upturned plastic drink bottles with the bottom cut off. Remove the lid to allow the water to drain freely, or put pin holes in the lid to turn the empty bottle into a drip feeder. The bigger the holes and the more of them there are, then the quicker the water drips out for your plant to use.

Tying Plants to a Stake

Plants such as tomatoes which will grow as vines along the ground, young trees and other delicate, taller plants, require tying to a stake while they establish their root system and can support themselves against the wind. Most tomato plants are permanently tied to stakes because only the bush or determinate varieties grow strong enough stems to support their own weight. Trees can need staking for a few years or for life, depending on their size and variety.

A tomato plant tied to a cane.

For most plants, the stakes are put in at right angles to the ground, i.e. straight up. Trees and larger plants require the stakes to be placed at an angle of 45 degrees to provide full support during windy weather. If the stake is upright, like the plant it is supporting, then it is relatively easy for the wind to blow it over. Having the stake at an angle, facing into the prevailing wind, braces the tree and stops it blowing over in high winds.

Garden twine is fine for tying most plants to a stake, though use a soft twine rather than a plastic one to avoid damaging your plants. Trees will need strong ties to ensure that they are securely tied. Tie the twine in a figure of eight around the stem of the plant and the stake so that the middle of the eight is between the plant and the stake. This prevents the twine from cutting into the stem of the plant and damaging it. Make sure the tie is tight enough to support the plant, but not so tight it damages it. As the plant grows, you may need to cut the tie off and replace it with another one as the stem thickens.

How To Save Seeds

Saving seeds is very easy to do and most allotment holders save some seeds for the following year as it saves money and lets them grow their favourite varieties. A lot of people will save garlic or beans for the following year because they are pretty simple to save, though you can save seeds from almost any plant. Some plants, such as carrots and parsnips, are biennial plants though, which means they do not produce seeds until the second year.

Before you start, you cannot save seeds from F1 (hybrid) plant varieties as they do not breed true to their parents. You must use open-pollinated or heirloom seeds. Over time, you will breed your own unique varieties that have acclimatised to the environment where you live. This is a great way for you to breed beneficial traits into your plants such as disease resistance, climate tolerance and so on.

As you read this section, you will learn about the different types of plants you can save seeds from, how to save seeds and even how to cross breed the seeds to make your own unique varieties. Note that if you are cross breeding plants, you must isolate them from insects and then pollinate the plants by hand to ensure you get the pollen from the plant you are expecting.

If you are just saving seeds to grow the follow year, then let a couple of plants go to seed, depending on how many seeds you want to keep. Harvest the rest of your plants as normal. Once the seeds have matured, they need to be dried in a warm (not hot) place with plenty of air circulation. Do not leave them anywhere damp and try to avoid larger seeds touching each other to avoid them rotting. Once they are dry, store them in a glass jar or paper bag in a cool, dark place until the following year. Most seeds are good for the following year, but after that, germination rates can deteriorate.

Broad Beans

Broad beans cross very easily with other varieties, though there are only a handful of different cultivars typically grown on allotments. In theory, to keep your variety pure, you need at least half a mile between varieties, which obviously is not practical on an allotment site. Growing in a greenhouse or polytunnel can help, but insects still get inside. A very fine netting will be enough to keep insects off, but remember to pollinate the flowers by hand, though most varieties are self-pollinating.

An easy way to do this if you are not concerned about the seeds being 100% pure is to save the seeds from the center of a block. These will be mostly pure as insects that reach the center of your broad bean patch will be carrying pollen from your broad bean plants and

little foreign pollen should remain.

Leave the bean pods that you want to mature on the bush and allow them to dry in situ. They will turn a dark brown colour and become dry and wrinkled. Pick the beans, shell them and check they are dry. A simple way to do this is to bite them gently. If your teeth leave a dent in the bean, then dry them further. Broad bean seeds have a good germination rate for several years when fully dry.

French and Runner Beans

Most allotment owners save the seeds from these beans as they are so prolific! Seriously, you will have so many of these that you will be overrun with them.

French beans usually self-pollinate, though insects can cross breed them with other varieties. If you are just saving seed, then any beans will be okay to save, though if you can plant them six to twelve feet away from any other French beans you are unlikely to experience any cross pollination.

Runner beans are pollinated either by the wind or by insects before the beans have set. These are very likely to cross with varieties grown nearby and, like broad beans, should be at least half a mile away from other varieties, which isn't practical. Usually, netting your beans is the best way to ensure they are not cross pollinated.

Seeds are collected by allowing pods to yellow and dry out on the plant. If the weather is wet, harvest the ripe pods and leave them somewhere dry until the pods are brittle and have completely dried. Then you can shell the beans and dry them completely. Runner beans are fully dry when they break when you bite them, rather than you just leaving a dent in them. Stored in an airtight container, fully dry, the dried beans will be viable for up to three years.

Should weevils be a problem in your area, put the bean container in the freezer for seven days to kill all the insect eggs.

Peas

Peas are usually self-pollinating, only occasionally cross pollinating with other plants. Save a few plants just for seeds rather than leaving a few pods on several plants. Check the plants as they are growing and any that are weak or not true to type should be removed.

Leave the pods to mature until they are brown and you can hear the seeds rattling inside. When the pods become too ripe, they will burst open, so you may end up harvesting the pods a few at a time. If the weather is really bad, pull up the whole plant and hang upside down in your shed to allow the pods to dry.

Once the pods are completely dry, shell the peas and leave them to dry further in a warm place before storing in a glass jar or paper bag.

Aubergines

These usually self-pollinate, but insects will cross pollinate them. If you want to save the seed, grow six to eight plants of the same variety to maintain genetic diversity.

Leave the fruits to mature, well past when you would eat them. The purple aubergines will turn a brown/purple colour while the green/white aubergines will turn a yellowish colour. You will only need to save a couple of fruits to have plenty of seeds, the rest of the fruits can be picked for eating.

Cut the aubergine into quarters lengthwise and pull apart, avoid the core. You will be able to see the brown seeds quite easily. Put the cut fruit into a bowl of lukewarm water and then rub the seeds away from the flesh with your fingers. Once done, add some more water, stir and wait for 5-10 minutes. The good seeds will sink to the bottom of the water. Remove the debris at the surface, repeat a couple more times until you are just left with the good seeds.

Sieve out the seeds and then dry in a single layer on a plate in a warm area. Stir them around occasionally so they do not stick together; the seeds are quite small so are hard to separate out by hand.

When fully dried and correctly stored, aubergine seeds can last up to seven years.

Peppers and Chillies

These plants are self-pollinating but will cross very easily with each other through insects. Ideally, you need to isolate your plants by 150 feet/50m from other pepper/chilli plants, which is not very practical. Isolating these in small plastic greenhouses with a single variety per greenhouse is probably the easiest way to prevent cross pollination.

Seeds are saved by cutting open ripe peppers and rubbing the seeds off the ribs and onto a plate. When deseeding chillies, always wear gloves as chilli oil is hard to get off your hands and can be painful if got in the wrong areas.

Dry the weeds in a warm area until they snap rather than bend.

Tomatoes

Many varieties of tomatoes are self-pollinating, though there are some that are insect pollinated. Look at the size of the stigma on the flower. If it is long, and protrudes beyond the anthers, then there is a chance of cross pollination. If the anthers are fused together, then they are unlike to cross pollinate.

Collect some tomatoes that are fully ripe before they split. Slice them in half and squeeze the pulp and seeds into a jar. This is then fermented for a few days to remove the jelly coating on the seeds and kill off any diseases that could be on the seeds. Put the jar somewhere warm for three days, stirring twice a day. It will develop a coat of mould and start to stink!

Then add lots of water and stir. The good seeds will sink to the bottom. Carefully pour the top layer of mould and debris off. Empty the good seeds through a sieve, and rinse well under running water.

Shake off excess water and then tip out onto a china plate (they stick to most other things) and dry somewhere warm, out of direct sunlight. When completely dry, store them in a cool, dry place where they will be viable for four or more years.

Beetroot/Chard

This technique works for beetroot, perpetual spinach, sugar beet and Swiss chard, all of whom will cross pollinate easily as they are members of the same family. These are biennial plants, meaning they flower and produce seeds in the second year. Most of these will overwinter outside ok, but in colder areas, beetroot benefits from being harvested in the autumn, storing over winter and replanting in the spring.

These plants are wind pollinated so any other plants without about two miles will cross pollinate them! To minimize cross pollination, plant in a block and take the seed from the middle plants. As few growers allow these plants to flower, your chances of cross pollination are fairly low.

To keep a variety true to type, it must be isolated. An easy way to do this is to cover the flowers with a shiny, rain proof paper bag or an agricultural fleece bag. Shake the bag regularly to distribute the pollen around the flower.

Harvest the seeds as they turn brown and dry. When dried completely, these will last at least five years.

Carrots

Carrots are also biennial plants and in a lot of areas can be overwintered in the ground. The leaves die back in the autumn and regrow in the spring. In colder areas, dig your carrots up in autumn, select the roots with the best shape and colour and twist off the foliage. Store in a box of dry sharp sand in a frost free area, ensuring they do not touch. Plant in the spring and they will sprout again and flower.

To maintain a carrot variety, you will need seeds from at least 40 roots to maintain genetic diversity. Too small a genetic base will result in small, low quality roots in just a few generations.

Carrots grow very tall when allowed to flower, often over waist height with some attractive umbels of flowers that attract lots of insects. They are insect pollinated and need to be about 1600 feet/500m from other carrot varieties. You may think this is not a problem as few people allow carrots to go to seed, but it does cross with wild carrot which results in very thin, white roots that are of no use. Isolate your carrots as best you can and remove any white roots from future generations.

When the umbels turn brown and dry, cut them off with secateurs. The best seeds are on the first and second flower umbels to appear, though the other flower heads are still viable. Dry the seeds indoors and then separate the seeds out in a sieve or by rubbing them between your hands.

Carrot seed will germinate well for up to three years providing it is stored properly.

Brassicas

Broccoli, cabbage, cauliflower, calabrese, kale and Brussels sprouts are all members of the brassica family and so will cross pollinate each other. They will not cross with swedes, turnips, mustard greens or oriental brassicas. In a lot of cases, brassicas are self-incompatible, meaning they need pollen from another plant, not just themselves.

To maintain purity, there should be no other flowering brassicas within a mile of your allotment. Typically, so long as your immediate neighbours do not have any, you should be fine. Usually at least one person on an allotment site will leave their brassicas to flower. To let the insects do their work efficiently, plant your brassicas in blocks rather than rows as this encourages the pollinators to remain in one place.

For genetic diversity, keep a minimum of six plants for seed. Do not save seeds from any weak plants or any that are not typical for the variety, these can be eaten instead.

Brassicas produce a tall flower stalk with an abundance of small, yellow flowers. The seed pods are slender and turn from green to a straw colour as they mature. As they dry, keep a close eye on them as they will split and drop the seed when they are too dry. It is best to cut the entire plant down when the majority of pods are dry. Leave the plant on a sheet or in a tray indoors for the pods to mature and dry. Once fully dry, the seeds are easy to remove from the pods.

You will get a lot of seeds from these plants and when stored properly, they are viable for up to five years.

Turnips and Oriental Brassicas

Pak choi and mizuna are members of the turnip family and will cross with each other but not with the brassicas described above. These are biennial plants and require overwintering. In some cases, a spring sown crop will bolt in the first year if it is too hot, though these seeds

are not necessarily the best to save as you could breed the trait of early bolting into your plants!

The best way to save these seeds is to sow after midsummer in a polytunnel or greenhouse. The semi-mature plants will overwinter well indoors and then can be planted out in the spring. Choose at least six of the best plants to keep for seed, the rest can be eaten over the winter months if you want. Once the plants flower, ensure that insects have access to the flowers to pollinate them.

The seed pods start out green and as they mature, turn a pale tan colour. When the majority of the pods are brittle and dry, the stalks of the plants can be cut and laid out on a sheet indoors to finish drying. Rub the seed pods between your hands to get the seeds out and sieve them to separate the seeds from the chaff.

Lettuce

Most lettuces are self-pollinating and it is rare for them to cross breed. If you are planning on saving the seed from multiple varieties, separate the crops by about 12 feet or plant a tall crop between the different lettuce varieties.

Choose three or four good quality lettuces to save for seed. Avoid saving seed from any that bolt early as that is not a trait you want to encourage. Head lettuces can need some help for the seed stalk to emerge by cutting the head open a bit with a sharp knife.

It only takes about two weeks from flowering for the seeds to be fully ripe. Harvest the seeds every day by covering the flower head with a paper bag and giving it a good shake. The ripe seeds will fall off the plant into the bag. Alternatively, you can harvest the whole plant if most of the seeds look ripe.

Separate the seeds from the chaff in a sieve and leave to dry fully before storing. The seeds should remain viable for up to three years.

Pumpkins, Courgettes, Squashes and Marrows

These are all members of the same family and will happily cross pollinate with each other. Gardeners often find some odd looking courgettes or deformed pumpkins, which is down to cross pollination. To save pure seed you need to hand pollinate the fruits.

These plants have male and female flowers, with the female flowers turning into fruit. It is very easy to spot the difference as the female flowers always have an immature fruit at their base whereas male flowers just have a long, straight stem.

To pollinate the flowers, transfer the pollen from a male flower to a female flower using a paint brush, cotton bud or anything else. Check your plants in the evening and find some flowers that are just about to open. Carefully put a thin rubber band over the end of the flower to stop it from opening. This stops insects from getting to the flower and pollinating it before you do. The following morning, pollinate your flowers and then shut the female flowers again to prevent insects from getting in.

You may not want to save seed from all the fruits on a plant, so just hand pollinate a few and mark the ones you have done. An easy way to do this is to tie a piece of wool loosely around the stem of the hand pollinated fruits.

Once the fruits have fully developed, harvest them and store them indoors for another month to finish ripening. Cut the fruit in half, scoop out the seeds and use the rest of the fruit for cooking as normal. Wash the seeds under running water in a colander, rubbing them between your fingers to get rid of the fibres and flesh. Shake off excess water and spread out on a kitchen plate or tray to dry. Fully dry seeds will snap rather than bend.

Melons and Cucumbers

All melon varieties will happily cross pollinate each other. Ideally, you need at least a quarter of a mile between varieties to prevent this, but usually if you are growing in a greenhouse or polytunnel, you will avoid cross pollination. Cucumbers do not cross with melons, but they do cross with other varieties of cucumbers, including gherkins. These also need around a quarter of a mile isolation to prevent cross pollination.

Both melons and cucumbers can be hand pollinated using a paintbrush. It is a little bit fiddly to do, but east enough. Grow the plants under fleece to keep insects off of them and pollinate between different plants to maintain genetic diversity.

Melon seeds are harvested when the fruits are ripe and you would eat them. Pick the fruits and store them inside for a couple of days to allow the seed to finish maturing. Cut the fruit open, scoop out the seeds and wash them under running water in a sieve. Spread the seeds out on a china plate and leave them to completely dry.

Cucumbers, however, need to ripen well beyond the point where you would eat them. They become much plumper and the green cultivars will turn a dark yellow/brown colour while the white varieties turn a paler yellow. Leave the cucumbers for about a week for the seeds to ripen, then cut open, scoop out the seeds and add them and the pulp around them to a glass jar. Add some water, stir well and leave on a sunny windowsill for two to three days to ferment.

Fill the jar complete with water, stir well and the good seeds should fall to the bottom of the jar. Scoop off the pulp and debris from the top of the jar, empty it carefully and then fill it again. Repeat the process a couple more times and you will be left with the good seeds in the bottom of the jar. Drain the water off and spread the seeds out on a plate to dry fully.

Both melon and cucumber seeds will last for several years if stored properly.

Making an Isolation Cage

Isolation cages are ideal for plants like peppers or aubergines. You can build larger versions of this to cover multiple plants, but a good quality horticultural fleece will do the job.

You will need four canes, some string, some garden wire and some cheap nylon flyscreen (or something similar) that is five times as long as it is wide. Old net curtains, scaffolding netting or anything with a tight weave net will work. A piece of screen 1m by 5m builds a cage large enough to cover three or four plants.

Cut a square piece of screen one metre square which will be the top of the cage. Fold the rest of the flyscreen around and sew the ends together. This is the sides of the cage. Sew the top square to the sides so you have a cube of flyscreen with the bottom missing.

Drive the four canes into the ground in a square slightly smaller than the cage top so they stick out of the ground a little less than the height of the cage. This may be easier to do before you sow the top on the cage.

Twist a piece of wire around the top of each of the canes and run the string around the tops of the cane, supported by the wires to prevent the string from slipping. Do the same about halfway down the cane to stop the screen from flapping against the plants in the wind.

Finally, slip the cage over the plants and weigh down the bottom with stones or earth. This will keep the insects off of your plants and prevent cross pollination.

Chapter 5 – Your Allotment Month By Month

This chapter will talk about how to manage your allotment throughout the year, discussing what you can plant when and what jobs to do each month. These are not set in stone and are a general guide. What you can do will depend a lot on the weather, which as we all know is variable, and where in the country you are located. Someone in the north of Scotland has a very different growing season to someone in Cornwall. This section gives you a general overview of what you can plant and do in a vegetable garden but adjust these as necessary for your local environment.

Seed Sowing Chart

Seeds are planted at various times of the year. They are either started indoors or under glass or planted direct in the soil, depending on the variety and time of year. Some seeds will be started indoors early in the year and then planted direct later in the year when it has warmed up.

This is a general guide as to when seeds should be planted and harvested, but the dates will vary depending on how far north or south you are. Planting dates will also vary from cultivar to cultivar. For example, Pea 'Kelvedon Wonder' can be planted direct from March to June, ready to harvest from May through to October whereas Pea 'Douce Provence' can be planted from October to November to overwinter or January to February for a harvest from May to October. Some other varieties of pea such as 'Little Marvel' can be planted as late as June.

As a general rule of thumb, tender plants which can be damaged by frost should not be planted out until the risk of frost has passed.

Key:

Sow Indoors	
Sow Outdoors	
Plant Out	
Harvest	

	Jan	Feb	Mar	Apr	May	Jun	Jul	Aug	Sept	Oct	Nov	Dec
Artichoke (Globe)			■	■	■	■	■	■	■	■		
Artichoke (Jerusalem)	■	■	■	■							■	■
Asparagus			■	■	■							
Asparagus Pea						■	■	■				
Aubergine		■			■	■	■	■	■			
Basil		■	■			■	■	■	■			
Bean (Climbing)				■		■	■	■	■	■		
Bean (Dwarf)						■	■	■	■	■		
Bean (Runner)						■	■	■				
Beetroot			■	■	■	■	■	■	■			
Broad Bean		■	■	■	■	■				■	■	
Broccoli			■	■	■	■		■	■	■		
Broccoli (Sprouting)		■	■	■	■	■	■	■	■	■		
Brussel Sprouts		■	■	■					■	■		
Butternut Squash				■	■			■	■	■		
Cabbage		■	■	■	■	■	■	■	■			
Carrot		■	■	■	■	■	■					
Cauliflower		■	■	■				■	■	■	■	■
Celeriac					■	■						

	Jan	Feb	Mar	Apr	May	Jun	Jul	Aug	Sept	Oct	Nov	Dec
Celery			■		■	■	■	■	■	■		
Chard	■	■	■	■	■	■	■	■	■	■	■	■
Chicory				■	■	■	■	■	■	■	■	■
Chinese Cabbage		■	■			■	■	■	■			
Coriander						■	■	■	■	■	■	■
Courgette				■	■	■	■	■	■	■		
Cucumber			■	■	■		■	■	■	■		
Endive		■	■	■	■	■	■	■	■	■		
Garlic	■	■				■	■	■		■	■	■
Kale	■		■	■	■					■	■	■
Kohl Rabi		■	■		■	■	■	■				
Leek	■	■	■	■	■			■	■	■	■	■
Lettuce			■	■	■	■	■	■	■			
Marjoram		■				■	■	■	■	■		
Marrow				■	■	■	■	■	■	■		
Mint			■	■	■	■		■	■	■		
Onion			■			■	■	■	■	■	■	■
Oregano		■		■	■	■	■					
Pak Choi				■	■	■	■	■	■			

	Jan	Feb	Mar	Apr	May	Jun	Jul	Aug	Sept	Oct	Nov	Dec
Parsley			▓	▓	▓	▓						
							▓	▓	▓			
Parsnip			▓	▓	▓							
	▓	▓							▓	▓	▓	▓
Peppers (Chilli)		▓										
						▓						
							▓	▓	▓			
Peppers (Bell)		▓	▓									
							▓	▓	▓			
Potatoes			▓	▓								
						▓	▓	▓	▓			
Pumpkin				▓								
									▓			
Radish		▓	▓	▓	▓	▓	▓					
								▓	▓	▓	▓	▓
Rocket				▓	▓	▓	▓	▓	▓			
										▓	▓	▓
Rosemary			▓	▓								
					▓	▓	▓	▓				
Sage			▓	▓								
					▓	▓	▓	▓	▓			
Shallot	▓			▓							▓	
							▓	▓	▓			
Spinach		▓	▓	▓	▓	▓		▓	▓			
	▓	▓	▓	▓	▓	▓			▓	▓	▓	▓
Spring Onion			▓	▓		▓						
Swede					▓							
									▓	▓	▓	▓
Sweetcorn				▓		▓						
Sweet Peas	▓	▓			▓							
Thyme				▓	▓	▓	▓	▓				
Tomato		▓	▓									
							▓	▓	▓			
Turnip			▓	▓	▓	▓	▓					
			▓						▓	▓	▓	▓

Allotment Jobs

It can be a bit overwhelming knowing exactly what to do at your allotment, particularly if you haven't grown much before. This section gives you a guide to what you can be doing each month of the year, including what you can harvest, what you can sow and general jobs around the allotment.

Of course, these is by no means an exhaustive list and not all jobs will apply to all people. This section will give you an idea of what you can do which could inspire you to grow some new plants or motivate you when you are wondering what is best to do, particularly during the winter months when there isn't normally much to do. Of course, these jobs and planting ideas will vary based on where you are in the country and the weather.

January

In most areas, it will be too cold and wet to sow much outdoors this month. However, indoors, particularly in a heated propagator, there are plants that can be sown. This can give you a head start on growing this year.

Snow can make it hard to work on your allotment!

What To Harvest

You can still harvest overwinter crops if you planned well last year.

- Brussels Sprouts - keep harvesting these from the bottom of the stalks up. Pick them before they get too big and the leaves unfold.
- Celeriac - harvest as and when you need it, but it will last in the ground for another couple of months. If the weather is very cold, spread a mulch of straw over the roots to protect them.
- Endive - this can still be harvested, though it needs covering with a cloche to protect it from the cold.
- Jerusalem Artichokes - leave these in the ground until you are ready to use them as they won't keep for long once lifted.
- Kale - the leaves can still be harvested this month. Many hardy kale varieties will thrive in winter and provide a welcome source of winter greens.
- Leeks - keep harvesting your leeks just before you need them as they do not store well once out of the ground.
- Parsnips - these can still be harvested or left in the ground until required.
- Sprouting Broccoli - some varieties of sprouting broccoli can be harvested now. Cut the spears when they are ready and you want to use them.
- Swede - lift any remaining swedes and store as

they will grow too big and become woody if left in the ground any longer.

- Winter Cabbages - these can be left in the ground and harvested as required, though make sure they are netted to protect them from pigeons.
- Winter Cauliflowers - the first of these should be ready now. Check the heads are covered by the leaves to protect them from the frosts.
- Winter Salad Leaves - plants such as land cress, winter purslane and corn salad are ready to harvest this month. They will need protection during the coldest weather.

Vegetable Plant Jobs

There is not too much to do in the vegetable garden. Mainly it is maintenance and keeping out of the cold this month! However, if you have a greenhouse, there are some plants you can start off.

- Broad Beans - if the ground isn't frozen, hardy broad beans can still be sown direct. If it is very cold, start the broad beans off in pots under cover.
- Garlic - if the weather is mild and the ground not waterlogged or frozen, you can continue to plant garlic bulbs.
- Leeks - sow leek seeds in pots in your greenhouse or cold frame.
- Onions - sow onion seeds in modules in your greenhouse or cold frame.

- Peas - hardy varieties can be sown in modules or pots and kept indoors until planting them out in March or April.
- Potatoes - potatoes can be chitted this month in egg boxes or seed trays. Put them somewhere light but cool and they will start to produce shoots in a few weeks.
- Radishes - as these germinate and grow quite fast, you can get an early crop by planting in modules or pots under cover.
- Winter Salad Leaves - these can be planted in a greenhouse or cold frame.

Fruit Tree/Bush Jobs

Beyond pruning and planting bare root trees/bushes, this is a quiet month for fruit.

- Bare Root Trees/Bushes - these can still be planted providing the ground isn't too cold or wet.
- Grapes - this is the last month to prune your outdoor grape vines before the sap starts to rise.
- Pruning - apples and pears can still be pruned this month. Fruit bushes can also still be pruned.
- Rhubarb - new sets can be planted this month and established plants can be divided. You can force rhubarb by covering a crown with a large bucket/bin so it produces shoots a few weeks earlier than normal. However, if you do this, rest that crown next year and do not harvest from it

General Jobs

This is a good month to maintain your allotment, though you can find you are fighting against the weather. However, on the odd sunny, but chilly, day get out and keep on top of as much as you can.

- Digging - keep digging your plot and adding well-rotten manure or compost to amend the soil.
- Pots and Containers - clean these using a weak solution of household bleach to prevent diseases and viruses passing on to this year's crops.
- Stakes, Ties and Wires - check all of these across your vegetable garden and make any replacements or repairs as necessary.

Greenhouse and Polytunnel Jobs

There isn't much to do in your greenhouse, but ...

- Hardy Annuals - plants such as cornflowers can be planted in modules in your greenhouse this month for some early flowers.
- Heating - if necessary, keep heating your greenhouse to keep it frost free and protect tender plants.
- Repairs - make any repairs that are required to your greenhouse, ensuring that doors and ventilation work and glass is securely in place. Add more glass clips if necessary, as the windy months that follow could blow out loose glass.
- Tidy - take advantage in the lull of activity to tidy up your greenhouse and remove any debris so there are fewer places for pests to hide.
- Ventilation - on sunny days, open vents or windows so the greenhouse does not become too humid.

February

February is usually a cold month for most us, with many in more northerly climates still with snow on the ground and frosts are frequent. It can also be a wet month in my areas, meaning seeds rot before they germinate.

This is a month where you really need to understand what the growing conditions are where you live. For some further south, planting will be possible, but for most of us, it is time to stay inside and lay the foundations for later in the year. It is not worth planting much in the ground as it is frozen and waterlogged, which means many seeds will rot.

However, do not dismay as there are plenty of things you could be getting on with!

It might be chilly, but you can still do something!

What To Harvest

There will still be some things to harvest at your allotment from last year. Keep a close eye on everything because the cold and wet weather can damage some of your plants.

- Brussels Sprouts - there should still be some sprouts left on the plants, if you haven't already harvested them all. If they are starting to get a bit big and look like they are going to blow, harvest them, then blanch and freeze them.
- Celeriac - lift these as and when you need them. Be careful when trimming the roots as slugs can hide in them.
- Endive - winter hardy endive will still survive if they are covered with cloches. Harvest entire heads or just the outer leaves.
- Jerusalem Artichokes - this is the last month to harvest these. Any tubers left in the ground are likely to start sprouting next month.
- Kale - this hardy plant will still be producing leaves for you. Keep harvesting them regularly to encourage the production of more leaves.
- Leeks - lift these as and when you need them.
- Parsnips - these should last in the ground until next month, but if the weather gets very cold,

cover them with 6"/15cm of straw to protect them.
- Sprouting Broccoli - keep harvesting the spears as this will encourage the production of more.
- Swedes - if there are any left in the ground, lift them this month. Check that they are not too coarse and woody to eat.
- Winter Cabbages - these can still be left in the ground or cut and brought indoors. Hang them in a cool place to store them.
- Winter Cauliflowers - these will have stopped growing by now and it is worth harvesting them to prevent damage to the curds. Blanch and freeze any excess.
- Winter Salad Leaves - you can still be harvesting your winter salad leaves providing you protected them from the cold.

Vegetable Plant Jobs

Work is starting to increase in the vegetable garden as you prepare for summer. Although it is still cold and wet, you should be able to get out more this month.

- Broad Beans - if the ground isn't frozen, sow direct outside, otherwise if the weather is cold, sow indoors in pots.

- Brussels Sprouts - early cultivars can be sown indoors in modules this month for planting out in April or May.
- Cucumbers - seeds can be sown indoors at a temperature of 21C/70F.
- Garlic - plant cloves now, but if the ground is frozen or waterlogged, wait until next month.
- Globe Artichokes - sow in pots and keep at a temperature of 18C/65F until they germinate. Keep them indoors until April or May when they can be planted out.
- Jerusalem Artichokes - plant tubers outside, taking into account where they will cast shade so other crops do not have their sunlight blocked. If it is very cold, cover with cloches.
- Kohl Rabi - early cultivars can be sown indoors in modules this month to plant out in April or May.
- Leeks - these can still be started off from seed this month.
- Lettuces - start seeds off indoors, then plant out under cover next month.
- Onions - seeds can be started off now at a temperature of 10C/50F for planting out in March or April.
- Potatoes - start chitting your potatoes. Place your potatoes in egg cartons, without the lid on. Make sure the side with the most eyes is facing upwards. These can chit for several weeks until you are ready to plant them outside. Chitting pre-sprouts the potatoes before planting which helps speed up the growing process when you plant them. The jury is out of whether this needs doing for all potatoes or just for main crop potatoes. It does not hurt and certainly helps in cooler climates.
- Peas - in milder areas, peas can be sown outdoors under cloches. Warm the soil up with a cloche before planting.
- Radishes - seeds can be sown in modules or pots indoors providing night-time temperatures remain above 5C/40F.
- Shallots - these can be planted in shallow drills with 7"/18cm between sets. Leave the tips slightly exposed above the soil.
- Spinach - a fast growing variety can be sown indoors now and planted out in March for harvesting in April or May.
- Sprouting Broccoli - early cultivars can be sown indoors in modules this month to plant out in April or May.
- Tomatoes - seeds can be sown indoors at a temperature of 21C/70F.
- Turnips - early varieties can be sown outdoors under cover.
- Winter Salad Leaves - these can still be sown in a greenhouse or cold frame.

Fruit Tree/Bush Jobs
It will still be quiet in the fruit garden due to the cold, but there are a few jobs you can do.

- Bare Root Plants - these can be put in the ground this month providing it is not frozen or waterlogged.
- Apricots - fleece your apricot trees to protect them from rain and frost. Be prepared to hand pollinate the flowers though.
- Blueberries - finish winter pruning your blueberry plants.
- Currants - finish winter pruning all your currant bushes.
- Feed - feed and mulch your fruit trees and bushes.
- Gooseberries - this is the last month to winter prune your gooseberries.
- Peaches/Nectarines - fleece the trees to protect the blossoms from the cold. If you can uncover them on warmer days, it will mean you don't need to hand pollinate the trees.
- Pruning - finish pruning your apples and pears this month as the sap will start rising at the start of March.
- Raspberries - prune your autumn fruiting raspberries this month by cutting them right down to the ground.
- Rhubarb - rhubarb can be forced, but remember if you force it this year, you need to rest it next year. Forced rhubarb is very sweet. Cover one or two crowns with a large black bucket to force the rhubarb, then insulate with straw or manure to help give it more heat.
- Supports - check all wires, ties and stakes to ensure they are in good condition. Replace or repair any that are damaged.

General Jobs
This month is all about preparing for the growing season by digging in compost and manure, warming the soil and finishing pruning trees and bushes.

- Asparagus - order new crowns now for planting in March or April. As this requires a permanent bed, think carefully about where you will put your new asparagus bed. Start preparing the ground now by digging in plenty of well-rotted compost.
- Raised Beds - top up the soil in your raised beds

using well-rotted compost or manure.

- Soil - prepare the soil for next year. Cover areas that you want to plant in next month to warm the soil. Dig in manure or compost to improve the soil.

Greenhouse and Polytunnel Jobs

Your greenhouse will start to fill up this month as you start seeds off. If your greenhouse gets too cold, you may want to keep seeds indoors until it warms up a little more.

- Cleaning - wash the glass to let more light into the greenhouse.
- Peaches/Nectarines - hand pollinate these if they are in your greenhouse using a soft paintbrush.
- Sweet Peas - start these off in deep pots and keep them frost free. You can use the cardboard insides of toilet rolls.

March

March is when it all starts to get busy in the vegetable garden as, hopefully, spring is on its way and the weather is warming. However, for many of us, March now means frosts and snow as the weather is colder and unpredictable.

Interestingly, in the UK, March 25th (The Feast of the Annunciation or Lady Day) used to be the start of the year, aligning with the spring equinox. When the Gregorian calendar was adopted in 1752, the start of the year moved to the 1st January.

A good month to tidy up ready for the planting season.

What To Harvest

March is a bit of a cross over month, where winter crops finish off and spring crops start, though there should still be plenty of eat on the allotment.

- Brussels Sprouts - late varieties should still be ready to pick.
- Celeriac - lift the last of your celeriac before the month is out.
- Kale - this can still be harvested.
- Lettuce - winter lettuces, protected from the cold by a cold frame or cloche, will be ready to harvest.
- Leeks - these will be looking a little battered after spending winter outdoors but are still usable. Harvest them and use them as soon as possible.
- Parsnips - any parsnips left in the ground need to be lifted before the end of the month otherwise they will start sprouting and become inedible.
- Rhubarb - you should be able to start pulling some stems now.
- Spring Cabbage - this is the last month for winter cabbage and the first where your spring cabbages are ready. Harvest them before the leaves form dense heads.
- Spring Cauliflowers - providing these have survived the winter, these will be ready to harvest this month.

- Spring Onions - seeds planted last August or September should be ready to harvest this month.
- Sprouting Broccoli - some cultivars will be producing spears this month. Keep harvesting them to encourage the production of new spears.
- Swiss Chard - the first of this year's Swiss chard, planted last summer, will be ready to harvest this month.

Vegetable Plant Jobs

In all but the coldest areas, March is a busy month sowing seeds, so hopefully you will have plenty of space on your windowsills and in your greenhouse!

- Asparagus - plant asparagus crowns in prepared trenches this month and next.
- Broad Beans - plant seeds outdoors now, but if it is too cold, cover them with cloches.
- Brassicas - sprouting broccoli, red cabbage and autumn cabbages can be planted indoors or outdoors.
- Brussels Sprouts - sow seeds indoors in pots.
- Carrots - sow outdoors but protect with cloches if it is too cold.
- Celery - sow outdoors but cover with fleece if it is too cold. Dig trenches for your celery in the same way as you do for runner beans.

- Celeriac - sow outdoors, but if it is too cold, cover them.
- Garlic - this is the last month that you can plant garlic cloves, so if you haven't already planted any, get them in the ground now.
- Herbs - at the end of the month, it will be warm enough to plant seeds that can tolerate cooler temperatures such as dill, coriander, chives and oregano. They can be sown direct but cover with fleece if a frost is predicted. Young plants of hardy herbs such as mint, thyme or rosemary can be planted out this month too.
- Kohl Rabi - sow indoors for planting out when it has warmed a little.
- Lettuce - salad crops can be sown indoors and outside this month.
- Onions - onion sets can be planted now for a summer harvest.
- Peas - peas can be planted outdoors, but if the weather is cold, cover them with cloches.
- Potatoes - first earlies can be planted now if the ground isn't frozen. Plant 6"/15cm deep with 12"/30cm spacing with the shoots pointing upwards.
- Radishes - sow under cloches or in cold frame.
- Rocket - sow seeds under cloches or in a cold frame.
- Runner Beans - start making runner bean trenches to give the plants the best start. Dig trenches 2-3'/60-90cm wide and 12"/30cm deep. Fill them with compost over the next few weeks so it can rot down and provide the rich, fertile soil your beans will need.
- Shallots - sow shallot sets this month with the tip of the set just above the surface.
- Spring Onions - sow spring onions under cloches or in a cold frame.
- Turnips - seeds can be sown now, but if it is too cold, cover to protect them.

Fruit Tree/Bush Jobs

The fruit garden will be waking up this month, though it is quieter than the vegetable garden.

- Bare Root Plants - this is your last month to plant bare root plants. From next month, you will only be able to plant container grown plants.
- Feed and Mulch - feed and mulch your fruit trees and bushes using a high potash fertiliser.
- Pollinate - apricots, peaches and nectarines flower early in the year and there aren't always enough insects around to pollinate them. You may need to hand pollinate your plants using a soft paintbrush.
- Protect - cherries, apricots, peaches and nectarines will flower this year, but the flowers are susceptible to frost damage. If the flowers die in the frost, then the tree will not produce fruit this year. If there is a risk of frost, fleece the plants to protect them.
- Raspberries - if you haven't already pruned your autumn fruiting raspberries, this is the last month you can do it. Cut them right down to the ground and new canes will appear that will bear fruit.
- Rhubarb - forced rhubarb can be harvested this month. Remember that once you have harvested from it, the crown needs to be left alone and not harvested next year so it can re-establish itself.
- Strawberries - cold stored runners can be bought and planted out this month and should crop later in the year. Existing plants can be covered with cloches to encourage them to flower earlier. Remove the cloches on warmer days to allow for pollination.
- Winter Pruning - finish winter pruning your blackcurrants, blueberries and gooseberries this month as they will be growing soon and it will be too late.

General Jobs

This month is mainly about sowing seeds, but you will be on frost alert, ready to protect delicate seedlings and blossoms from frosts. Continue preparing beds for planting next month.

- Feed - overwinter plants such as onions, kale, cabbages and so on will be looking a bit tired now and will benefit from a feed. A top dressing of seaweed fertiliser, chicken manure or blood fish and bone will perk your plants up.
- Fertilise - apply fertiliser to your soil. You can use pelleted chicken manure, seaweed or fish, blood and bone. Scatter it over the soil and let it break down naturally.
- Herbs- perennial herbs such as rosemary and sage can be trimmed to tidy them up. Herbs such as mint and chives can be dug up, divided and replanted. Remember, avoid planting mint in the ground as it is incredibly invasive.
- Seedbeds - rake seedbeds, removing stones and other debris from the soil. Keep beds covered until you are ready to plant in them.
- Weeding - the warming weather will cause the weeds to spring to life as they too benefit from your hard work feeding your plants. As you turn the soil, you will also expose new weed seeds to the light, causing them to germinate. Dig out

perennial weeds and hoe regularly to kill annual weeds.

Greenhouse and Polytunnel Jobs

These should be warming up nicely now but will still be cold at night and there is a risk or frost. You can plant some vegetables directly into the soil in your greenhouse or polytunnel. Just be aware that many of these will not ripen until June or July. If you are planting tomatoes or cucumbers as well, make sure you leave space for them as June/July is too late to plant these vegetables.

- Aubergines – plant 5 seeds in a 3"/7cm pot and transplant when large enough to handle.
- Basil – plant 4 seeds per cell in a seed tray, later in the month.
- Celeriac - start this off in trays or modules in your greenhouse.
- Celery - start off in modules in your greenhouse.
- Chillies – plant 5 seeds in a 3"/7cm pot, early in the month and transplant later.

- Courgettes – plant 1 seed per 3"/7cm pot.
- Dwarf French Beans - start off in a large container for an early indoor crop in June.
- Insulation - once the temperatures start to rise, insulation such as bubble wrap can be removed from your greenhouse so more light can get in.
- Lettuces - these can be started off in trays in your greenhouse.
- Peppers – plant 5 seeds per 3"/7cm pot and transplant when later enough to handle.
- Pumpkins – plant 1 seed per 3"/7cm pot.
- Squashes – plant 1 seed per 3"/7cm pot.
- Sweet Peas - sow more sweet peas in your greenhouse in deep pots.
- Tomatoes – plant 5 seeds per 3"/7cm pot and transplant when later enough to handle.
- Ventilation - open vents on sunny days to prevent the humidity getting too high.

April

April is a fun time in the allotment or vegetable garden. Things are starting to grow, but not just the things you want … the weeds start to grow including the dreaded mares or horse tail. This will send up shoots with pods on the end that release spores to spread the plant. If you see any of these, pull them up and put them in a plastic bag and then get rid of them. All the other weeds are going to be growing well but leave the flowers on the dandelions as these are a vital early season food source for bees. Many of these weeds are actually edible and could make for some free food!

We are starting to get serious now with our planting, it is full steam ahead with getting seeds in the ground and starting off plants like pumpkins and courgettes.

Your greenhouse may start filling up with seedlings!

What To Harvest

There will be some harvesting on the allotment this month from overwinter crops and early spring plantings.

- Asparagus - April is an exciting time as it is the first month where your asparagus is really at its best. Harvest the spears when they are as thick as your index finger by cutting them with a sharp knife just below the soil. Asparagus is best eaten within a few hours of harvesting when they are at their sweetest.

- Kale - this is probably the last month to harvest kale planted last year. Don't plant kale again in the same location this year.

- Leeks - this will be the last chance to harvest leeks from last year. You may have to trim a few layers off, but they will still be edible. Lift them by the end of the month and blanch and freeze any you can't use.

- Lettuce - lettuces such as cos varieties sown last autumn should be ready to harvest now.

- Rhubarb - rhubarb is ready to harvest too. Hold on to the base of each stalk and pull with a twist. Cut the leaf off and compost it. The stalks can be used fresh or frozen.

- Rocket - start harvesting young leaves when they are the length of your thumb.

- Salad Leaves - sown earlier in the year, these will be ready to harvest.

- Spring Cabbage - some spring cabbages will be ready to harvest. For pointed cabbages, you can either wait until the heads are fully formed or pick them when the leaves are still a little loose.

- Spring Cauliflowers - keep harvesting these while the heads remain firm.

- Spring Onions - those sown last autumn should be ready to harvest now. Pick them before they grow too big and their flavour becomes overpowering.

- Spinach - if the weather hasn't been too bad, you may well get the first of your spinach ready to harvest. The young leaves are great in salads.

- Sprouting Broccoli - this is probably the last month to harvest sprouting broccoli.

- Swiss Chard - harvest your Swiss chard and leaf beets. Young leaves are best, but older leaves can be eaten if you strip the tough stalk away.

Vegetable Plant Jobs

In April, the vegetable garden starts to get busy this month as there is a lot to get planting as the weather is warming and the risk of frost is minimal in many areas. Just keep your eye on the weather as sudden frosts can still happen. If there is a frost warning or you feel the temperature is getting too cold, fleece your plants to protect them. A lot of your planting will be done under cover. Even though the weather is improving and feels warmer, avoid the temptation to plant direct unless the seed packet instructions say so.

- Asparagus - asparagus crowns must be planted by the end of the month otherwise it will be too late.
- Aubergines - this is the last month for sowing aubergines as otherwise they will not have enough time to mature and fruit before the end of the growing season.
- Beetroot - you can plant beetroot outdoors this month, though if the soil is cold and wet, cover them with cloches.
- Broad Beans - sow direct outdoors and protect with cloches if it is too cold.
- Broccoli - sow indoors or outdoors, depending on the variety.
- Brussels Sprouts - sow indoors or outdoors, depending on the variety.
- Cabbages - sow indoors or outdoors, depending on the variety.
- Carrots - these can be planted direct.
- Celery - sow indoors to plant out in June.
- Chillies/Peppers - keep sowing these indoors.
- Courgettes - plant indoors ready to plant out next month.
- Cucumbers - keep sowing cucumbers indoors.
- French Beans - sow these in containers in your greenhouse for planting out next month.
- Globe Artichokes - offsets from established plants can be cut off and planted to produce new plants.
- Herbs - keep sowing herbs; most herbs can now be sown outdoors.
- Jerusalem Artichokes - plant new tubers by the end of the month.
- Kohl Rabi - transplant young plants started off in the greenhouse.
- Leeks - sow direct outdoors or in containers for planting out later.
- Lettuces - lettuces and leafy salad vegetables can be planted direct now. If the weather is still cold, cover the seeds until it warms.
- Melons - sow in pots in your greenhouse or indoors and cover with a plastic bag.
- Onions - this is the last month for transplanting seedlings outside or to plant onion sets.
- Parsnips - April is the last month to plant parsnips.
- Peas - plant peas direct, covering them with cloches if it is still cold. Put pea sticks in place now, before the plants become too large.
- Potatoes - second early and maincrop potatoes can be planted now. First early potatoes need to

be earthed up to ensure the tubers do not get exposed to the light.

- Pumpkins/Squashes - plant in pots in your greenhouse ready to plant out next month.
- Runner Beans - plant in pots in your greenhouse to get a head start on the growing season. Put the cane supports in place now while the plants are young to avoid damaging the roots later on.
- Sweetcorn - as sweetcorn has a long growing season, it can benefit from being started indoors. Use deep pots to start the seeds off; the cardboard insides of toilet rolls are ideal.

Fruit Tree/Bush Jobs

The fruit garden is starting to burst into life. Check plants such as blackcurrants for aphid infestations as this pest will start to gather on new growth.

- Blackcurrants - feed your blackcurrant bushes with a high nitrogen feed and some blood, fish and bone.
- Blackberries - feed your blackberries in the same way as blackcurrants. Also weed around the canes.
- Planting - although you cannot plant bare root trees or bushes, you can still plant container grown plants. These will be making their way into the shops, so it is a good time to buy some and get them in the ground.
- Pollination - continue to hand pollinate your apricots, peaches and nectarines.
- Pruning - once the leaf buds have opened, cherry, plum, apricots, peaches and nectarines can be pruned.
- Raspberry - weed around your raspberry beds.
- Strawberries - strawberries can be fed and covered to stimulate fruit production. New strawberry plants can have flowers removed to allow them to establish themselves fully.

General Jobs

There is a lot to do this month preparing for the busy

- Frost Protection - there is still the risk of frost, so be prepared to cover your plants if there is a frost warning.
- Harden Off Plants - plants raised indoors must be hardened off before planting out otherwise they will struggle to grow or even die with shock from being moved outdoors.
- Pot On Plants - plants that are becoming too large for their pots need to be moved into bigger pots so they can continue growing until they can be put in the ground.
- Seedbeds - continue to prepare your seedbeds,

breaking up lumps of earth.

- Seedlings - seedlings in trays or modules can be pricked out and planted in their own pot when they have two leaves. Be very careful when handling young seedlings as they can easily be damaged. They need to be moved into their own pots before they grow too large and become difficult to separate. Handle by the leaves rather than the stem.
- Weeding - keep on top of the weeds as they will be growing like crazy as the weather warms.

Greenhouse and Polytunnel Jobs

Your greenhouse will be filling up with seedlings this month as it is still too cold for many plants outside.

- Cleaning - clean the glass in your greenhouse to let in as much light as possible.
- Guttering - fix guttering to your greenhouse if you haven't already got some so you can catch water in a water butt. Check your guttering and clean it out of dead leaves and other debris.
- Microgreens - you can grow microgreens in your greenhouse for a tasty treat in just a few weeks.
- Sweet Peas - plant sweet peas in deep pots and keep them frost free.
- Ventilation - open vents, doors and windows on warm days for good air circulation.

May

May is a busy month in the vegetable garden. The days are getting longer, the weather warming and the risk of frost in most areas diminishing to close to zero. Many seedlings started in the last month or two are straining to get out of their pots, keen to be in the ground so they can really grow. Plus, some early crops will even be ready to harvest now.

Definitely one of the joys of May.

What To Harvest

There will be vegetables to harvest this month, and it is the start of the 'fun' part of running a vegetable garden. Surprisingly, there is quite a lot you can harvest, including:

- Asparagus - cut the tips when they are 5-7"/13-18cm long and no fatter than your forefinger. Use a sharp knife and cut just below the surface of the soil. Fresh asparagus is best eaten as soon as possible after harvesting, otherwise store wrapped in plastic in your refrigerator. Unfortunately, this crop cannot be left in the ground until you are ready to harvest it and must be picked when it is ready.

- Garlic - the first of your garlic can be lifted this month while the leaves are still green. They will be milder and are considered 'wet'. Store them in your refrigerator and use them as you need them.

- Globe Artichokes - although these will be small, pick a few and use them this month as it will encourage the plant to produce more.

- Oriental Leaves - mizuna and other Oriental leaves will be ready to harvest for salads. Pick the leaves when they are small and use as soon as possible. They will store for a couple of days in plastic in your refrigerator.

- Lettuce - lettuces sown as cut-and-come-again crops can be harvested.

- Radish - some early sown radishes will be ready to harvest this month. Pull them before they grow too big and become woody.

- Rhubarb - these are best harvested when the stalks are about 12"/30cm long as larger stalks can become a bit stringy. Harvest the stalks as and when you need them, remembering not to take too much from a single plant.

- Spinach - pick as a cut-and-come-again crop. The young leaves are used in salads and the older leaves are best cooked.

- Spring Cabbage - this may be the last month you can harvest your spring cabbages. Blanch and freeze any excess for longer term storage.

- Spring Onions - the first of these may well be ready to harvest, so pick them and enjoy them.

- Spring Cauliflower - this is the last month for harvesting your spring cauliflowers. The summer ones should be ready from next month, but any excess can be blanched and frozen.

- Turnips - the first baby turnips will be ready to harvest. They are at their best when they are still small, before they grow too large and become woody. The leaves, 'turnip tops', can be steamed or used in stir fries.

Vegetable Garden Jobs

There is a lot to sow and plant in May, it is probably one of the busiest months for putting things in the ground, so hopefully you will have spent some time conditioning and preparing your soil for planting season.

- Brassicas - Brussels sprouts, cauliflower, cabbage and broccoli can all be planted out this month.

This is the last month to get Brussels sprouts in so they are ready for Christmas. Sprouting broccoli and calabrese can be planted until July for harvesting over winter and into the New Year. As these plants can grow quite large, give them plenty of space.

- Broad Beans - tall plants need to be staked, particularly in windy areas, to prevent the plants being damaged in the wind or by the weight of the pods.
- Celery - plants that has been started indoors can be planted out, though take care to protect them from the first.
- Chillies/Peppers - best sown indoors, though in many areas it will be too late for them to grow to maturity this year. If you are keeping them under cover, they can still be planted for a later harvest.
- Cucumbers -sow indoors, though they can be sown outdoors in sheltered areas under a cloche or in a cold frame. If it has warmed towards the end of the month, cucumbers started off indoors can be moved outside.
- Florence Fennel - sow outdoors if the soil is warm enough.
- French/Runner Beans - sow outdoors if the soil has warmed and the risk of frost passed, otherwise continue to start them off indoors for planting out towards the end of the month and start of June. Young seedlings can be protected from cold snaps with plastic bottles or cloches.
- Globe artichokes - feed with a high potash feed and covered with a rich, organic mulch.
- Kohl Rabi - sow outdoors, providing the soil is warm enough.
- Leaf Vegetables - leafy vegetables such as spinach, kale, chard and the Oriental leaves including mizuna, mustard greens and Chinese broccoli can all be sown outdoors, though keep your horticultural fleece to hand to cover them on cold nights.
- Lettuce - sow directly, though if the weather is chilly, sow them under cover. Most herbs can be planted directly, though tender herbs such as basil will benefit from protection from the cold.
- Peas - both main crop and sugar snap peas can still be planted outdoors, though be prepared to protect them from the cold with cloches if necessary. Provide supports to keep them off the ground and protect the pods from mice, slugs and snails.
- Potatoes - these will be showing their heads above soil. Keep earthing them up and covering them to prevent the tubers being exposed to light

and turning green. If there is a risk of frost, earth up or otherwise protect your potatoes as the stalks and stems are not frost hardy and will die off if they get too cold.

- Root vegetables - all root vegetables including turnips, swedes, beetroot and carrots can all be planted outdoors now. If it is still a bit chilly, cover the beetroot seeds with fleece to aid germination.
- Seeds - those sown last month such as carrots, beetroot, lettuce and parsnip will benefit from being thinned out. The thinnings can be eaten in green salads.
- Squashes - all squashes including pumpkins and courgettes are planted indoors or under glass this month to improve germination, then planted out next month.
- Sweetcorn - plant directly outside. Remember to plant this crop in blocks rather than rows to improve germination. Young seedlings benefit from protection from frost and slugs too.
- Sweet Potatoes - if the weather has warmed, these can be planted at the end of the month. This is also the last month to get your seed potatoes in the ground.
- Weeding - keep the weeds down around your onions and garlic. They hate competition and can quickly get crowded out by faster growing weeds.

Fruit Tree/Bush Jobs

The fruit garden will still be quiet this month, but there are plenty of jobs to get on with, as there always is!

- Apple/Plum - pheromone traps can be hung in apple and plum trees to reduce the risk of codling moth and plum fruit moth.
- Cape Gooseberries - plant out this month but be prepared to protect the plants from frost.
- Cherry/Plum - these can be pruned this month. Trained trees such as peaches, nectarines and apricots can be thinned or new shoots can be tied in. On trained apples and pears, leaders and side shoots can be shortened.
- Fruit Bushes - weed around the base and apply a good mulch. This will help the soil retain moisture and suppress weed growth.
- Gooseberries - thin fruits out so that those left on the plants can grow larger. These are unlikely to be mature enough to eat raw but can certainly be cooked. Also check the centre of your gooseberry bushes for signs of gooseberry sawfly caterpillars. These will strip your plants of leaves and reduce your yield significantly. Remove the caterpillars by hand or use an appropriate

treatment.

- Melons - start off indoors as it will be too cold in many areas to plant outside. Keep them warm and sheltered from the frost.
- Raspberries - check for suckers and new shoots, as they can be a little over-eager. Pull them up or cut them off so that your raspberries don't get overcrowded.
- Rhubarb - young plants, started from seed, can be transplanted outdoors, as can strawberries.
- Strawberries - remove runners from strawberries so they concentrate on producing fruit. Keep the plants covered in the cold to help the plants flower earlier. Remember to remove the cloches during the day to allow for pollination. New strawberry plants need the flowers pinching off so that they do not produce a crop in their first year and can fully establish themselves.

General Jobs

There are plenty of things to do at your allotment, though keeping on top of weeds and pests is likely to be one of them as they are all emerging after the cold of winter. Make sure you keep the weeds down around your vegetable plants so they don't crowd out what you are trying to grow. Some of the jobs to do this month include:

- Frost Alert - keep paying attention to the weather news this month. Although the weather is warming, there is always the risk of a sudden frost. If the temperature looks like it will drop too much, then cover your tender plants to protect them from cold/frost damage.
- Tender seedlings - start hardening off and plant out this month once the risk of frost has passed. Be prepared though to go outside if there is a risk of frost and cover them to protect them.
- Watering - keep watering young plants and seedlings, particularly those that are kept under cover or in a greenhouse as they do run the risk of drying out.

- Weeding - keep weeding as the weeds will be bursting into life too this month. Use your hoe to take the heads off the weeds and this should help reduce the problems with weeds later in the growing season.

Greenhouse and Polytunnel Jobs

The greenhouse will be a hive of activity this month as your seedlings continue to grow and main crops such as tomatoes and cucumbers are planted. Jobs to do include:

- Potting on - tomatoes, cucumbers, peppers, chillies and aubergines can all the planted on into larger containers now. Put supports in place while the plants are still young to prevent damage to the roots later on.
- Repotting - any plants that are growing too big for their containers need to be repotted into larger containers so they can continue to grow until they can be planted out.
- Tidying - keep your greenhouse tidy and clear of any debris to avoid pests lurking in it. Because it is a busy time of year, it is very easy for your greenhouse to get cluttered and filled up with spilt soil and other odds and ends.
- Tidying - keep your greenhouse tidy and clear of any debris to avoid pests lurking in it. Because it is a busy time of year, it is very easy for your greenhouse to get cluttered and fill up with spilt soil and other odds and ends.
- Ventilation - open vents, windows and doors during the day to encourage pollinating insects in and for the air to circulate.
- Watering - keep plants, particularly seedlings, well-watered as they can dry out and wilt very easily in the warmer weather. Tomatoes, cucumbers, peppers, chillies and aubergines can all the planted into larger containers now. Put supports in place while the plants are still young to prevent damage to the roots later on.

June

June is all hands to the pump as it is one of the busiest months in the vegetable garden. The risk of frost has passed now for almost everyone, so all those tender plants you have been carefully looking after can be planted out. Many of the crops you have nurtured through the colder weather will now be ripening and ready to harvest, and let's not forget the weeds will be enjoying the warmer weather and your efforts watering/feeding your plants.

Delicious when harvested small.

What To Harvest

This is a good month to harvest fruit and vegetables, so make sure you have plenty of room in your fridge and freezer for everything. You may be busy cooking with a lot of what you harvest as it is truly a glorious month at the allotment.

- Asparagus - keep harvesting your asparagus shoots. Traditionally, harvesting was stopped on the longest day, 21st June, but most people will continue to harvest into July while the plant is still producing spears.
- Beetroot - pick when they are about the size of golf balls as they are tender and tasty. Once they grow too large, they become woody and hard to eat. The leaves can be eaten raw in salads or added to stir-fries.
- Broad Beans - autumn sown broad beans will be ready to harvest this month, as will those started earlier in the year under cover. Pick while the beans are still small as they have the sweetest flavour. These beans can be blanched and frozen for longer term storage.
- Broccoli - summer sprouting broccoli and calabrese should be ready to harvest from this month. Cut while the buds are tight and the heads firm. Check your broccoli regularly as they can quickly become too ripe.
- Carrots - early carrots, sown in March or April, should be ready to pull this month. The small,

baby carrots are great in salads or stir-fries.
- Cauliflowers - early summer cauliflowers, planted in March, should be ready to harvest now. Harvest when the heads are firm and before the bolt. Check them regularly as they can very quickly turn. Cauliflower can be blanched and frozen for long term storage.
- Cherries - if you have netted your cherries to protect them from the birds, some may be ready towards the end of the month.
- Florence Fennel - this is the first month to harvest fennel. The smaller bulbs are great in salads whereas the larger bulbs are better cooked.
- Globe Artichokes - the young, tightly budded globes are delicious cooked and eaten whole. Larger globes are best steamed or boiled and then picked apart for the heart.
- Gooseberries - thin the crop again by picking alternate fruits. These may not be ripe enough to eat raw, but certainly can be cooked.
- Garlic - the leaves will start to yellow and wilt when your garlic is ready. Traditionally, it is harvested on the longest day, but pick when you are happy it is ready. Dry thoroughly with the leaves on before storing.
- Kohl Rabi - these should be ready to harvest this month. If you are eating them raw, pick them when they are the size of a golf ball.
- Lettuces - Little gem type lettuces sown in March

or April will be ready to harvest. Other cut-and-come-again crops can still be regularly harvested which encourages new growth.

- Onions - overwintered onions will be ready to harvest this month. Dry them thoroughly with the leaves on before storing.
- Peas - pick the peas when they are young and sweet. Eat as soon as you can after picking before the sugars turn to starch. Peas can be blanched and frozen.
- Potatoes - new potatoes will be ready to harvest this month. Dry these out in the sun before storing in hessian sacks or paper bags. Do not wash potatoes that you plan to store, just rub the dirt off when they have dried.
- Radishes - those sown in April or May should be ready to harvest this month. Do not allow them to grow too large otherwise they become woody and difficult to eat.
- Rhubarb - continue harvesting your rhubarb, making sure you do not take too much from a single plant. The harvest can continue for a month or two.
- Spinach - pick spinach leaves as a cut-and-come-again crop. Keep them well watered and shade them from the hottest weather if you can. Spinach has a tendency to bolt once the temperature rises and they get too dry.
- Spring Onions - crops sown in the spring should be ready to harvest this month.
- Strawberries - you know summer is here when the strawberries are ready. Check the plants daily for ripe strawberries and keep them netted to prevent birds from damaging your crop.
- Swiss Chard - harvest regularly and, like spinach, keep it well watered to prevent it from bolting. Harvest as a cut-and-come-again crop. Young leaves can be eaten raw whereas older leaves need to cooked.
- Turnips - many modern varieties are ready to harvest just five or six weeks after sowing. Harvest when they are the size of golf balls and have a sweet and nutty taste. When they grow too big, they become woody and tough to eat.

Vegetable Garden Jobs

The vegetable garden is very busy this month. There is a lot to do, not least of which is keeping on top of the weeds. The hoe is your friend this month. Knock the heads of the weeds and leave them in the sun to dry and rot, providing nutrients back into the soil. Regularly hoeing your soil will keep the weeding manageable. There is still lots to plant this month.

- Asparagus - feed your asparagus with a general purpose fertiliser when you have finished harvesting the spears. Leave the plants to grow and don't cut them down until the autumn when they have turned brown.
- Aubergines - plant these outdoors now, if you are going to, so they have as much time as possible to fruit.
- Beetroot - keep sowing seeds this month for harvest in September and October.
- Broccoli - late sprouting broccoli seeds can be planted now for an autumn or spring harvest. Calabrese can also be sown direct this month.
- Brussels Sprouts - plant these out, firming them down into the ground well so they don't suffer from wind rock. Stake these plants if you are in an exposed or windy area. Net the plants to protect them from butterflies and birds.
- Carrots - this is the last month to sow main crop carrots that will be ready in September or October.
- Cabbages - plant these out but use cabbage collars to deter cabbage root fly. Net them immediately to protect them from cabbage white butterflies and birds.
- Cauliflower - spring sown seedlings can be planted out. Again, net these plants to protect them.
- Celeriac - this is the last month you can plant out celeriac. It is a slow growing plant and needs plenty of time to mature.
- Celery - plant out into a rich, fertile soil. Self-blanching varieties need to be planted in closely spaced blocks otherwise plant in celery trenches.
- Chicory - plant out seedlings this month, being very careful not to disturb the roots.
- Chillies / Bell Peppers - young plants can be transplanted outdoors this month but may benefit from being covered if the weather is cool.
- Cucumbers - sow directly or plant out those grown earlier.
- Endive - this can be sown directly for harvesting in autumn to early winter. Note that in hot weather, germination can be tricky.
- Florence Fennel - traditionally, this is sown after 21st June as the plants are less likely to bolt, though modern cultivars are a bit more forgiving. Sowing now will produce a crop in early autumn.
- French Beans - sow a second crop of French beans this month. Seedlings can be planted out.
- Herbs - most herbs can still be sown this month for a late summer or early autumn harvest.

- Kale - sow more kale in seed trays for planting out next month. Transplant out seedlings when they are 4"/10cm tall, disturbing the roots as little as possible.
- Kohl Rabi - continue sowing more seeds this month, thinning out rows where required. These are best netted to protect them from birds, but also watch for slugs which will damage the roots.
- Lettuces - sow direct but note that they do not germinate well in high temperatures. According to folklore, lettuce should be planted towards the end of the day as the soil cools.
- Oriental Leaves - pak choi, mizuna and more can still be sown this month.
- Peas - this is probably the last month to sow snap peas, main crop peas and mangetout. Towards the end of the month, plant early varieties that mature quicker.
- Pumpkins / Winter Squash - these will have been started off earlier in the year but can be planted out this month. Prepare the planting area by digging in plenty of well-rotted manure or compost.
- Radishes - continue to sow radishes to ensure a constant crop.
- Runner Beans - this is the last month to sow runner beans which should continue to fruit until October or the first frosts. Seedlings started indoors can be planted out.
- Salad Leaves - continue to sow salad leaves such as rocket and so on to use as cut-and-come-again crops.
- Spring Onions - sow more seeds this month so you have a continuous supply through the autumn.
- Squashes - all squashes, including courgettes, marrows and pumpkins, can be planted out this month. Allow plenty of space, particularly for vining squashes like pumpkins. These are greedy plants and will need plenty of water and food.
- Swedes - thin out those sown last month and cover to protect from birds and root fly.
- Sweet Potatoes - this is the last month to plant out sweet potato slips. They need a rich soil that has been earthed up into ridges. Put plastic bottles with the big end cut off, cap end down, in the soil by each slip so you can water directly to the roots.
- Tomatoes - transplant any tomatoes you plan to grow outside. Remember to support vining tomatoes. As they grow, pinch off side shoots to prevent the plants growing out of control.
- Turnips - sow more this month for harvesting in August to September.

Fruit Tree/Bush Jobs

Some fruit will be starting to ripen, so there will be some to pick, but there are plenty of jobs to keep your plants healthy and growing well.

- Apples/Pears - towards the end of the month, your apple and pear trees will experience "June drop", where they naturally thin out some of their crop. Check your trees and thin out excess fruit by hand. This allows the remaining fruit to grow to a good size and helps prevent branches breaking under the weight of the fruit.
- Berries – berries such as redcurrant and gooseberry will benefit from a pruning. Cut back the new lateral shoots to five leaves, unless you want them to develop into new branches next year.
- Blackberries - vining berries, such as blackberries, need the new canes tying in to supports. These will produce fruit next year while the canes that have produced fruit this year will be cut down in the autumn.
- Cape Gooseberries - the young plants can be planted out this month. Choose a sunny, but sheltered spot for them.
- Figs - the trees need the tips of new shoots pinching out so they only have five leaves left.
- Grapes - vines need side shoots pruned and thin the fruit.
- Melons - in warmer areas, these can be planted outside, otherwise raise them under cover. They need a rich, fertile soil in a sheltered position in full sun.
- Peaches, Nectarines and Apricots – thin the fruit to about 6-8"/15-20cm between fruit on peach and nectarine trees. Apricots need to be 3"/7.5cm apart. On wire trained trees, tie in new shoots.
- Plums, Gages and Damsons – these can all be thinned, both at the start of the month and then at the end. At the start of the month, thin to 1"/2.5cm between fruit and at the end of the month, increase the gap to 3"/7.5cm.
- Raspberries - keep removing raspberry suckers from around your plants and compost them.
- Strawberries - new runners can be planted this month and they should produce fruit in a couple of months. If you are keeping any strawberry runners, pot them up for some new plants.

General Jobs

There is a lot of jobs to do in the vegetable garden this month. Weeding and watering is going to take a lot of your time. Spreading a mulch around your plants will help prevent water from evaporating, feed the plants and keep the weeds down. However, there is lots of other jobs to do as well.

- Netting - net plants such as peas, brassicas and soft fruit to protect them from birds and butterflies.
- Peas / Beans - when you have finished harvesting peas and broad beans, cut the plants down just above soil level and compost the greenery. Leave the roots in place as they will release nitrogen into the soil.
- Potatoes - keep earthing up your potatoes to keep the tubers out of the light.
- Supports – build supports for your climbing beans, making sure they can support the weight of the fully grown plants.

Greenhouse and Polytunnel Jobs

The greenhouse will be bursting to life this month, but you need to ensure nothing dries out in the hot weather.

- Feeding - feed your tomatoes, chillies, peppers and aubergines weekly with tomato food to ensure they produce a good crop.

- Humidity - if it is getting too dry in your greenhouse during the day, soak the floor (known as damping down) in the morning so that the water evaporates during the day. This also helps to keep the greenhouse slightly cooler. Leaving buckets of water in your greenhouse can also help.
- Shading - if the weather is getting too hot, install some greenhouse shading to protect delicate plants from too much sun.
- Tomatoes - pinch out any side shoots from your tomato plants so they can concentrate on growing tall and producing fruit. Otherwise, the plants end up producing lots of greenery and very few fruits. Tomatoes will need regular watering throughout the summer which will help to prevent blossom end rot and split fruits.
- Ventilation - open vents, windows and doors to keep the air circulating and to prevent it getting too hot in your greenhouse.
- Watering - keep all your plants well-watered as they will dry out quickly in the warmer weather. Some plants will benefit from being watered twice a day. An irrigation system may make your life easier if you can install one.

July

J uly is another busy month in the vegetable garden. Planting will be slowing down, but harvesting is going to be occupying a lot of your time. Weeding and watering will be another time consuming task but mulching your plants can help reduce the amount of work you have to do here.

Start harvesting before they grow too big.

What To Harvest

July is a great month for harvesting as lots of things will be ready for you to pick and enjoy. Remember to check your plants regularly and harvest everything when it is at its peak. Many plants can go from ripe to overripe very quickly, so visit your vegetable garden daily and pick everything that is ripe. Store it, use it or freeze it.

- Apricots - some early varieties may be ready to harvest if the conditions have been favourable.

- Aubergines - in warmer areas, you may get some ripe aubergines towards the end of the month.

- Beetroot - continue to harvest your beetroot before they grow too large. If you have a lot of beetroot ready at one time, they can be picked for long term storage.

- Blackberries - the first blackberries will be ready to harvest this month, as will other hybrid berries such as tayberries.

- Blackcurrants - these will start to ripen this month. Newer varieties will ripen at all once whereas traditional varieties ripen gradually. Pick and use the ripe berries, though they can be frozen if necessary.

- Blueberries - this month should see the first of your blueberries ready to harvest. Pick the largest, softest berries that are a dark blue/black colour.

- Broad Beans - check these daily as they will ripen rapidly. Harvest from the bottom of the plant upwards and compost finished plants, leaving the roots in the ground. Harvest the beans before they grow too big and become tough and bitter.

- Broccoli - harvest your broccoli regularly when it is ready. Note that this plant can quickly become overripe, so when they are ready, do not leave the on the plant.

- Carrots - early carrots are best eaten when young, whereas main crop carrots are good when they are larger.

- Celery - some celery could be ready this month. Water them before harvesting to help keep them crisp for longer.

- Cherries - providing you netted your cherries to protect them from birds, they should be ready to be picked.

- Chicory - this can be picked now for baby salad leaves or left to form hearts.

- Chillies / Bell Peppers - if you have grown these undercover, these may be ready to harvest this month.

- Courgettes - June sees the start of courgette (and summer squash) season. These need harvesting regularly when they are the same size as those found in the shops. Harvest daily as they can literally double in size overnight!

- Cucumbers - harvest outdoor cucumbers when they are 6-8"/15-20cm long. Any longer and the seeds become too large and unpleasant tasting.
- Florence Fennel - Cut these about 1"/2.5cm above the ground and leave the remains in the ground. In a few weeks, feathery leaves will have sprouted from the stump which are delicious in stir-fries.
- French Beans - dwarf bush varieties will be ready to harvest this month. These are best picked every day when they are at their best.
- Garlic - continue to harvest garlic as the leave wilt and turn yellow. Allow them to dry fully before storing.
- Globe Artichoke - keep harvesting these before the purple flowers start to show.
- Gooseberries - these should be ripening nicely this month. Sweet ones can be eaten raw whereas other can be cooked or made into jam.
- Kohl Rabi - continue harvesting this plant before the roots are larger than a tennis ball.
- Lettuces - keep harvesting lettuces once they form hearts. Cut-and-come-again crops are likewise harvested by taking the outer leaves.
- Marrows - these can be picked now while still relatively small or left for next month when they are larger.
- Onions - most of your onions will be ready to harvest by now. Dry them with the leaves still on and then store.
- Peaches and nectarines - this is the first month that these can be harvested from trees grown in sheltered areas.
- Peas - pick peas regularly before they grow too large. They are best eaten straight away while still sweet or blanched and frozen the same day.
- Plums - some early season plums could be ready to harvest towards the end of the month. Harvest when they are slightly soft but before they become squishy.
- Potatoes - second earlies will be ready to lift now. When the flowers appear, scrape away the soil from the base of a plant and check the potatoes to see if they are ready. Salad varieties should be harvested before they grow too big and used as soon as possible.
- Radishes - harvest while small for the best flavour. As they grow larger, they become hotter and woody.
- Raspberries - check your summer fruiting raspberries daily and pick those that are ripe. They will quickly become overripe if left. Harvest

when they are the correct colour and pull away from the plant easily, leaving the 'plug' behind.

- Red/White Currants - as these ripen, cut off the whole strig (truss) and strip the berries at home.
- Rhubarb - this is the last month where you can harvest rhubarb. After this month, leave the plant alone so it can store energy for winter.
- Rocket - keep harvesting rocket as a cut-and-come-again crop as the plant will continue to produce more leaves.
- Runner Beans - harvest your runner beans before they grow too large and become stringy. These can be chopped, blanched and frozen for long term storage.
- Shallots - the first shallots will be ready when the leaves have died down. Dry them fully before removing the leaves and storing them.
- Spinach - keep watering this plant to stop it from bolting and harvest as a cut-and-come-again crop.
- Spring Onions - continue to harvest these and sow more seeds for another crop later in the year.
- Strawberries - harvest these regularly while they are still at their best. Remove any that are overripe or mouldy.
- Tomatoes - outdoor tomatoes can be ready to harvest this month, though only pick them when they are fully ripe.
- Turnips - keep harvesting your turnips before they grow too big. They are best when around the size of a golf ball.

Vegetable Plant Jobs

There are still some vegetables to plant out this month for cropping later in the year. Some seedlings raised in your greenhouse or under cover can be planted out now too.

- Beetroot – these can be planted this month.
- Brassicas – net all your brassicas to protect them from birds, butterflies and other pests.
- Broccoli - some varieties can be planted now for a late autumn crop.
- Brussel Sprouts, Cabbages and Cauliflowers – these can be planted now for harvesting next spring, though make sure you plant an overwinter variety. Autumn cauliflowers, cabbages and Brussels sprouts that you have been raising from seed can be planted out now too. All brassicas will benefit from the earth being piled up around the stalks and firming down to prevent wind rock.
- Broad Beans - these need to be cut down when the harvest is finished. Cut them just above the

surface, leaving the roots in the ground. The greenery can be composted while the roots are left in the ground where they release nitrogen.

- Carrots – these can be sown direct this month.
- Cauliflower - cover the heads otherwise they will turn yellow in the sun. An easy way to do this is to pull outside leaves over the heads and tie them in place.
- Celery - trench celery needs earthing up to keep the stems out of the light.
- Climbing Beans – these generally keep on climbing until the frosts finish them off. In July, you can pinch the tops off them otherwise they will continue to grow and when they reach the top of your canes, they get tangled and top heavy, i.e. more susceptible to wind damage.
- Florence Fennel – this can be sown in July for a late autumn crop before the first hard frosts.
- French Beans – this is the last month for planting French beans so they will produce a crop before the frosts set in.
- Kohl Rabi – continue planting this month for a late autumn to early winter crop.
- Leaf Vegetables – leafy vegetables such as kale, mizuna, Chinese broccoli and Swiss chard can still be planted out and will last well into the autumn and even into winter.
- Leeks - these should all be planted out into their final growing position by the end of this month. Cover with a fine netting to protect them from leek moth.
- Onions, Shallots and Garlic – these must be fully dried before they go into storage. Check them carefully and any suffering from white rot, mould or any damage, should be used immediately and not stored. Lay the bulbs on the ground in sunny weather to dry or put them in the greenhouse or shed to dry. The more they dry, the longer they will keep. Once they are fully dried, remove and compost the leaves.
- Peas – net your peas to protect them from birds. Make sure they are raised up off the ground to protect them from mice. You can continue to plant peas and they will produce a crop before the first frosts.
- Potatoes - keep earthing up your potatoes as required to prevent the tubers being exposed to the sun.
- Tomatoes/Peppers – these need regular watering and feeding this month as soon as the flowers appear. Tomato plants should have the side shoots pinched off. When tomatoes form four or five trusses, pinch the growing tip off the plant so it concentrates on ripening the fruit.
- Turnips – sow these direct now.

Fruit Tree/Bush Jobs

Your fruit trees and bushes will need some attention this month and will start to be producing a harvest for you. Some of the jobs you can be doing this month include:

- Apples/Pears – thin fruit if required.
- Apricot – thin fruit if required.
- Blackcurrants - lightly prune either just before or just after harvesting the fruit. Red and white currants and gooseberries can also be pruned in the summer after they have fruited.
- Blackberries – both blackberries and hybrid berries such as tayberries have new canes tied in so that old canes can be cut back in the autumn.
- Cherries/Plums – both cherries and plums can be pruned once the fruit has been harvested. Note that stone fruit trees are pruned in the summer months, not the winter.
- Grapes - vines have the fruit thinned and side shoots pruned. Some of the leaves can be removed around clusters of grapes to give them more sun and speed ripening.
- Raspberries - when you finish picking summer fruiting raspberries, cut the canes that have produced fruit back to ground level as they will not produce fruit next year.
- Strawberries - tidy up your summer strawberries by removing old foliage and runners as well as any debris such as straw around the base of the plants.
- Trees - all wire trained trees need to be checked to make sure the ties are secure, but not constricting the tree. New growth can be lightly pruned or tied in.

General Jobs

This month you are going to be concerned with watering, weeding and mulching, particularly if the weather is very hot and dry. Even though, there are other jobs to do too.

- Mulching - mulch your plants to help conserve moisture and keep the weeds down.
- Propagate Herbs - perennial herbs such as rosemary, sage and thyme can be propagated with softwood, stem or semi-ripe cuttings.
- Watering - water everything regularly but be careful not to overwater plants. Water direct to the base of the plant and avoid getting water on the leaves of the plant. For many plants, such as spinach, rocket and cauliflowers, regularly

watering them can help to stop them from bolting.

- Weeding - keep the weeds down across your vegetable garden as they will be enjoying the warm weather and benefiting from you feeding and watering your plants.

Greenhouse and Polytunnel Jobs

The greenhouse will be full of plants now but will also be getting very hot. You will not want to be spending too much time in the greenhouse in the heat of the day!

- Damping Down – damp down your greenhouse in the morning by soaking the floor to help keep the humidity up.
- Tidying - tidy up the greenhouse from all the activity earlier in the year, removing any potential hideouts for slugs and snails.
- Tomatoes - greenhouse grown tomatoes can often be allowed to grow to 5-7 trusses before the ends are pinched out.
- Ventilation - open windows, vents and doors to help air circulation and to encourage pollinating insects into the greenhouse.
- Watering - water plants in the greenhouse regularly, sometimes twice a day, to prevent them from drying out. Tomatoes, in particular, must be regularly watered otherwise they end up with blossom end rot and split fruits.

August

The vegetable garden quietens down a little in August, surprisingly enough, giving you a bit of time to enjoy the weather and the fruits of your labour. Your main jobs will still be weeding and watering, but now you will be busy harvesting everything and wondering what on earth you will do with it all (or is that just me?). It's an enjoyable month on the vegetable plot as the sun should be out and you can take some time to enjoy watching the world go by as you work.

Makes a great jam.

What To Harvest

Sowing and planting in August has slowed right down this month as very little will have enough time to ripen before the onset of winter frosts. Some fast growing root vegetables or lettuces will survive, but not much else. As you harvest other crops, so you can plant out overwintering vegetables such as spring cabbages and winter cauliflowers.

- Apples - early apples will be ready to harvest this month. It can be hard to tell when apples are ripe, though finding more on the ground can be an indication. In some varieties, the colour deepens or changes. Generally, picking one and eating it is the best way of telling. Pick apples by lifting the apple slightly and twisting it, rather than pulling. It should come off the tree easily if it is fully ripe.

- Apricots - these are ready to harvest when they are slightly soft and can be removed from the tree with little resistance.

- Aubergines - when they are black and glossy, they are ready to harvest. Store in your refrigerator and use as soon as possible.

- Beetroot - harvest these regularly otherwise they grow too big and become woody and hard to eat. Store in your refrigerator with the leaves removed (leave 1" of stalk though) or pickle for longer term storage.

- Blackberries - blackberries and other hybrid berries such as loganberries, tayberries and so on will all be ready to harvest this month. Store in your refrigerator, freeze or make into a jam for longer term storage.

- Blackcurrants - these turn a shiny blue/black when they are ripe. Pick them as soon as you they are ripe and store in your refrigerator. They can be frozen whole or made into jams for longer term storage.

- Blueberries - these ripen at different times, so check regularly and harvest a couple of times a week. Store in your refrigerator, freeze or process for longer term storage.

- Broad Beans - there should still be some pods left on the plant that can be harvested this month. When you have harvested the last pods from a plant, cut it down to root level, compost the foliage and leave the nitrogen rich roots in the ground.

- Broccoli - keep harvesting both sprouting broccoli and calabrese before the flower buds start to open.

- Cabbages - summer and red cabbages should be ready to harvest this month. Pick them when the heads are solid and dense. Store in your refrigerator or blanch and freeze.

- Carrots - the last of the early carrots and the first of the main crop carrots will be ready to harvest this month. Store wrapped in plastic in your refrigerator or blanch and freeze for longer term storage.

- Cauliflowers - both summer and autumn cauliflowers should be ready to harvest. Store in your refrigerator or blanch and freeze for long term storage.

- Celery - harvest before the leaves turn yellow otherwise the stalks become stringy.

- Chillies/peppers - start harvesting these this month. Generally, though this does not apply to all varieties, peppers become sweeter and chillies hotter as they ripen.

- Cucumbers - harvest before they turn yellow. Any yellow cucumbers found on your plants should be removed and composted to encourage the production of new fruits.

- Figs - the first of the figs are ready this month. Pick when the colour darkens and they are slightly soft. Often there is a bead of nectar at the base when the fruit is ripe.

- Florence Fennel - bulb fennel will bolt in dry weather, so harvest the bulbs before they elongate and become too tough to eat. The stumps can be left in the ground and they will produce new shoots. The feathery leaves can be used in stir-fries and salads.

- French Beans - both dwarf and climbing varieties will be ready this month. Pick while small to eat the pods whole or leave to swell to eat the beans or save them to plant next year.

- Garlic - the last of your garlic is harvested this month. Hang it up to dry for use over the winter months.

- Globe Artichokes - keep picking the globes as they are ready, working from the top of the plant down.

- Kohl Rabi - keep harvesting kohl rabi and eating them raw or cooked.

- Lettuces - keep your lettuces well-watered and shade them if you can otherwise they will bolt. If the temperatures are too high, new seeds will struggle to germinate. Harvest as and when you need them.

- Marrows - harvest as they reach the size you prefer, though don't leave them too long otherwise the seeds become large and a bit chewy to eat.

- Onions - harvest the last of your onions and dry them thoroughly before storing.

- Pak Choi - harvest the young leaves as a cut-and-come-again crop.

- Peaches and Nectarines - these will be ripe this month. Pick the fruits when they are a little bit soft and pull away from the tree easily.

- Pears - these are very difficult to tell when they are ripe because they ripen from the inside out. It is better to pick when under-ripe and ripen off the tree.

- Peas - pick the pods while they are still young for the sweetest peas. Keep them netted to protect them from birds.

- Plums - most plums and gages will be ready to harvest this month. They do not store well, so use soon after harvesting, freeze, or make into a jams or sauces.

- Potatoes - there will still be potatoes ready to harvest. Allow them to dry thoroughly and then store in paper bags or hessian sacks. Do not wash any potatoes that you plan to store and put any damaged potatoes to one side for immediate use.

- Radish - you should be harvesting these now. Remember to harvest them while they are small before they become woody and difficult to eat. Store without the leaves, wrapped in plastic in your refrigerator.

- Raspberries - summer fruiting raspberries will finish this month and autumn fruiting ones should be starting towards the end of the month. Harvest regularly as they very quickly become overripe.

- Red/White Currants - harvest these berries when they are ripe but before they become too soft. Cut the entire strig (or truss) off and use a fork to remove the berries when you get home.

- Runner Beans - harvest your beans every day or two otherwise they will become too big and stringy. Unless you are allowing some pods to ripen to save seeds, remove overripe pods and compost to encourage the production of more pods.

- Shallots - lift the last of these and dry them before storing.

- Spinach - this will bolt if the weather is hot and dry, so water regularly and shade if you can. Harvest the leaves regularly.

- Spring Onions - keep harvesting spring onions before the bulbs grow too large. The large the bulbs become, the stronger the taste of the onion.

- Squashes - harvest the squashes every few days as they will grow very quickly and can become too large for eating.

- Strawberries - keep harvesting strawberries as and when they are ripe.
- Sweetcorn - when the tassels or silk turn brown or black, the cobs are generally ready to harvest. The juice from the kernels should be milky not clear when they are right. Harvest as soon as they are ready otherwise animals such as rats, squirrels and badgers will eat them.
- Tomatoes - keep harvesting your tomatoes as they ripening. Fresh tomatoes do not store well, so use them as soon as you can or process them for longer term storage.
- Turnips - the roots are best eaten while still relatively small. The young leaves can be eaten like spring greens or spinach.

Vegetable Garden Jobs

There is not a great deal to plant at this time of year, but as you are clearing space as other crops finish, you can plant overwinter crops such as winter cauliflower and cabbage. You will still be watering and weeding this month, paying particular attention to crops like lettuce and spinach that bolt if the weather gets too hot.

- Beetroot - you can still sow some beetroot for an autumn harvest.
- Broccoli - sprouting broccoli can be planted out this month for harvest next spring.
- Cabbage - sow more cabbages for a spring harvest, remembering to keep them covered to protect them from pests and birds.
- Carrot - this is the last month of the year you can sow carrots. Try to sow a fast maturing variety for an autumn crop.
- Cauliflowers - winter and spring cauliflowers that were started off earlier in the year can be planted in their final position now for a harvest early next year.
- Kale - plant out any overwinter kale plants, sown earlier in the year.
- Lettuce - some varieties can still be sown, though if temperatures are too high, they may struggle to germinate.
- Onions - Japanese onion seeds can be sown this month. Mark drills with string and sow seeds and leave them until spring to thin out. They will be okay overwinter as they are hardy and will be ready to harvest next summer.
- Radish - keep sowing radishes which should be ready to harvest before the winter frosts.
- Spinach - some varieties can be planted this month for an autumn harvest.
- Swiss Chard - sow this for an autumn/winter harvest.

- Turnip - this is the last chance you have to sow turnips to harvest before winter sets in.

Fruit Tree/Bush Jobs

August is a good month for fruits as many of them will be ripening. Remember to harvest fruits regularly as many of them can become overripe very quickly. A lot of soft fruits do not store well, even in your fridge, so freeze them or turn them into a jam or similar for longer term storage.

- Blackberries - your blackberries and hybrid berries need the new canes tying in ready for next year whereas old canes are removed in the autumn.
- Currants - summer prune all currant bushes once the fruits have been harvested.
- Fruit Trees - heavily laden fruit trees need to be propped up with rope or supports as branches can break under the weight of the fruit.
- Gooseberries - summer prune your gooseberry bushes once they have finished fruiting.
- Grapes - prune side shoots and remove some leaves so the fruit gets some sun.
- Strawberries - the runners you pegged down earlier in the year will have roots by now and can be planted out into a sunny location and kept well-watered.

General Jobs

There are a lot of jobs in the vegetable garden other than watering and weeding. Keep debris under control as slugs and snails will take the opportunity to hide anywhere and decimate your plants when you are not looking. This is also a good month for painting sheds and other woodwork as it is generally dry.

- Brassicas - earth up brassicas to support them as they do not like being blown in the wind.
- Celery - earth up your non-self-blanching celery to protect the stems from the light.
- Climbing Beans - pinch out the tops of climbing beans so they don't become top heavy and concentrate on growth lower down.
- Cucumbers - continue to tie up your cucumber plants, using additional canes when necessary.
- Mulch - mulch your plants, ideally after rain, to keep the moisture in the ground.
- Peppers - tie up and feed your pepper plants.
- Potatoes - keep earthing up potatoes to prevent the tubers being exposed to the light.
- Pumpkins - feed your pumpkins once a week with a high potash tomato fertiliser. If the weather is damp, lift them off the ground using planks of wood or bricks to prevent them from

rotting.

- Tomatoes - keep feeding, pinching out and tying up your tomato plants.

Greenhouse and Polytunnel Jobs

The greenhouse or polytunnel will be getting very hot this month, so you will need to keep doors, windows and vents open. Your plants may need to be watered two or three times a day, depending on the temperatures.

- Damping Down - each morning, on hot days, pour water over the floor of your greenhouse to increase the humidity.

- Pests - check your plants regularly for pests and diseases. Take action the moment you spot a problem to prevent it from spreading.
- Potatoes - cold stored potato tubers can be planted in containers for a Christmas harvest.
- Shade - delicate plants in the greenhouse will benefit from some shading to protect them from sun scorch.
- Tomatoes - remove the lower leaves from vining tomato plants to allow air and light to reach the fruit. Make sure these are kept well-watered and there is sufficient air flow between the plants.

September

September generally sees work on the allotment calming down a little. The weather will start to become cooler and the days shorten. There will be less to harvest and plant, giving you more time to work on longer term or structural projects on your plot. However, there is still plenty to keep you occupied!

Cape gooseberries.

What to Harvest

Although harvesting will slow down this month, there should still be plenty to harvest throughout the month.

- Apples - the last of the early season apples and the first of the mid/late season varieties can be harvested this month.
- Apricots - the last of the apricots can be harvested this month. After the end of the month, any fruit left on the tree is unlikely to ripen any further.
- Aubergines - harvest while the fruit have a glossy shine to them. Once the shine starts to fade, the fruits can develop a bitter taste.
- Beetroot - keep picking the beetroot. As well as pickling them, try roasting them doused in balsamic vinegar and olive oil!
- Blackberries - late season blackberries are ready to harvest. Mark the canes that have produced fruit (tie some ribbon or string to them) as they will need cutting back soon.
- Blueberries - late season varieties will still have a few berries on them to harvest.
- Broccoli - this can still be harvested this month when the heads are tightly formed.
- Brussels Sprouts - this month you can start harvesting these, though they could still be small.
- Cabbages - autumn and red cabbages should be ready to harvest from this month through to November.

- Cape Gooseberry - also known as physalis, these should be ripe this month. Harvest when the husks dry and turn brown and papery. The bright orange fruit will be visible inside.
- Carrots - lift your carrots, being careful not to snap the roots (use a hand fork). Keep them covered with a tightly woven mesh to prevent carrot root fly damage.
- Cauliflower - harvest when the heads are tightly curled and before they bolt. Blanch and freeze for long term storage.
- Celeriac - you can lift some of these this month, though they are likely to be a little small.
- Chillies and Peppers - as they turn red, they will be hotter or sweeter. Harvest as and when required.
- Courgettes - the last of the courgettes should be ready to harvest this month. Remember to check your plants often as they can quickly become too large.
- Cranberries - the first of the cranberries will be ripe this month, though you can leave them on the bush until they are all ripe.
- Cucumbers - harvest these before they grow too large. If grown outside, the plants will die in the frosts.
- Damsons - most damsons will be ready to harvest now as they can be picked slightly unripe as they are usually cooked. Damsons are often found growing in the wild.

- Figs - harvest these towards the end of the month. The ripe fruits will store for 2-3 weeks covered in a cool place.
- Florence Fennel - this can still be harvested this month.
- French Beans - harvest to eat or leave in place to dry.
- Globe Artichokes - you may get a second crop of edible flower heads, but they will need to be harvest by the end of the month.
- Grapes - some of these will be ripe this month, though the longer you can leave them, the higher their sugar content will be.
- Kohl Rabi - these will still be harvestable this month.
- Leeks - the first of the leeks should be ready this month if they were planted early. Baby leeks are good to harvest and use.
- Lettuce - keep harvesting as required.
- Marrows - the last of your marrows can be harvested as the plants will die in the cold and frosts. Leave the fruit in the sun to cure so the skins harden and they store better.
- Peas - keep harvesting peas and remove any overripe pods unless you are saving seeds.
- Pears - these can still be harvested still. Check them like you would apples.
- Plums - plums and damsons are ready to harvest.
- Potatoes – main crop potatoes are ready to harvest this month. Dry them thoroughly before storing over winter. In some areas, providing pests and wet weather aren't a problem, the tubers can be left in the ground until required.
- Pumpkins - you can start harvesting these when they are ripe this month.
- Radishes - winter radishes can be harvested when the roots are larger than salad varieties.
- Raspberries - autumn fruiting raspberries will still be fruiting. Harvest regularly as they will become overripe very quickly.
- Runner Beans - keep harvesting the young, tender beans before they grow too large.
- Spinach - Keep harvesting the leaves from any plants that haven't bolted.
- Spring Onions - this is probably the last month you can harvest spring onions, though depending on how mild the weather is, some may still continue to grow into next month.
- Strawberries - perpetual strawberries will continue to ripen this month and possibly into October providing there are no early frosts.
- Sweetcorn - harvest any cobs that are ripe, eating them as soon as possible before the sugars turn into starches.
- Sweet Potatoes - the first of your sweet potatoes will be ready to dig up this month.
- Swede - the first swedes will be ready to harvest this month. They will continue to grow larger, so harvest a few as and when you need them, leaving the rest for later.
- Swiss Chard - keep harvesting the leaves before they grow too large. New leaves will appear in the centre. This plant does get attacked by slugs and snails, so check regularly for these pests and compost any damaged leaves.
- Tomatoes - you can still harvest tomatoes as they ripen, particularly the larger, beefsteak tomatoes that take longer to mature.
- Turnips - keep harvesting these while the roots are still relatively small.
- Winter Squashes - these can start to be harvested this month, though cure them (dry) before storing and they will last some time.

Vegetable Plant Jobs
There are plenty of jobs in the vegetable garden, including sowing winter salad leaves and lettuces plus some of the Oriental leaves. Overwintering onion sets can also be planted this month as they will survive the cold of winter.

- Cabbages - transplant spring cabbages into their final growing position. Ensure they are firmed into the ground well and protect them with netting and cabbage collars.
- Lettuce - winter lettuces and salads such as corn salad, winter purslane and rocket can be sown this month under cloches.
- Mizuna - Oriental leaves such as mizuna and mibuna can be planted now, though the young plants may benefit from covering on colder nights.
- Onions - plant overwintering onion sets. Bury the sets 3-4"/7-10cm apart with the tips either just above or below the surface of the soil. Check these regularly as they are often dug up by curious animals and left on top of the soil.
- Radishes - you may be able to sow a last crop of radishes early in the month to harvest before the end of the year.
- Spinach - this is your last chance to sow spinach, though cover them on colder nights.
- Spring Onions - these can be sown in September to overwinter for a spring harvest.

Fruit Tree/Bush Jobs

The fruit garden will still have a lot to harvest, but there are a few jobs to do. Bare root trees shouldn't be planted until winter, but they can be ordered now from suppliers for later delivery. Container grown fruit bushes and trees can be planted now.

- Cranberries - new plants can be sown from now until November, though remember they need an acidic soil. For most people, these are best grown in containers of ericaceous compost.
- Peaches and Nectarines - container grown plants can be put in the ground now, though wait until November to plant bare root trees. These trees need a sunny, sheltered, south facing position.
- Strawberries - plant new strawberries so they have plenty of time to establish themselves ready for a good crop next year.

General Jobs

September is very much a tidying month where you clear away dead or dying leaves and plants, keep on top of weeds and generally keep your vegetable plot tidy after the rush of the summer.

- Asparagus - once the foliage has started to turn yellow, cut it down to about 1"/2.5cm above the surface and put it on the compost heap.
- Blackberries - prune blackberries and other hybrid berries, removing canes that have produced fruit. New canes, which will produce fruit next year, need tying in place.
- Brussels Sprouts - earth up and stake your Brussels sprouts and other brassicas to stop them rocking in the wind. In more exposed areas, tie them to stakes to stop them being damaged.
- Celeriac - feed regularly with a liquid feed and remove any damaged leaves.
- Celery - earth up your celery plants so the sun cannot get to the stems.
- Compost - turn your compost heap a couple of times this month and aerate it regularly to help speed up decomposition. It is likely to be quite full from the summer. If the compost becomes too dry, water it but do not soak it. It will benefit from covering to keep it warm, which also helps the composting process.

- Grapes - prune side shoots and remove some leaves so the sun can get to the fruits.
- Green Manure - start sowing green manures such as phacelia, field beans and annual ryegrass. These will all overwinter and can be dug into the soil next spring.
- Pumpkins - keep feeding and watering your pumpkins, particularly the larger varieties. Carefully remove leaves from around the fruits so the sun can get to them.
- Seeds - collect and save any seeds this month from heirloom varieties. Seeds from F1 varieties are not worth saving as they will not grow true to the parent plant.
- Water - keep watering your plants during dry weather. Squashes, and particularly pumpkins benefit from plenty of water so that the fruits can keep growing.

Greenhouse and Polytunnel Jobs

Like outside, many jobs here will involve tidying up, but many plants will still be ripening and producing fruit.

- Dead Leaves - remove dead or damaged leaves from your plants and compost them. Do not allow plant debris to remain on the greenhouse floor as this can harbour pests and diseases.
- Frosts - watch out for early frosts and bring any tender plants in from outside if there is a risk of frost.
- Heaters - check your greenhouse heaters are in good working order, so that any repairs can be made before you need to use them.
- Pests - keep checking for pests and diseases, making sure there is sufficient space between your plants for air circulation.
- Shading - now light levels are dropping, shade paint can be washed off and shade netting removed and cleaned.
- Ventilation - vents and windows will need to be closed on cooler nights now to protect your tender plants.

October

In October, the allotment gets quieter, though you can find plenty to do. Sowing will be slowing down, but there is still lots of harvest and eat. Many of your plants will not survive a frost, so they need to be harvested before a frost hits. You will not be watering as much, but there is plenty of tidying up and putting parts of your plot 'to bed' for winter.

To be blanched and frozen for use later in the year.

What To Harvest

Even though it is getting cooler, there is still quite a lot to harvest, though much of it will be tailing off as the month progresses. With the risk of frost increasing, many fruits will need to be harvested before the cold damages them.

- Apples - the rest of your apples should be harvested by the middle of the month. Any damaged fruit should either be discarded or used immediately, depending on what is wrong with it while the rest of the fruits can be stored or used.
- Aubergines - plants grown in your greenhouse may still be producing aubergines. Outdoor plants are likely to have finished by now.
- Beetroot - finish harvesting your beetroot before they become too large and woody.
- Broccoli - this is usually the last month for harvesting calabrese broccoli, but the sprouting varieties normally crop until spring.
- Brussels Sprouts - start harvesting these before they 'blow' and the leaves unfurl. Harvest from the bottom of the plant up. Blanch and freeze if you can't use them all.
- Cabbages - keep these netted and start harvesting autumn cabbages.
- Cape Gooseberries - leave the berries on the plant for as long as you can as they will become sweeter. However, they need to be harvested before the first frost.

- Carrots – main crop carrots can still be harvested this month. Providing they are not being damaged by slugs, they can be left in the ground (with the foliage cut off) for later in winter.
- Cauliflowers - continue harvesting your autumn cauliflowers.
- Celeriac - these should be approaching full size now, so can be harvested when needed. For those left in the ground, remove the outer leaves around the crowns to reduce the risk of slug damage.
- Celery - harvest your celery before the frosts arrive.
- Chillies / Peppers - you may still be harvesting these from the greenhouse, though outdoor plants are unlikely to still be producing.
- Courgettes - harvest the last of the courgettes and summer squashes before they are killed off in the first frost.
- Florence Fennel - this plant can survive light frosts, but any bulbs left in the ground will benefit from having a cloche put over them.
- French Beans - any beans dried on the plant for storage will be ready to harvest. Once removed from the pods, check for damage and store in airtight containers.
- Grapes - mid-season grape varieties are harvested around the middle of the month whereas late-season varieties will be picked at the

end of the month.

- Kohl Rabi - those sown in the summer will be ready to harvest.
- Leeks - harvest leeks as and when you need them.
- Lettuces - summer sown lettuces can be harvested now, though will benefit from protection from the cold.
- Marrows - some marrows may still be on the plants. Make sure they are harvested before the frosts, which will kill the plant.
- Parsnips - these are left in the ground until after the first frost that turns the starches into sugars, making them sweeter. Lift after the first frost and use. They can be left in the ground until needed providing they are not being damaged by pests or the ground is not waterlogged.
- Pears - Any pears left on the tree need picking. Damaged or bruised fruit should be used immediately, whereas intact fruit can be stored.
- Peas - harvest the last of the peas before the frosts arrive.
- Plums and Gages - late ripening varieties may still have some fruit on. Damsons can also be harvested and sloes can be picked towards the end of the month after the first frost.
- Pumpkins - pumpkins and winter squashes are harvested before the frosts kill the plants. Cure them in the sun so the skin hardens and they store longer. Bring them indoors before the first frosts.
- Radishes - some may still be ready to harvest from a summer sowing. Do not leave them to grow too large as they become inedible.
- Raspberries - autumn fruiting raspberries will still be cropping and often continue to do so until the first hard frost.
- Runner beans - pick any beans left on the plant.
- Spinach - keep harvesting spinach as and when you need it. Autumn cultivars, sown in late summer, should be ready to harvest.
- Strawberries - if there are any strawberries left on the plants, harvest them before the first frost as they will not survive.
- Swede - this month, and next, swedes are at their best, so harvest them as and when you need them.
- Sweet Potatoes - dig up the last of your sweet potatoes as they will be attacked by slugs if they remain in the ground. Dry them in the sun before storing.
- Tomatoes - if the weather is mild, outdoor tomatoes may still be ripening, though you may need to bring unripe fruit indoors to ripen completely. The plants will not survive the frost.
- Turnips - lift them before they get too large, though they can be left in the ground until required providing pest aren't damaging them.

Vegetable Garden Jobs

Most of the jobs in the vegetable garden involve tidying up and preparing for winter. This month you can sow and plant crops that don't mind the cold such as garlic, onion sets and rhubarb.

- Broad Beans - early varieties can be planted this month or next and should overwinter fine in most areas.
- Brussels Sprouts - keep earthing up all your brassica plants to stop them from rocking in the wind. Any yellowing leaves should be removed and composted.
- Cabbages - spring cabbages are planted out into their final position. Firm the ground down well and protect them from birds with nets.
- Chillies - outdoor chillies will die in the frosts. If you want to keep them through winter, lift them, put them in containers, prune and store in a frost free greenhouse or polytunnel over winter.
- Clay Soil - dig in manure and organic matter to help break up clay soil over winter.
- Cover Beds - any unused beds should be covered with a woven weed membrane. This allows water to penetrate through to the soil while suppressing weeds and keeping the soil warm, allowing for earlier planting in the spring. Note that although you can use tarpaulins, the water will pool on top of the plastic and not get into the soil below.
- Garlic - garlic cloves are planted from now until the end of the year. They need cold weather to form bulbs. They will survive the winter, though they struggle if they become waterlogged.
- Green Manure - green manures that will not overwinter need to be dug into the soil.
- Heavy Soil - break up heavy soil that has become compacted over the year.
- Jerusalem Artichokes - cut these down to just above the ground and compost the leaves.
- Leeks - earth up leeks that are left in the ground and protect from allium leaf miner with a tight weave mesh.
- Onions - overwintering onion sets can still be planted.
- Parsnips - mulch your parsnips with straw to protect them so they last longer in the soil.
- Peas - sow overwintering peas in a sheltered spot.

The plants will need protecting with cloches over winter.

- Plant Supports - canes, stakes and pea sticks can all be removed, cleaned and stored under cover for use next year.
- Vegetation - remove all dead foliage and dying plants. These can be composted, providing they are not diseased.

Fruit Tree/Bush Jobs

There may still be a few apples and pears to pick, but generally, harvest time will be over in the fruit garden. There is still some work to do, but mainly it is tidying up and preparing your plants for winter.

- Currants - bare root currant bushes can be planted.
- Gooseberries - bare root bushes can be planted.
- Grapes - bare root vines can be planted this month or next, though traditionally, they are planted in March.
- Ordering - order new fruit trees and bushes for planting next month.
- Rhubarb - new plants can be put in the ground whereas old plants can be divided and re-planted.
- Strawberries - new plants can still be put in the ground, though they may not produce a large crop next year.

General Jobs

The allotment is quiet this month and there isn't a lot of other jobs to do at the moment.

- Compost - turn your compost heap a couple of times throughout the month and aerate it regularly with a fork to speed up the decomposition process.
- Digging - now is a good time to dig your allotment. Many people will turn the soil and leave it to break down over winter.
- Leaves - fallen leaves can be collected and piled in a corner of your allotment. Over the next year or two, they will break down to form leaf mould that can be used to improve your soil.
- Log Pile - build a log pile in a sheltered corner of your allotment for wildlife to shelter in over winter.
- Manure - fresh manure can be spread on beds where it will break down over winter and can be dug in sometime in early spring.

- Painting - if the weather is dry for a few days, sheds and other wooden structures could benefit from a coat of preservation paint to protect them through winter.
- Pots - empty and clean any pots that have finished for the season.
- Sheds - check that your shed is watertight. Check the roof, windows and door. You may be storing some of your harvest in here over winter and you must protect it. Make any repairs that are required.
- Water Butts - clear fallen leaves from water butts and clear gutters.
- Weeding - clear away any weeds, digging up all the young perennial weeds to prevent them from getting established.

Greenhouse and Polytunnel Jobs

Work in the greenhouse will have quietened down this month as most plants will be finished for the season. If you have a polytunnel, make sure it is securely fixed to the ground to protect it from the winter winds. So long as nothing is growing in your polytunnel, you can remove the plastic sheeting and replace it in the spring.

- Citrus Plants - move citrus plants inside as they do not tolerate frosts.
- Debris - clear any debris out of your greenhouse so that pests have nowhere to overwinter.
- Glass - check the glass is secure in its frames, replacing any damaged panels and fixings.
- Melons - melons may still be ripening, though the weather will be cooling too much for the plants to survive much longer, even indoors. Harvest the melons as soon as they are ripe, removing immature fruits so the larger fruits ripen.
- Microgreens - sow microgreens in your greenhouse for harvest in a few weeks.
- Onions and Garlic - these can continue to dry in the greenhouse before storing.
- Sweet Peas - start sweet peas off now to plant early in spring.
- Wash - wash the glass to remove any dirt and let as much sun as possible in.

November

It is now getting quieter at the allotment as the harvest draws to a close and the days shorten, making it harder for many people to get time to work on their allotment. The weather will be colder and winter storms will be coming in. It's a lot of tidying up and general maintenance, preparing for next year.

Great in winter stews.

What To Harvest

There will still be some crops ready to harvest and most of what is left will be winter hardy, so there is no need to hurry and pick them. Keep an eye on the weather as if your ground becomes too waterlogged it could rot root crops. Above ground crops can suffer in high winds, so secure them as required.

- Brussels Sprouts - the young leaves at the top of each plant, known as sprout tops, can be harvested and eaten like spring greens. Sprouts taste better after the first frost, so keep harvesting them before they 'blow', working from the bottom of the plant to the top.
- Cabbages - autumn and winter cabbages are ready to harvest now.
- Carrots - keep lifting your carrots or leave them in the ground providing they aren't being damaged by pests. They can benefit from a straw mulch to protect the roots from the frost and weather.
- Cauliflowers - harvest these as and when you need them. They will have stopped growing now, so unless it has gone really cold, leave them in place until you need them.
- Celeriac - dig the whole root up as and when you need them and trim them before use.

- Celery - this can be harvested.
- Cranberries - once the berries darken to a deep red, they are ready to harvest.
- French Beans - the beans that you have been saving to dry can be left on the plant until they dry. However, if the weather is too wet, you may need to remove them and dry them indoors otherwise they could rot.
- Jerusalem Artichokes - the first of your artichokes are ready to dig up this month. Dig up what you need and leave the rest in the ground for now.
- Kale - this is an extremely hardy plant that you can start to harvest what you can use as a cut-and-come-again crop. Leave the plant in the ground and keep harvesting throughout winter.
- Kohl Rabi - most cultivars will withstand some frost, but if it gets particularly cold, protect the plants with fleece or cloches.
- Leeks - dig forks up with a fork otherwise you risk breaking the stem. Harvest what you need and keep them covered to protect them.
- Lettuces - the first of the autumn lettuces will be ready to harvest.
- Oriental Leaves - plants such as mizuna, Chinese broccoli and so on will be ready to harvest.

- Parsnips - keep harvesting parsnips or leave them in the ground until you need them.
- Raspberries - you may find some autumn fruiting raspberries are ready to harvest in sheltered areas.
- Salad Leaves - many salad leaves will still be ready to harvest, particularly if you protect them against the frost.
- Spinach - most spinach varieties will be harvestable now, though protect this crop in bad weather.
- Sprouting Broccoli - pick any spears that are left before harvesting the hardier varieties next year.
- Swedes - if the roots are not too large, they can be left in the ground, otherwise you can harvest them.
- Swiss Chard - these are a hardy plant and will keep cropping throughout winter. Harvest leaves from the outside as and when you need them.
- Turnips - if the ground is going to freeze, lift the turnips and store them for use over winter.

Vegetable Plant Jobs

There isn't a huge amount to do in the vegetable garden this month as there is very little sow. Mainly it is about removing established weeds, tidying up and preparing for next year while keeping out of the bad weather.

- Brassicas - net your brassicas to protect them from pigeons who will strip the leaves as there isn't a lot of other food for them.
- Broad Beans - overwintering varieties can still be sown now either directly or in a cold frame.
- Cauliflowers - bend leaves over the heads and tie them in place to protect them from potential frost damage.
- Garlic - garlic cloves are best planted this month. Although you can plant them in December, the ground is often too hard or wet.
- Globe Artichokes - mulch the crowns with straw or bracken to protect them from frost damage over winter.

Fruit Tree/Bush Jobs

November is one of the main months for planting bare root fruit trees and bushes as they have a little time to establish themselves before winter sets in with a vengeance.

- Apples - start winter pruning apple trees once the leaves have fallen and the tree becomes dormant.
- Bare Root Trees - plant bare root cherries and plums between now and January and bare root apples and pears between now and March. November is considered the best time to plant bare root trees, particularly in areas where the ground freezes solid.
- Blackberries - plant bare root canes now, ideally in holes with plenty of well-rotted compost dug in.
- Currants - plant bare rooted plants. Blackcurrants can be pruned, opening up the bush so that air can circulate. Remove weak, diseased or older branches.
- Figs - any unripe figs larger than a cherry should be removed. Leave the tiny, embryo figs in place as they will be next year's fruit.
- Fruit Cages - remove the nets from your fruit cages to allow birds in so they can eat pests and their eggs. Removing the nets also prevents heavy snow or high winds damaging your cages.
- Gooseberries - continue to plant bare rooted plants. Prune established plants, cutting away damaged, diseased, dead or crossing branches.
- Grapes - bare rooted vines can be planted this month, otherwise it is best to wait until next March to plant them. Vines can be winter pruned from this month until January.
- Pears - when the leaves have fallen and the trees are dormant, start pruning the trees.
- Raspberries - bare root raspberry plants can be planted.
- Rotten Fruit - remove rotten fruit from your fruit trees. This is best destroyed rather than composted.
- Rhubarb - this is dormant now, so new sets can be planted or established plants divided and propagated. Spread well-rotted compost around the stems to feed the plants, but do not cover the crowns.
- Weed - weed around your fruit trees and bushes, then apply a good mulch.

General Jobs

There are a lot of other jobs to do, but mainly it is tidying up and preparing for next year. It's not the time of year when you want to spend hours outside, so get out when you can.

- Improving Soil - now is a good time to dig in well-rotted compost and manure to improve your soil. It can be spread on top of the ground and the worms left to pull it down into the ground.
- Leaf Mould - continue to gather fallen leaves to make leaf mould. Put them in cages or bags so they do not blow away.
- Lime - before the soil becomes too wet, apply lime to any areas of your allotment that need it.

Avoid adding lime at the same time as you add manure because they react with each other.

- Raised Beds - if you have raised beds, top them up with compost or manure as the soil level does drop over time. If you are not planting until late spring, you can fill the beds with fresh manure and cover them so it breaks down over winter.

- Tidying - remove any debris and other odds and ends from your growing area so that the plot if clean and tidy. This reduces the possible places that pests such as slugs and snails can overwinter.

Greenhouse and Polytunnel Jobs

The greenhouse will be quiet this month as most plants will be finished. Tomatoes are unlikely to still be fruiting unless the greenhouse is heated and chillies will have either died or you will have cut them back to overwinter them.

- Cleaning - scrub down your greenhouse staging, glass and framework if you haven't already done this.

- Herbs - potted herbs such as chives and parsley should be brought into the greenhouse overwinter so you can continue to harvest them.

- Insulation - if you are overwintering plants in your greenhouse, insulate it with bubble wrap. Tape this to the inside of the windows and doors, then remove it next spring when the weather warms. This helps to keep the greenhouse frost free over winter and protect tender plants.

- Pests - check your greenhouse regularly for overwintering pests and treat them appropriately.

- Rocket - leafy vegetables such as rocket can be sown in trays and grown in the greenhouse to be harvest over winter.

- Tidy - remove spent plants from your greenhouse and compost them.

December

December is a cold and wet month when many of us feel quite down that we can't get outside and enjoy our allotment or garden. Despite the frost and snow there is still plenty that can be done both outside and in the warmth of your home.

The cold weather is surprisingly useful to you as a gardener. It kills off pests and diseases so that they do not build up. When winter isn't cold enough there is always a big problem with diseases and pests the following year. The frost can also help break down soil that you have dug over and is necessary for some plants to germinate or fruit.

So, what can you do in the cold month of December?

Beds covered and filled with manure for winter.

What To Harvest

Even though it is cold, wet and frost outside, there is still things to harvest!

- Brussels Sprouts - these will be in peak production this month, so get harvesting. You can cut the entire stalk and stand it in a bucket of water or harvest the sprouts from the bottom of the plant up. These can be blanched and frozen for longer term storage or left in place to be harvested nearer to Christmas.

- Carrots - if the ground is in danger of freezing, harvest your carrots. Store those that are in good condition and the rest can be blanched and frozen.

- Cauliflowers - protect the curds from frost by wrapping the outer leaves around the curds. Harvest as and when you need them.

- Celeriac - leave them in the ground until you need them, removing any dead of dying leaves. If the temperatures are low, mulch with straw to protect them.

- Celery - providing you have protected your late celery from the frosts, it can be harvested this month.

- Jerusalem Artichokes - dig up any remaining

Jerusalem artichokes. Make sure you get all the tubers out of the ground, otherwise the plant will be back in the same place next year.

- Kale - this is a great vegetable to have overwinter as some varieties such as Cavolo Nero can survive almost any weather. Keep harvesting leaves from the plants as and when you need them.

- Kohl Rabi - harvest the last of these before the end of the month.

- Leeks - harvest as and when you need them as they do not store well. However, they can be blanched and frozen.

- Parsnips - lift as and when you need them. They can be stored in shallow boxes covered with moist sand if required.

- Savoy Cabbages - harvest your savoy cabbages as and when you need them. They can be chopped, blanched and frozen or used straight away.

- Swedes - harvest the rest of your swedes this month. After the end of the month, they will start becoming woody and difficult to eat. Swedes can be stored over winter once they have been lifted.

- Turnips - harvest the rest of your turnips this

month otherwise they grow too large and woody. Store them indoors in boxes filled with sand.

Vegetable Plant Jobs

This is probably the quietest month on the allotment as there is very little to sow and the weather isn't usually very cooperative. Try to get out and finish off preparations for next year, particularly as January is usually another cold and wet month.

- Garlic - if the weather is mild and the soil is not frozen or waterlogged, garlic can be planted this month. If the soil conditions are not right, plant your garlic in February or March.

Fruit Tree/Bush Jobs

It is quiet in the fruit garden this month too. Your main job will be winter pruning trees.

- Bare Root Plants - get these into the ground, digging in plenty of well rotten compost before planting.
- Blackberries - bare root blackberries and hybrid berries can still be planted this month.
- Grapes - winter prune outdoor grape vines before the end of next month and the sap starts to rise again.
- Pruning - winter prune your apples and pears, unless it is very bold. Fruit bushes can also be pruned this month.
- Raspberries - bare roots plants can be planted this month.
- Rhubarb - plant new sets or divide and propagate existing plants.
- Weed - keep the weeds down under your fruit trees.

General Jobs

This is mainly a month for housekeeping. If the soil is too wet or the weather too cold, avoid digging your soil as it disturbs the worms and micro-organisms living underground.

- Cleaning - clean your pots, tools and seed trays using a disinfectant to ensure diseases and viruses do not survive through the winter.
- Compost - keep turning your compost to encourage it to break down. Cover it to keep it warm and stop it getting waterlogged.
- Cover Beds - any beds that are not going to be used need to be covered to keep weeds down. You can spread some well-rotten manure or compost on the bed first to improve the soil.
- Digging - avoid digging if the soil is waterlogged or frozen. Basically, if when you walk on the soil, it sticks to your boots, it is too wet. Try to avoid walking on the soil and compacting it too much. Lay planks to distribute your weight.
- Soil Improvement - add organic matter to your beds, digging extra into any beds that will grow beans or peas.

Greenhouse and Polytunnel Jobs

It will be quiet in the greenhouse this month. Keep an eye on the temperatures and, if you can, heat the greenhouse on the colder days to keep frosts away from any plants. Otherwise, keep vents and windows shut, particularly at night.

- Pests - check overwinter plants for pests, particularly the red spider mite and treat appropriately.
- Watering - water plants sparingly through winter and keep the greenhouse as dry as possible to avoid diseases.

Endnote

Whether you have an allotment or have set aside part of your garden as a vegetable plot, there is a lot of information in this book designed to get you started and help make growing vegetables easier for you.

There is a lot of information in this book to digest, so you may find it easier to use it as a reference manual, referring to the various sections as and when you need them. You will find Chapter 5, the seed sowing chart and monthly job list a useful resource for knowing what you can be doing.

Raised beds make for a lower maintenance allotment.

There are no hard and fast rules for growing vegetables, a lot of it comes down to your local environment such as your soil and weather conditions. In some areas you can grow plants at times of the year when they would otherwise die, whereas in other areas, you can find it a struggle to grow anything.

To start with, you need to understand the area where you want to grow. What is the soil like? How much sun does it get? Is it exposed or sheltered or in a frost pocket? All of this will determine what you can plant and when. If the area is exposed, then planting taller vegetables or plants around the perimeter will act as a wind break and protect your vegetable garden. If it is a frost pocket, you know to protect your delicate plants at the slightest hint of a chill.

I had an allotment many years ago in a village that was downwind from a power station; you could see the chimney stacks from the site. This created a very odd microclimate that meant it stayed slightly warmer than the surrounding area meaning you could grow some more unusual plants, including ginger, successfully. However, it was also on the side of a hill in the middle of fields, meaning the wind howled across the allotments. I remember visiting after one particularly bad storm and finding one person's shed in a tree, another in the middle of the field next door and someone's shed roof in the middle of my onion patch!

Understanding your environment and working with it, changing it over time to meet your needs, allows you to turn even the most inhospitable area into somewhere you can grow vegetables. Perhaps you have a heavy clay soil that is good for little other than making pots. Over several years, with patience, if you dig in organic matter, you will adjust the soil in your vegetable garden and turn it into something you can grow anything in. You may be stuck growing potatoes or using raised beds for a few years, but the soil quality will change over time.

A lot of people forget that owning an allotment and growing vegetables at home is not a sprint, but is a marathon. It is a long-term project and although you may want to get your allotment under control in a few weeks, it can take months or even years before it is how you want it. I have had my current allotment for four years now and it still isn't quite finished. I've been putting raised beds and paths in over the years and getting the mare's tail under control, but I will get there. There is always a lot to do and many of us are busy with families and jobs. Therefore, you have to be patient and realise things will get done when they are done. However, do remember that most allotment committees expect to see progress, so follow my advice on how to make your allotment look good for the committee. I remember one allotment holder who did nothing but fill his allotment with potatoes for a couple of years because he was so busy with work he didn't have time to do anything else.

Growing your own fruits and vegetables is an incredibly rewarding and fun thing to do. If you have children, then they often enjoy this too, though be patient with them as they are not going to be as enthusiastic as you about many of the jobs that need doing. For me, the most important thing about my allotment is that it gets me away from electronic items and out into the fresh air. When you are busy with your home life and job, getting away from it at the allotment is a great opportunity for you to recharge your batteries.

Have fun growing your own, whether it is at home or at an allotment. In the rest of this series, you will learn in more detail about growing fruits, herbs and vegetables, plus I will share with you many of my favourite allotment recipes. There will also be a book all about how to store and preserve your crops. You will find that you are sometimes overwhelmed with fresh fruits or vegetables and it can be difficult using it all before it goes off. Therefore, learning to preserve or store your harvest will help you waste less of what you grow.

Enjoy growing and please, let me know how you get on!

Appendix A - Useful Resources

This is a list of useful resources when you are growing vegetables. There is no preference to any of them, but they are here for ease of reference for you:

More about me: www.GardeningWithJason.com

Seed and Plant Suppliers:

Thompson and Morgan – www.thompson-morgan.com

Suttons – www.suttons.co.uk

DT Brown – www.dtbrownseeds.co.uk

Mr Fothergill's – www.mr-fothergills.co.uk

Kings Seeds – www.kingsseeds.co.uk

Allotment Information:

National Allotment Society - https://www.nsalg.org.uk/

Federation of City Farms and Community Gardens - https://www.farmgarden.org.uk/

Appendix B – Glossary of Gardening Terms

Annual
A plant that completes its entire lifecycle, i.e. from germination to flowering to producing seeds and to dying in a single growing season.

Bareroot
Plants that have been grown in a nursery by a supplier and are provided as dormant plants with no soil on the roots, e.g. roses, current or raspberry bushes.

Biennial
A plant that completes its entire lifecycle over two years. In the first year, it grows and in the second it produces seeds and dies, e.g. foxglove.

Bolting
To flower and go to seed prematurely.

Broadcast sowing
Scattering seeds, usually by hand, over the soil rather than planting in drills or rows; usually done with wildflower or grass seed.

Calyces
The sepals of a flower, usually green and forms a whorl enclosing the petals and provides protection to a flower in bud.

Chitting
Performed on potatoes. Seed potatoes are placed on a tray or egg box in a bright, cool, frost-free location so they sprout before planting. The aim is to speed the harvest by having the potatoes part grown before planting.

Cloche
A structure, usually glass or plastic, but can be made from horticultural fleece. These are placed over plants or seeds to protect the plant from frost and keep the soil warm.

Cold Frame
An unheated glass or plastic frame, sometimes half made from kids, that is used to start seeds off and to harden off outdoor plants.

Cordon
A plant trained to grow as a single main stem, though occasionally refers to plants with two or three main

stems such as apple trees or tomato plants. Usually you have to prune the side shoots.

Corm
Similar to a bulb, this consists of a stem base, usually with a fibrous outer layer such as begonias and saffron.

Crown
The growing point where new shoots emerge, either at or just below the soil level, e.g. asparagus.

Cultivar
A variety of a plant specifically grown for its unique flowers, foliage colour, disease/pest resistance, growing habit and so on. It has different characteristics from the original species.

Deciduous
A plant that sheds its leaves at the end of the growing season and renews them at the start of the next.

Direct Sow
To sow seeds in the position where you want them to flower or crop outdoors, i.e. in their final positions.

Drill
A straight, narrow furrow in the soil in which you sow seeds or plant seedlings.

Evergreen
Plants that keep the majority of their leaves all year round.

Earth Up
Piling soil up around a plant to keep the light out, protect from frost of to encourage the stem to develop roots. This is usually performed on potato crops.

Ericaceous
Describes plants that do not like alkaline soils and need an acidic soil to grow, e.g. blueberries.

Everbearing
Refers in particular to strawberry plants that yield a small crop at the start of summer, a few berries during the rest of summer and then the main, heavy crop in late summer.

F1 Hybrid
The first generation plant bred from two distinct pure-bred lines. Usually they are uniform and vigorous plants, often with a degree of disease resistance and good for exhibiting. F1 seeds are not true to their parents so are not worth saving.

Feathered Maiden
A one-year-old tree, usually fruit, that has several feathers or side branches.

First Early Potatoes
Potatoes that normally produce new or baby potatoes that are ready around 10 weeks after planting. These are commonly grown in areas affected by blight to avoid the disease which is prevalent in July or August.

Floricane
Canes that fruit on the previous year's growth, i.e. grow for a year and then produce fruit and flowers. Typically, this refers to blackberries and summer-fruiting raspberries. The growth that had the fruit on is pruned over winter to make way for fresh growth.

Foliage
Refers to the leaves of a plant.

Genus
A taxonomic category used in plant and animal naming. Always capitalized and ranks above species and below family.

Germination
The act of a seed turning from a seed into a plant.

Grafting
Artificially joining the rootstock of one plant with a piece of wood from another to create a single plant with the rooting properties of the rootstock and the fruiting properties of the other piece of wood. Commonly down with fruit trees to create dwarf cultivars.

Half-Hardy Annual
A plant that completes its life cycle from germination to seeding and death in a single growing season. It can be grown outside but does not tolerate temperatures below 32F/0C and requires protection from frosts.

Half-Hardy Biennial
Tolerates cold in the same way as the above, but as it is a biennial, it grows in the first season, reproduces and dies in the second, providing the winter does not kill it.

Half-Hardy Bulb/Corm/Rhizome/Tuber
Grows like a normal bulb/corm/rhizome or tuber, usually supplied dormant with no top growth. These can be grown outside, but will require protection during winter from temperatures below 32F/0C and from frosts.

Half-Hardy Perennial
A perennial plant that requires protection during winter from temperatures below 32F/0C and from frosts.

Harden Off
Acclimatising young plants that have been grown indoors or under glass to being outside. Achieved by moving plants outside during the day and then bringing them back under cover at night.

Hardy Annual
An annual plant that can tolerate outdoor winter temperatures as low as 5F/-15C.

Hardy Biennial
A biennial plant that can tolerate outdoor winter temperatures as low as 5F/-15C.

Hardy Perennial
A perennial plant that can tolerate outdoor winter temperatures as low as 5F/-15C.

Haulm
Refers to the leaves and stems of the potato plant.

Herbaceous Plant
A non-woody perennial, usually dies back in winter to become dormant. Grows back from a woody base or underground rootstock in spring.

Lime
A calcium compound applied to the soil to make it more alkaline (i.e. lower the pH level). Useful to prevent brassicas from contracting club root diseases.

Medium
A growing material for plants.

Maiden Tree
A tree, usually under a year old, that can be trained into whatever form you desire.

Main Crop Potatoes
Usually larger potatoes, good for roasting, mashing and baking that are harvested up to 20 weeks after planting. Main crop potatoes store well over winter.

Mulch
A layer of compost, gravel, well-rotted manure or plastic sheeting, placed on top of the soil around the base of plants. This helps to improve the soil, feed the plants (in the case of compost and manure), suppress weeds and help the soil retain moisture.

Organic Matter
Plant or animal matter such as leaf mold, manure or compost, that is dug into the soil to feed the plants and improve the soil.

Perennial
A plant that lives for three or more years, e.g. asparagus

Pinching Out
Removing the growing tips of a plant to encourage side shoots and bushier growth. This results in more flowering stems and ultimately, more fruit.

Pollination
Transferring pollen between flowers. Usually performed by insects, animals or the wind (e.g. sweetcorn), it is performed by hand when breeding plants or sometimes when growing in a greenhouse if there is a lack of pollinating insects near the plant.

Pot On
Removing a plant from one pot, usually because it has outgrown the pot, and moving it to a large container so it can continue to grow.

Pot Up
To put cuttings or seedlings into a container to allow them to grow on.

Prick Out
To remove seedlings from a seed tray and transfer them to modules or pots so they have more space to grow. Done to prevent overcrowding and stunted growth.

Primocane Variety
Refers to fruit canes that produce fruit on the current year's growth, e.g. autumn(fall) fruiting raspberries.

Propagate
To grow more of one plant, either from saving and planting seeds or through cuttings or grafting.

Raceme
A flower cluster that has separate flowers attached for short stalks of equal length at equal distances on a central stem. Typically, the flowers at the base of the central stem are the first to develop.

Rhizome
A mass of roots such as those found in ginger and turmeric. Can usually be divided and new plants grown from the rhizomes.

Rootball
The roots and soil around the roots when a plant is lifted from the ground or removed from its container.

Rosette
A cluster of leaves, usually at ground level, radiating out from roughly the same point.

Rootstock
The roots of a plant. In grafting, the scion (plant) is grafted on to a rootstock, which is the roots and a length of main trunk.

Rose End
The end of a seed potato that has the most eyes, usually this is the widest ends. Chit your potatoes with the rose end facing upwards.

Runner
A trailing stem, growing above ground, that produces roots at the nodes and as multiple baby plants on, such as those found on strawberries. Some plants produce underground runners.

Scarifying
Damaging the coating of the seed to help encourage germination. This could be scratching it with sandpaper, soaking it in water or a number of other methods.

Second Cropping Potatoes
Also referred to as Winter Potatoes, these are planted late summer or early fall and harvested around 14 weeks after planting.

Second Early Potatoes
Harvested around 14 weeks after planting, these are good for everything from salad potatoes to chipping, roasting and mashing. Often grown in areas prone to blight.

Seed Potatoes
A potato tuber that has been grown specifically for gardeners to plant. These are usually certified disease and pest free.

Self-Fertile
Refers to a plant that does not require pollination from another plant.

Semi-Evergreen
A plant that keeps all or some of its leaves all year round.

Semi-ripe Cutting
Where the cutting has not reached seasonal maturity, but is too mature to be used as a softwood cutting. The base of the cutting will be turning woody (lignifying) and the tip will still be soft.

Senescence
The period of a plants life where it has passed maturity but before it dies off. The plant has lower levels of chlorophyll, which means carbohydrate production reduces. In annual plants, this takes place within a year and in biennials, it takes place in the second year. This often results in fewer flowers and fruits, but some plants increase production to ensure survival of the species. Senescence is not reversible. This can be triggered by temperature, day length, water supply and more.

Slips
Cuttings from a sweet potato plant or sweet potatoes that have been rooted.

Standard
A tree or shrub, such as bay or roses, that has been trained to certain height with a long, bare stem and the foliage at the top.

Stratification
The process of treating seeds to emulate natural conditions to encourage germination such as putting them in the freezer

Tender Annual
An annual plant that cannot tolerate temperatures below 41F/5C.

Tender Biennial
A biennial plant that cannot tolerate temperatures below 41F/5C.

Tender Perennial
A perennial plant that cannot tolerate temperatures below 41F/5C.

Thin
Refers to the act of removing seedlings, shoots, flowers, fruit or buds to improve the viability, growth and quality of those you leave. For example, you thin your carrots which are difficult to sow with sufficient space between them, eat the thinnings and then the remaining carrots have the space to grow to maturity.

Other Books By Jason

Please check out my other gardening books online, available in ebook and paperback formats. For an up-to-date list of published books and information, visit www.GardeningWithJason.com.

A Gardener's Guide to Weeds - How To Use Common Garden Weeds For Food, Health, Beauty And More

Ever wondered about the weeds that take over your garden? You may be surprised to know that these weeds are the ancestors of many of the crops we regularly eat and used to be the staple diet for humans. This book teaches you all about weeds including how to use them in your garden and kitchen and their traditional medicinal uses as well as the folklore and myths associated with them. A fascinating insight into the gardener's foe!

An Introduction To Smallholdings – Getting Started On Your Smallholding

Thinking about getting a smallholding? Find out everything you need to consider from the best location to what equipment you need. Talking about everything relating to a smallholding such as how to make an income, what to grow and sell, keeping animals and more, this guide will walk you through everything you must know before living the smallholding dream.

Berry Gardening – The Complete Guide to Berry Gardening from Gooseberries to Boysenberries and More

Who doesn't love fresh berries? Find out how you can grow many of the popular berries at home such as marionberries and blackberries and some of the more unusual like honeyberries and goji berries. A step by step guide to growing your own berries including pruning, propagating and more. Discover how you can grow a wide variety of berries at home in your garden or on your balcony.

Canning and Preserving at Home – A Complete Guide to Canning, Preserving and Storing Your Produce

A complete guide to storing your home-grown fruits and vegetables. Learn everything from how to freeze your produce to canning, making jams, jellies, and chutneys to dehydrating and more. Everything you need to know about storing your fresh produce, including some unusual methods of storage, some of which will encourage children to eat fresh fruit!

Companion Planting Secrets – Organic Gardening to Deter Pests and Increase Yield

Learn the secrets of natural and organic pest control with companion planting. This is a great way to increase your yield, produce better quality plants and work in harmony with nature. By attracting beneficial insects to your garden, you can naturally keep down harmful pests and reduce the damage they cause. You probably grow many of these companion plants already, but by repositioning them, you can reap the many benefits of this natural method of gardening. Find out more about how you can enjoy the benefits of companion planting here.

Container Gardening - Growing Vegetables, Herbs & Flowers in Containers

A step by step guide showing you how to create your very own container garden. Whether you have no garden, little space or you want to grow specific plants, this book guides you through everything you need to know about planting a container garden from the different types of pots, to which plants thrive in containers to handy tips helping you avoid the common mistakes people make with containers. Click here now to preview this book.

Cooking With Zucchini - Delicious Recipes, Preserves and More With Courgettes: How To Deal With A Glut Of Zucchini And Love It!

Getting too many zucchinis from your plants? This book teaches you how to grow your own courgettes at home as well as showing you the many different varieties you could grow. Packed full of delicious recipes, you will learn everything from the famous zucchini chocolate cake to delicious main courses, snacks, and Paleo diet friendly raw recipes. The must have guide for anyone dealing with a glut of zucchini. Click here (UK courgette version here) now to preview this book.

Environmentally Friendly Gardening - - Your Guide to a Sustainable Eco-Friendly Garden

A guide to making your garden more environmentally friendly, from looking after beneficial insects and wildlife, to saving water and reducing plastic use. There is a lot you can do to reduce your reliance on chemicals and work in harmony with nature, while still having a beautiful and productive garden. This book details many things you can easily do to become more eco-friendly in your garden.

Greenhouse Gardening - A Beginners Guide to Growing Fruit and Vegetables All Year Round

A complete, step by step guide to owning a greenhouse. Learn everything you need to know from sourcing greenhouses to building foundations to ensuring it survives high winds. This handy guide will teach you everything you need to know to grow a wide range of plants in your greenhouse, including tomatoes, chilies, squashes, zucchini and much more. Click here now to preview this book and find out how you could benefit from a greenhouse today! They are more fun and less work than you might think!

Growing Brassicas – Growing Cruciferous Vegetables from Broccoli to Mooli to Wasabi and More

Brassicas are renowned for their health benefits and are packed full of vitamins. They are easy to grow at home, but beset by problems. Find out how you can grow these amazing vegetables at home, including the incredibly beneficial plants broccoli and maca. Includes step by step growing guides plus delicious recipes for every recipe! Click here now to preview this book.

Growing Chillies – A Beginners Guide to Growing, Using & Surviving Chillies

Ever wanted to grow super-hot chillies? Or maybe you just want to grow your own chillies to add some flavour to your food? This book is your complete, step-by-step guide to growing chillies at home. With topics from selecting varieties to how to germinate seeds, you will learn everything you need to know to grow chillies successfully, even the notoriously difficult to grow varieties such as Carolina Reaper. With recipes for sauces, meals and making your own chilli powder, you'll find everything you need to know to grow your own chilli plants. Click here now for a free preview of this book.

Growing Fruit: The Complete Guide to Growing Fruit at Home

This is a complete guide to growing fruit from apricots to walnuts and everything in between. You will learn how to choose fruit plants, how to grow and care for them, how to store and preserve the fruit and much more. With recipes, advice, and tips this is the perfect book for anyone who wants to learn more about growing fruit at home, whether beginner or experienced gardener. Click here now for a preview of the book.

Growing Garlic – A Complete Guide to Growing, Harvesting & Using Garlic

Everything you need to know to grow this popular plant. Whether you are growing normal garlic or elephant garlic for cooking or health, you will find this book contains all the information you need. Traditionally a difficult crop to grow with a long growing season, you'll learn the exact conditions garlic needs, how to avoid the common problems people encounter and how to store your garlic for use all year round. A complete, step-by-step guide showing you precisely how to grow garlic at home. Click here now to find out what is in this book.

Growing Giant Pumpkins – How to Grow Massive Pumpkins At Home

A complete step-by-step guide detailing everything you need to know to produce pumpkins weighing hundreds of pounds, if not edging into the thousands! Anyone can grow giant pumpkins at home, and this book gives you the insider secrets of the giant pumpkin growers showing you how to avoid the mistakes people commonly make when trying to grow a giant pumpkin. This is a complete guide detailing everything from preparing the soil to getting the right seeds to germinating the seeds and caring for your pumpkins. Click here now to preview the book and order your copy.

Growing Herbs – A Beginners Guide To Growing, Using, Harvesting and Storing Herbs

A comprehensive guide to growing herbs at home, detailing 49 different herbs. Learn everything you need to know to grow these herbs from their preferred soil conditions to how to harvest and propagate them and more. Including recipes for health and beauty plus delicious dishes to make in your kitchen. This step-by-step guide is designed to teach you all about growing herbs at home, from a few herbs in containers to a fully-fledged herb garden. Click here now to preview the book and find out more.

Growing Lavender: Growing, Using, Cooking and Healing with Lavender

A complete guide to growing and using this beautiful plant. Find out about the hundreds of different varieties of lavender and how you can grow this bee friendly plant at home. With hundreds of uses in crafts, cooking and healing, this plant has a long history of association with humans. Discover today how you can grow lavender at home and enjoy this amazing herb. Click here now to peek inside the book!

Growing Tomatoes: Your Guide to Growing Delicious Tomatoes At Home

This is the definitive guide to growing delicious and fresh tomatoes at home. Teaching you everything from selecting seeds to planting and caring for your tomatoes as well as diagnosing problems this is the ideal book for anyone who wants to grow their own tomatoes. You will learn the secrets of a successful tomato grower and learn about the many different types of tomato you could grow, most of which are not available in any shops! A comprehensive must have guide. Click here now for a preview of this book.

How to Compost – Turn Your Waste into Brown Gold

This is a complete step by step guide to making your own compost at home. Vital to any gardener, this book will explain everything from setting up your compost heap to how to ensure you get fresh compost in just a few weeks. You will learn the techniques for producing highly nutritious compost that will help your plants grow while recycling your kitchen waste. A must have handbook for any gardener who wants their plants to benefit from home-made compost. Click here now to preview this book.

How to Grow Potatoes - The Guide To Choosing, Planting and Growing in Containers Or the Ground

Learn everything you need to know about growing potatoes at home. Discover the wide variety of potatoes you can grow; many delicious varieties you will never see in the shops. Find out the best way to grow potatoes at home, how to protect your plants from the many pests and diseases and how to store your harvest so you can enjoy fresh potatoes over winter. A complete step by step guide telling you everything you need to know to grow potatoes at home successfully. Click here now to preview this book.

Hydroponics: A Beginners Guide to Growing Food without Soil

Hydroponics is growing plants without soil, which is a fantastic idea for indoor gardens. It is surprisingly easy to set up, once you know what you are doing and is significantly more productive and quicker than growing in soil. It doesn't even have to be expensive to get started, and the possibilities are endless. This book will tell you everything you need to know to get started growing flowers, vegetables and fruit hydroponically at home. Click here now to preview this book.

Indoor Gardening for Beginners: The Complete Guide to Growing Herbs, Flowers, Vegetables and Fruits in Your House

Discover how you can grow a wide variety of plants in your home. Whether you want to grow herbs for cooking, vegetables or a decorative plant display, this book tells you everything you need to know. Learn which plants to keep in your home to purify the air and remove harmful chemicals and how to successfully grow plants from cacti to flowers to carnivorous plants. Click here now for a preview of this book.

Keeping Chickens for Beginners – Keeping Backyard Chickens from Coops to Feeding to Care and More

Chickens are becoming very popular to keep at home, but it isn't something you should leap into without the right information. This book guides you through everything you need to know to keep chickens from decided what breed to what coop to how to feed them, look after them and keep your chickens healthy and producing eggs. This is your complete guide to owning chickens, with absolutely everything you need to know to get started and successfully keep chickens at home. Click here now to preview this book.

Raised Bed Gardening – A Guide to Growing Vegetables In Raised Beds

Learn why raised beds are such an efficient and effortless way to garden as you discover the benefits of no-dig gardening, denser planting and less bending, ideal for anyone who hates weeding or suffers from back pain. Easy to build and lasting for years I cannot recommend this method of gardening enough for its many benefits! You will learn everything you need to know to build your own raised beds, plant them and ensure they are highly productive. Click here now for a preview of this book.

Save Our Bees – Your Guide to Creating a Bee Friendly Environment

Find out how you can help save the bees and protect this insect that is vital to your food production and environment. Our modern lives have disrupted the bees to a point where many are dying off. Learn what you can do to help the bees no matter how much space you have at home! Discover what bees need, how you can provide it and all about the different types of bees! These misunderstood creatures are pretty much harmless and are fascinating insects. Click here now to preview this book and start helping to save the bees!

Square Foot Gardening – Growing More in Less Space

Learn about this unique gardening style which enables you to grow more in less space. This dense planting method using nutrient rich soil to produce fantastic yields. You will learn exactly how to create your own square foot garden, how to create the perfect soil mix and exactly how to space your plants for maximum yields. You will find out what you can grow in a square foot garden as well as what to avoid growing plus helpful advice so you can make the most of your growing area. An in-depth guide to getting you started with your first square foot garden. Click here now to preview this book.

Vertical Gardening: Maximum Productivity, Minimum Space

This is an exciting form of gardening allows you to grow large amounts of fruit and vegetables in small areas, maximizing your use of space. Whether you have a large garden, an allotment or just a small balcony, you will be able to grow more delicious fresh produce. Becoming more popular not just amongst gardeners but even with city planners, this is a fantastic gardening technique that significantly boosts your yield. Find out how I grew over 70 strawberry plants in just three feet of ground space and more in this detailed guide. Click here now to find out how you can grow more in less space!

Worm Farming – Creating Compost at Home with Vermiculture

An in-depth guide to one of the hottest topics on the market as you learn how you can use worms to turn your kitchen scraps into a high quality, highly nutritious compost that will help your plants to thrive! Easy to set up, low cost and able to be done in a small corner of a shed or garage this is a fantastic way for anyone to make their own compost or even scale it up to create a highly profitable business. Discover how you can make one of the best composts on the market with kitchen waste and worms! Click here now to learn how you can get started with worm farming today; it's easier than you thought!

About Jason

Jason has been a keen gardener for over twenty years, having taken on numerous weed infested patches and turned them into productive vegetable gardens.

One of his first gardening experiences was digging over a 400 square foot garden in its entirety and turning it into a vegetable garden, much to the delight of his neighbors who all got free vegetables! It was through this experience that he discovered his love of gardening and started to learn more and more about the subject.

His first encounter with a greenhouse resulted in a tomato infested greenhouse but he soon learnt how to make the most of a greenhouse and now grows a wide variety of plants from grapes to squashes to tomatoes and more. Of course, his wife is delighted with his greenhouse as it means the windowsills in the house are no longer filled with seed trays every spring.

He is passionate about helping people learn to grow their own fresh produce and enjoy the many benefits that come with it, from the exercise of gardening to the nutrition of freshly picked produce. He often says that when you've tasted a freshly picked tomato you'll never want to buy another one from a store again!

Jason is also very active in the personal development community, having written books on self-help, including subjects such as motivation and confidence. He has also recorded over 80 hypnosis programs, being a fully qualified clinical hypnotist which he sells from his website www.MusicForChange.com.

He hopes that this book has been a pleasure for you to read and that you have learned a lot about the subject and welcomes your feedback either directly or through an Amazon review. This feedback is used to improve his books and provide better quality information for his readers.

Jason also loves to grow giant and unusual vegetables and is still planning on breaking the 400lb barrier with a giant pumpkin. He hopes that with his new allotment plot he'll be able to grow even more exciting vegetables to share with his readers.

Want More Inspiring Gardening Ideas?

This book is part of the Inspiring Gardening Ideas series. Bringing you the best books anywhere on how to get the most from your garden or allotment.

You can find out about more wonderful books just like this one at www.GardeningWithJason.com.

Follow me at www.YouTube.com/OwningAnAllotment for my video diary and tips. Join me on Facebook for regular updates and discussions at www.Facebook.com/OwningAnAllotment.

Follow me on Twitter and Instagram as @allotmentowner for regular updates, news, pictures and answers to your gardening questions.

Thank you for reading!

Printed in Great Britain
by Amazon

39950646R00093